HOMER FOR REAL:

A Reading of the *Iliad*

Also By Eric Larsen

An American Memory, a novel
I Am Zoë Handke, a novel
A Nation Gone Blind:
America in an Age of Simplification and Deceit
The End of the 19th Century, a novel

HOMER FOR REAL:
A READING OF THE *ILIAD*

The First in a Series Called:
Great Literary Works
for Regular People:

A Course of Readings Drawn from
a Life in the Classroom

by
Eric Larsen

The Oliver Arts & Open Press

Quotations from Richmond Lattimore's *The Iliad of Homer*
are reprinted by the generous permission of the
University of Chicago Press.

Quotations from Robert Grudin's *American Vulgar: The Politics of
Manipulation Versus the Culture of Awareness* are made with permission
from Counterpoint Press

Library of Congress Cataloging-in-Publication Data
Larsen, Eric, 1941-
Homer for Real: A Reading of the Iliad. *Volume One of Great Literary Works for
Regular People–A Course of Readings Drawn from a Life in the Classroom*

ISBN: 978-0-9819891-2-9

The Oliver Arts & Open Press
2578 Broadway (Suite #102)
New York, NY 10025
http://www.oliveropenpress.com

For my Students
Then and Now

CONTENTS

Introduction

I was twenty-one years old, in what I remember as the particularly fragrant spring of 1963, when I taught my first college class. This was in Minnesota, at Carleton College. A conflict had come up to prevent Wayne Carver from meeting the Friday fourth-hour session of his sophomore survey course, and, instead of finding a colleague to cover for him, he graciously turned to me, a last-semester senior, and asked if I would fill in for the period. His request seemed to me a bit unreal and very flattering.

The day was sunlit and cool, with the smells of earth and moist greenery drifting in through big open windows. The preceding hour, at 10:00 a.m., I sat in Owen Jenkins' History of Literary Criticism, and, when that adjourned, I walked across to the other end of the building, still on second-floor Laird, to Wayne Carver's waiting class. The day's subject was Yeats, I remember, though how much work we covered I can't say. I do know that we went through "Among School Children" and "A Prayer for My Daughter," but anything else now escapes me.

I suppose I actually was, if barely, qualified to lead such a class. The term was at its end. I'd finished my six-hour written comprehensives, had passed my orals, and had submitted and defended my senior thesis. And I'd read a fair lot of Yeats.

It felt strange, though, to be at the front of the class instead of in it. I stood up through the hour instead of sitting at the chair and table in front not just because it felt more natural to me but because I'd observed the law of academics that, with rare exceptions, the more interesting instructors remained on their feet while the less interesting did not.

During the year after that, 1963-1964, I went to Iowa City for my Master's and spent no time in front of a class. Through the four decades from 1964 through 2005, however, not a year passed but that I spent at least part of it "in front." I was a teaching assistant in Madison, Wisconsin, for a year, an assistant professor in Wayne, Nebraska, for another, then a teaching assistant back in Iowa City for two more. From the fall of 1968 through the spring 1970 I taught in Europe with the University of Maryland. Then it was back to Iowa City for 1970-1971, and for the unbroken years from 1971 through 2005 I was at John Jay College of Criminal Justice in the City University of New York.

Two—maybe three—things about John Jay are pertinent to this Introduction. The first is that when New York City all but went broke, in 1976, most of John Jay's traditional liberal arts majors were stripped away, including its English major, which at that time was but newly born. This denuding of the curriculum was done for economic reasons—other CUNY colleges could go on teaching the traditional liberal arts while John Jay would be required to focus solely on its own "mission" of criminal justice. It didn't seem to matter that no one knew or—at least not in my hearing over the next thirty-five years—was able to define exactly what "criminal justice" was or what it really consisted of.

But that couldn't be allowed to stand in the way of academic planning, and so our English major was taken away—as were the college's majors in history, philosophy, art, and so on. This meant that for the three decades that still lay stretched out ahead of me at John Jay, I would be relegated to freshman composition and sophomore surveys of literature, teaching these to students whose interests, generally speaking, lay far afield from either the humanities or from the art of writing.

I was extremely lucky, though, that one of the college's central founders—and its humanities head—had been Robert C. Pinckert, a powerfully educated traditionalist *and* a graduate of Columbia College, where, as a first-year student, he had gone through Columbia's famous "Lit Hum" courses. When Bob was designing the humanities part of what would be the "core" required of all students at John Jay, he constructed the literature surveys on the model of what he himself had studied at Columbia.

And so, thanks to Bob Pinckert, it came about that bare, homely John Jay was to be my Harvard and my Yale—and my Columbia, too. English major or no, I still had the great luck of being able to make my living by reading and teaching great stuff—real, substantive, interesting, historically and aesthetically important works of literature from Homer through Samuel Beckett.

It was not a life exotic or varied, but it was certainly rich. How can Hamlet, Dante, Chaucer, Homer, Milton, and Virginia Woolf *not* be rich? Admittedly, it wasn't the same as teaching Lit Hum two-and-a-half miles uptown would be, since the students at John Jay were very, very different from their Morningside Heights counterparts. I'll say more about my students in a moment, but first another word or two about the Pinckert and Columbia legacy.

Bob Pinckert was an exceptionally sure and perceptive judge of character, and as a result his early faculty appointments at John Jay were excellent. Not only did we have a strong department, but we also enjoyed a generally shared view that the literature survey courses, as written, were solid, durable, worthwhile, rewarding both to us and to the students, and in need of no defense. They were not only a life raft, but the very best kind of life raft This state of general agreement, however, came under attack in the early 1990s when two things happened. Bob retired, for one, and the disease-flood of "political correctness" at last rose high enough to crest our own walls, sending ankle-deep water through the corridors.

And then it started getting deeper. New appointments to the English staff, as the decade wore on, came from what seemed to have become a different world entirely–and from a different kind of education entirely–than those of us from the Bob Pinckert generation had come from, been familiar with, and valued. I've written at length about these kinds of changes in my book *A Nation Gone Blind: American in an Age of Simplification and Deceit* (2006), and, as I point out there, it wasn't a matter of the new people not being smart–many of them were very, very smart indeed–but it was simply a matter of their not being literary.

As *A Nation Gone Blind* points out also, these were highly idealistic young people, impelled by extremely strong desires to do good in various social, cultural, and political ways–but, to repeat, they were neither literary in their thinking nor had they absorbed *literary* educations. Aesthetics or aesthetic judgment or aesthetic history or aesthetic pleasure meant nothing to them other than that they considered such things elitist and suffocating at worst and, at best, of absolutely *no* social, political, or cultural value or importance in the framework of their own reformist programs.

For reasons like these, the last fifteen years or so of my time at John Jay were defensive ones and by no means especially pleasant. Suddenly, a strong and highly contentious battle against the Lit Hum model was being mounted, and year by year, as ever more of the original Pinckert appointments reached retirement, fewer and fewer of us remained to mount and sustain a defense.

What was it like? Well, the experience is described fully in *A Nation Gone Blind*, although here I can say that in great part it was a battle against intellectual–and most certainly literary–simplification. Books like Toni Morrison's *Beloved* were to replace *The Oresteia* of Aeschylus, Chinua Achebe's *Things Fall Apart* to replace Joseph Conrad's *Heart of Darkness*, and Art Spiegelman's *Maus* Samuel Beckett's *Waiting for Godot*. The problem wasn't necessarily that these "replacement" works were "bad,"[1] though without question they were simple. And their simplicity revealed clearly that they had been chosen by instructors not on the basis of their unique or historical literary importance but on the basis of their providing evidence or undergirding for agendas of one social, political, or cultural sort or another. That the books favored by the "New Professors," as I privately named them, tended more and more to be current, recent, or contemporary works further underscored their intended use as agenda-supports–but, even more important, it also showed the new instructors' willingness to jettison history altogether in anything remotely akin to the deep sense of pastness that underlay the very formation of the Lit Hum sequences.

Up until I left John Jay, I was able to keep my own literature sections within the tradition they'd come from, but the effort to keep them that way put me into a state of social segregation from the rest of the teaching staff and I felt ostracized and quite alone–except for the company of one other fellow-laborer, Ira Bloomgarden. Ira dated back to the earliest of the Bob Pinckert days, was himself also profoundly educated–he, too, was a graduate of Columbia College–and by this time had become my longest-term remaining colleague and increasingly my closest friend. At the end, the two of us didn't so much bow out of the department or out of the college as merely disappear from both, our departures generally unremarked and unlamented by those we were leaving behind.

Times change. Still, during the three-and-a-half decades of my own academic career, they *really* changed. What's become of things at the college since I left, I don't know. But, in some sense, it doesn't matter, since what I want to do here, in this first volume of the several others that I hope will follow it, is not to lament what may have happened *since* I left teaching, but, instead, to re-create the things that *did* happen in my own classrooms during the time when the tradition of Lit Hum was still their guiding spirit.

I said a moment ago that I would say something about my students, who, unquestionably, were very different from those on the famous Morningside Heights campus a couple of miles uptown. Students at John Jay were of every age, from those just out of high school to those in their sixties or even more. Some were policemen, some worked in city or federal agencies, there were a good many young mothers, and, taken all together, I would estimate that more than half of my students held down jobs. Close to half, I would say, came from blue-collar neighborhoods in the five boroughs or in northern New Jersey or the nearer reaches of Long Island. Something close to the other half came from what some would call the projects, others the ghetto, still others el barrio.

Excepting, on average, what I'd guess to be one to two percent of the overall population, my students were most, most clearly under-prepared for college-level work. Again, with the few exceptions I've mentioned, their writing abilities, in the main, ranged from the barely adequate to very weak to all but non-existent. As for backgrounds in reading—again, with that tiny number of exceptions—it seemed that in high school they had done virtually no reading and had been encouraged to do even less. In a class of forty-five students, three or four hands would go up if I asked how many had read *1984* or *Animal Farm*. In the case of *All Quiet on the Western Front*, I got maybe one hand a year, and it was the same for *any* book of Ernest Hemingway. As for the "classics," the books and works making up the courses I was about to teach, not only had they gone almost universally unread, but the recognition *most* familiar to me over the years was the recognition that almost none of my students had ever even *heard* of the books that we were now about to read.

Nevertheless, these were my students, I was their instructor, and Lit Hum formed the basis on which we were about to proceed. The work–from day one through day 1,960^2–was never easy, for me or for them. For them, the assignments were hard, the style and language often difficult, the essays and the exams equally so. For me, *those* things weren't so hard, but plenty of other things *were*. Imagine what I faced, and how many things I invariably had to do at once. Most of the students were intimidated, and I had to charm every single one of them, in one way or another, into feeling equal to the work and to the books rather than dismally inferior to both. This feeling of intimidation among the students took many forms. Some students went sullen, and I had to reach out to them in any way I could. Others fell asleep–half due literally to too many hours on jobs, and half as a means of escape or insolence, the results of intimidation–and I had to reach out to *them*. Some, admittedly, were bored to death, and I had to reach out to *them*. Still others began catching on more quickly than the rest, and they'd begin to dominate or "act out," and I had to reach out to them to bring *them* back into the class as a coherent group.

It was like being an actor playing six roles at once, or a juggler doing what it is that jugglers do. How much easier it would have been–as, indeed, it later became for others–simply to teach easy books, like the ones I mentioned earlier, then to fit each book to an agenda, and get your students to feel at home with "literary" things *that* way.

But in exactly what sense would that really be literary? Toni Morrison, for example, is as much, and perhaps more, a *bad* example of a novelist as she is a good one.[3] As for the other "easy" books mentioned earlier—yes, it would be nice to encourage students to become readers, but, once encouraged, *those* were all books they could easily read by and for themselves, at least far, far more so than they could Homer, Dante, Milton, or Aeschylus by or for themselves. And, too, even if a course made up only of "contemporary" works *could* be called "literary," it couldn't conceivably be a course claiming literary *history* as any central part of its substance or structure.

Among the important considerations of semester-long, or year-long, readings modeled on the Lit Hum courses is that they're fully intended to give readers some awareness of the three- or four-thousand-year *story* of literature. I myself call it the story-within-the-stories. The works of literature themselves have their own stories. But as you follow these onward, from one age to another—from as far back, say, as the epic of Gilgamesh, near 2,000 BC, up to Samuel Beckett, near 1945 AD—the story of the world itself gets told, the story of the changing world as it's reflected in and by those works.

I always felt that to *simplify* what I was able to offer to my students would amount in no uncertain terms to deprivation. In fact, it seemed to me that it would amount, really, to a betrayal. Almost none of these people had ever before been given a shot at the history of literature, or ever before been given a shot at the "classics" of literature. And if they weren't given a shot at those things *now*, at a time when there were means, motive, and opportunity—then, after that, when *would* they get a shot?

There were ancillary concerns, too, that had to do not with the students but with me. Conscience, for example, and what I thought of as honesty. I'd made the choice to get the education I'd gotten, and the choice to be trained to do what I now, furthermore, had contracted with the Department of Higher Education of New York State *to* do.

There'd be no living with myself if I didn't do all I could, if I didn't fulfill the terms of my contract.

And so I set out trying to imitate the actor playing six or more roles at once–professor, comedian, disciplinarian, reader aloud, explainer of syntax, teller of anecdotes, builder of vocabulary, heroic advocate of literature and of its history. In class above all, I did everything possible to prevent there *ever* being a dull moment, or *ever* a moment of the least hesitation on my part about where to go next, what page to turn to, what next step to take. In every class, too, there had to be a structure of some kind that rose to a natural climax at the end, or to a perfect cliff-hanger, so as to link the day's work to the next day to come. All of this had to be done, too, within the self-imposed terms of my own inner clock, whose rule was that, at a minimum, ninety-five percent of each class period *had* to be spent in active and productive involvement with the day's material. If anything more than five percent of the period went unused, or was used unprofitably, I considered it a personal failure. It was hard work, yes, but when it went well–which wasn't always–the effect was glorious. By the end of those classes, I would have had almost the equivalent of a physical workout, my shirt well soaked as evidence. And thus went my decades-long effort to make the reading of these ancient, remote, often difficult books become no longer intimidating to my students, to make them seem a part of our own world while at the same time trying never, ever to lose the other vital essence of those books, which is that they really *are* remote and distant from our own world, that they really *are* very, very old.

As the era of the New Professors progressed in the early 1990's, I more and more regularly saw and heard other instructors addressing their students (and vice versa) on a first-name basis. This was something I could not and would not do. It had nothing whatsoever to do with affection for my students–I became extremely fond of many of them, you can be quite sure–but in class I explained to them that I was *not* their friend. I was instead something quite different altogether:

I was their *instructor*. I would then provide an illustrative example (or I would "put a case," as Jaggers would say in *Great Expectations*). Suppose a person were injured in a bad accident or suffered the sudden onset of a very serious disease. If this person went to a doctor for help, would he or she prefer that that doctor be a friend to the patient, or that the doctor be a *good doctor*?

Who, after all, would want emergency treatment, in even the most remote or least conceivable way, to be dependent upon the question of whether or not the doctor *liked* you?

Still, it was clear that I did need some way of being less formal in class than the instructors of my own ancient day had been–back when they'd called on us by preceding our surnames with Mr. or Miss.[4] Obviously *that* would no longer work–even though the truth is that I had actually done it myself in my first decade-and-a-half or so at John Jay. Later, though, it was obvious that I needed an alternative, and so I began adjectivizing each student's last name and following the result with the word "One." Kelly Cramer, by this method, became "the Cramerian One," Anthony Stefenese "the Stefenesian One," Mike Macdougal "the Macdougalian one" (accent on third syllable), Judy Berniay "the Berniayvian One," and Tony Santiago "the Santiogovian One" (accent on fourth syllable), and so on. I liked it, the students *very* much liked it, and it had the added merit of building pronunciation skills, of building up practice in the tripping of the tongue.

•

I've written this introduction as a means of suggesting exactly why it is that I'm embarking on this series of books about "great literature," books that I'm saying are intended "for all readers." But I've written the introduction also as a way of suggesting what I hope the quality and tone of those books will be–starting here, with *Homer For Real*. What I hope is that, to the best of my ability, I can transfer to the printed page the content and at least some part of the atmosphere of what took place inside those three-and-a-half decades' worth of classroom hours–at least when they, I, and the students were all at their–or our–best.

If someone has never read the *Iliad*–well, conceivably it's possible that this little book may be a way for that person to get a start on it. If someone else remembers simply and passionately hating the *Iliad* because it was taught by the most boring instructor that the imagination of all of the gods could ever have produced–well, this book may offer a second shot at the poem that will work out better this time. And if yet another person is, yes, faintly or even *more* than faintly interested in the *Iliad* but is–yes again–sufficiently intimidated by the "great classic" so as to hesitate to take it off the shelf or to pay actual *money* for it–well, again, maybe *Homer For Real* will be useful in helping that person make up her mind to take the book down, go ahead and read it, doing so along with *Homer For Real*.

Anyway, I know that I hope so, in all those cases.

The great old books are good ones. And I've tried with this book of my own, as I will with the others that are to come, to write a good book, and a true one, about *that* book.

Something entirely unexpected happened to me one day last winter. I was at my computer, reading email, and I found that the "in" folder contained this:

Date: Tue, 16 Dec 2008
From: R. M.
Subject: John Jay College
To: ericlarsen@ericlarsen.net

Prof Larsen,

I have wanted to say this to you for about the past 10 years. Your obsession in making sure that my mind opened to a world that I never knew existed has helped me tremendously. I could not write, had no interest in literature, and had a hard time enunciating words. I had a very hard time articulating a thought in words and I didn't have a vocabulary. I felt like an idiot.

I grew up in the inner city and attended inner city schools. Stereotypical Latino household and stereotypical inner city neighborhood in many regards. But it was a white guy from Minnesota who taught me how to read with an analytical skill that helped me beat the stereotype and taught me that I don't have to be that way.

I live today with many of the teachings that were learned as a result of the readings in your classroom. I live with humility, awareness, vocabulary, and understanding. I could go on but this is an email, not a dissertation. Thank you. God bless. And if it means anything to you– you made a difference in my life and I thank you for igniting my stale mind.

R. M.

Ten *years!* And to be called, blessedly and openly and factually, "a white guy from Minnesota"! What a wonderfully open and honest tag, and what a wonderful piece of mail to get, as any devoted instructor, or coach, or mentor knows very, very well. I faintly remembered R. M.'s name, though I remembered nothing else about him. So I opened my bottom left desk drawer and, from the darkness in the very back, drew out all of my old grade books. It turned out that "about the past 10 years" was actually eleven years. And it also turned out that R. M. hadn't passed the course. He'd gotten an "F."

I was crushed to think of it, and sorry. But then I re-read the email he'd sent, and then I read it yet again. It was a strong letter, and, even more, it was a confident one. And so, taking heart, I concluded that even though R. M. may have failed the course, the course, thank god, had not failed *him*. And, thank god again, he'd wanted to let me know about it.

---

[1] Although in the case of *Beloved* I'm a follower of the views of Stanley Crouch in his "Aunt Medea," from all the way back in 1987 (*Notes of a Hanging Judge: Essays and Reviews 1979-1989* [Oxford University Press, 1990]).

[2] A very rough number, derived by multiplying the number of class meetings in each semester (28) by the number of semesters (70). Assuming that a person taught four courses each semester, the total of classes met over thirty-five years would be 7840.

[3] Again, see Stanley Crouch (footnote, p. xiii).

[4] In truth, this old custom was a secret delight to me back then, in 1959, since it was rare but incontrovertible evidence that I had at last managed to leave high school behind.

Day One

Assignment:
Be in class with your copy of the *Iliad*[1]

Usually, we took up Homer in the fall semester, when late summer still hung dreamily outside the windows. Because I've always found it a dullish business to hear very much about a book before reading it–like hearing gossip about someone you haven't met–I preferred to begin a new work whenever possible simply by reading it, a bit like beginning a swim by jumping in.

Very few of my students had read Homer, some had scarcely heard of him, and almost none were sure when the *Iliad* dated from. I allowed that much–a rough dating of the poem–to precede a reading of the first lines. Our working-determination was that Homer had been active circa 850 B.C.,[2] and that therefore the pool we were about to take a swim in was drawing close to being three thousand years old.

Why lose still more time, then, by hesitating to jump in? So we came to the first seven lines of the *Iliad*, translated by the famous and, to my view, great Richmond Lattimore.[3] Thus:

> Sing, goddess, the anger of Peleus' son Achilleus
>
> and its devastation, which put pains thousandfold upon the Achaians,
>
> hurled in their multitudes to the house of Hades strong souls
>
> of heroes, but gave their bodies to be the delicate feasting
>
> of dogs, of all birds, and the will of Zeus was accomplished
>
> since that time when first there stood in division of conflict
>
> Atreus' son the lord of men and brilliant Achilleus. (I, 1-7)

There's much more to talk about in just these few lines than can easily be folded into a single class period if even the least bit of that time is wasted. For that reason, let me mention a few more matters that we'll skip—for now. One of these is the "story"[4] of the *Iliad*. As for that, all a reader need know right now is that the *Iliad* takes place in Troy[5] and that it's set in the tenth and last year of the Trojan War (more later); that its four chief characters are the following: 1) Agamemnon, great warrior and commander-in-chief of the allied Greek forces; 2) Priam, aged king of the walled city of Troy, too old to fight; 3) Hektor, a son of Priam and the greatest of all the Trojan warriors; 4) and the hot-tempered Achilleus, greatest of all the fighters on the Greek, or Achaian, side.

Yes, I know that there are lots of other characters—top among them Helen and Paris—but let's not talk about them now. It will be much more fun if we do it later, particularly when we get to Book Six[6] of the poem. Meanwhile, though, here's a tip: In the back of the book, Lattimore has provided a convenient glossary of every character-name and every place-name in the poem. If you want to know *right now* who Helen was, or who Paris was, just flip to the back and look each up in the glossary. Not only will you find who or what they are, but you'll find out how to pronounce their names.[7]

But let's get back to those seven lines. They raise a good many interesting questions.

Why, for example, is the first word of the poem "sing," instead of, say, "talk about" or "tell" or "narrate" or "reveal" or "repeat"? And, for that matter, why is the second word of the poem "goddess"?

Straightaway, we get into interesting matters. Who that "goddess" is or what Homer may think of her, let's take up later. But we do know that "sing" is absolutely the right choice of word for Homeric epics, since they were, in fact, not read, but instead they were sung. Everyone knows the words "rhapsodic" and "rhapsody," but not everyone may know that those words all come from the Greek word "rhapsode," which is the word designating a certain kind of professional in antiquity: Namely, a person who memorized the great epics, then went around to the homes of the rich or noble and sang the poems for after-dinner entertainment, accompanying himself on the lute, all of this in exchange for food, money, or hospitality.

What a thought! Just try imagining your way back almost three thousand years, and then imagine an after-dinner scene in some nobleman's house, how incredibly quiet everything would be—no cars, no planes, no radios, no stereos, no highways, dynamos, turbines, engines, fans—and what the sound of it would be like as the rhapsode, amid all that surrounding vastness of night-time silence, began plucking at the lute and singing—well, singing perhaps the first seven lines of the Iliad, and then after those lines, the remainder of the poem's 15,693[8] lines, though hardly all of them in one night, god knows, and maybe not even all of them at just *one* nobleman's house before time came for him to be moving on.

It might well be, too, that an audience would request the singing just of a favorite *part* of the poem for a night's entertainment—like Book VI, with its fine psychological close-up of Helen, or maybe the comical part of Book XIV, where Hera borrows Aphrodite's "magic" waist-scarf so as to seduce Zeus, who, like all men, falls asleep right after love-making, thus providing Hera the opportunity she wanted all along–to change the course of the war so it would go *her* way rather than her husband's way.

Amazing as it seems to us, none of all this was written down–not by Homer and not by anyone else, at least not until a good length of time after Homer. The poems were composed in the oral tradition rather than the written, or, more accurately, in the "oral-formulaic" tradition, though, again, let's let that subject wait a minute or two before we say more about it.

So Homer, not writing anything down, composed the epics orally, while the rhapsodes memorized them and sang them aloud for their life's work. It wasn't until later that the idea of writing them down occurred to anyone–or, for that matter, became possible. The novels of Mary Renault offer a wonderful way to learn about both Greek antiquity and mythology, and on this particular subject–of memorization as opposed to the writing down of literature–*The Praise Singer* (1978) is especially apt. That novel is about the poet Simonides (556-468 BC), who recites the Homeric songs for kings–until writing replaces the oral tradition. Believe it or not, according to Mary Renault's treatment of the subject, figures like Simonides were strongly opposed to the writing down of the epics, or of any other literary works. But opposed *why*? Well, for one thing, it would mean a loss of work for Simonides. But, much more important, he and others were desperately afraid that if the poems weren't memorized, they'd far more certainly be lost. Paper–or papyrus–after all, was far more fragile, more subject to loss or destruction or ruin by fire or water or a multitude of other dangers than were things that could be stored in the powerful security of living human memory.

And maybe he had a point. If Simonides had had his way, possibly we'd still have *all* the plays of Aeschylus, Sophocles, and Euripides, or even the second part of Aristotle's *Poetics*, the lost part on comedy.[9] But, it hardly need be said, there's no going back now.[10]

●

And here we are, already almost out of a class-worth's of time, and how far have we gotten through those seven opening lines? We've covered the first word, "Sing." Better get moving.

Let's leave the "goddess" until later–it will be more fun to talk about her when, very soon, we'll meet Athene and see a goddess actually at work. In the case of the first line, I myself, personally, very much doubt–doubt completely, in fact–that Homer believed literally that a divine muse was necessary as help for him to compose his poem. But nevertheless he goes through the motions of observing what was once almost certainly a belief but that in his own mind has become a literary convention, not altogether unlike beginning fairy tales with the phrase "Once upon a time." But don't worry: We'll talk plenty about the gods later, and about how, whether, and in what way Homer "believes in" them.

And the central subject of the poem? Well, there it is, the fourth word–"anger"–in this case the awful anger of Achilleus against his commander Agamemnon in their quarrel over–well, over a girl. We don't have much time right now for synopsizing the story, but a little re-telling may be helpful in getting you started with your own reading.

So. In previous battle, Agamemnon abducted the lovely girl Chryseis as war booty–a risky thing, we quickly learn, since Chryseis' father, Chryses, is a priest of Apollo. In fact, Agamemnon's offense to Chryses, and through Chryses to Apollo, is the cause of the plague that's about to visit the Achaian armies–a plague thought to[11] come by means of the malevolent arrows of Apollo himself, he "who strikes from afar."

Again, let's save the gods for later. The point right now is that Chryses arrives and asks that Agamemnon return Chryseis to him. Urged by his men to comply ("Then all the rest of the Achaians cried out in favor / that the priest be respected and the shining ransom be taken"

[I, 22-23]), Agamemnon refuses, and for nine days the Achaians suffer under the plague. Only after Kalchas the soothsayer points out the cause-and-effect relation between Apollo's anger and the coming of the disease does Agamemnon relent. He agrees to returns Chryseis to her father Chryses, the priest of Apollo, although Agamemnon won't return the girl happily and certainly not without a good deal of anger of his own–in a wonderful scene that we'll look at in detail next time.

But what is this trouble that will make for his anger? It's that Agamemnon remains firm that he alone, leader of all the Achaians, must not be the only major warrior who goes without a woman taken as a prize of war.

In a nutshell, he advances the notion that he be given Briseis, the lovely woman belonging to Achilleus, having been taken by *him* as his own prize of war.

The very thought of losing Briseis to Agamemnon makes Achilleus *really* angry–and more than just angry, as we'll see later. It makes him so crazy that he swears to withdraw from the war, go to his tent, and do no more fighting for the Achaians. Given Achilleus' great superiority over everyone else as a warrior, the devastating effect of his withdrawal might be something like what might have happened if General Eisenhower had stomped off in a huff a couple of days before June 6, 1944, dropping his position as supreme commander and letting the whole gigantic apparatus of D-Day more or less fall apart, ensuring that the Nazis be allowed to maintain complete control of all greater Europe.

And so it is, as we return to our seven lines, that the poem is going to be not just about Achilleus' *anger*, but about the immeasurable pain, devastation, death, and loss his anger will bring to those who continue in the fight, with their–that is, the Greek–side so radically weakened. So it is that the poem will not be just about (the emphases are mine, of course) "the anger of Peleus' son Achilleus," but *also* about "*its devastation,* which put pains thousandfold upon the Achaians,"

> hurled in their multitudes to the house of Hades strong souls
> of heroes, but gave their bodies to be the delicate feasting
> of dogs, of all birds, and the will of Zeus was accomplished
> since that time when first there stood in division of conflict
> Atreus' son the lord of men and brilliant Achilleus. (I, 3-7)

What will Homer conclude, over the length of the epic, *about* this great subject of Achilleus' anger? We'll have to read and find out. But meanwhile, let's take a quick look at something deep inside the book, something relevant to that wonderful phrasing in lines four and five above, about leaving "their bodies to be the delicate feasting / of dogs, of all birds. . . " If any single word stands out in those two half-lines, certainly it's "delicate," isn't it? A curious choice, one might think–or perhaps not. In any case, let's go all the way to Book XXII, "The Death of Hektor,"[12] and, in that book, let's go all the way to line 328 (p. 444). Here, near the end of the poem, Achilleus has re-entered the battle, swearing to seek vengeance for Hektor's having, by this time, slain Patroklos, Achilleus' dearest and closest friend.[13] And, indeed, Achilleus' fierce retribution is successful, as, in these lines, he has succeeded in slaying Hektor, who has only a breath or two of life remaining.

We have a minute or two left ourselves, so let's read enough of the passage to get the context. Achilleus sees the chink in Hektor's armor (actually in Achilleus' own armor, which Patroklos was wearing at the time when Hektor slew him, then stripped and took it), and that's where he aims:

> He was eyeing Hektor's splendid body, to see where it might best
> give way, but all the rest of the skin was held in the armour,
> brazen and splendid, he stripped when he cut down the strength

> of Patroklos;
> yet showed where the collar-bones hold the neck from the shoulders,
> brilliant Achilleus drove the spear as he came on in fury,
> and clean through the soft part of the neck the spearpoint was driven.
> Yet the ash spear heavy with bronze did not sever the windpipe,
> so that Hektor could still make exchange of words spoken.
> But he dropped in the dust, and brilliant Achilleus vaunted[14] above him:
> 'Hektor, surely you thought as you killed Patroklos you would be
> safe, and since I was far away you thought nothing of me,
> o fool, for an avenger was left, far greater than he[15] was,
> behind him and away by the hollow ships. And it was I;
> and I have broken your strength; on you the dogs and the vultures
> shall feed and foully rip you; the Achaians will bury Patroklos.'
> (XXII, 328-336)

We'll return to this passage later, but, for now, let me just ask whether you notice anything curious in these lines, in comparison with our reading of those first seven lines in Book I.

And of course you do. Back there in Book I, the phrase "delicate feasting" described the manner in which dogs "and all birds" ate the flesh of the battlefield dead. Here, on the other hand, most differently, Achilleus says to Hektor that "'on you the dogs and the vultures / shall feed and foully rip you. . .'"

Now, it's perfectly true, as students always hastened to point out, that Achilleus is speaking in a state of high excitement, rage, and fierce vindictiveness. And it may very well be true that Homer chose these words precisely to reflect that emotional state.[16] And yet doesn't there still remain a question, and a serious one? Homer also chose which words to use back in the first seven lines of Book. I, and there he used the words "delicate feasting." If you were asked whether the birds and dogs in the first case would or wouldn't be likely to eat any differently than they'd eat in the *second* case, what would you answer? I mean, aren't dogs dogs, and aren't birds birds? Do they really have different table manners depending on time, place, or occasion? In the wild, is a dog or wolf going to eat one way one time and another way another time?

Certainly, your answer will be no, your reason being that wild animals generally are going to eat dead bodies in precisely the same manner at one time as at another, and they're going to do it whenever they get the chance.

So our great problem can be posed in this question: "Why on earth did Homer ever think it right or proper to use those words 'delicate feasting' in the *first* place?"

And that question can be re-posed in these questions: "Which way *do* wild animals actually eat their meat? Do they eat it "delicately"? Or do they eat it in such a way as to be accurately describable as "foully ripping," or as "mauling and mangling"?

Which is it? Are they "delicate" or are they "foul" and "mangling"?

And here we come to the biggest and greatest question of all, the one that will bring our first hour to an end:

Doesn't Homer know the difference? Aren't good writers—let alone great ones—supposed at the very least to be consistent? And, finally, is the eating performed by these animals *ugly* or is it *pretty*?

We won't answer this question now. But maybe, when we finally do get around to answering it, we'll find that it holds an important key to the essence of Homer and his world.

Day Two

Assignment: *Iliad,* Book I

Well, have you read your assignment? Here's quiz one:

1) In Bk. I, this goddess pulls Achilleus by the hair:

a) Aphrodite b) Thetis c) Hera d) Athene e) Iris

2) When Kalchas the soothsayer explains the cause of the plague, he says it has come:

a) Because Zeus is angry b) Because Ares is angry c) Because Apollo is angry d) Because Aphrodite is angry e) Because a hecatomb is owed to Poseidon

3) When Agamemnon agrees to return his war-prize, Chryseis, to her father, he notes:

a) That, soon, he will need a replacement for her b) That a fierce storm will ensue c) That Poseidon is soon to punish the Achaians by means of an earthquake d) that the army's low morale must be raised e) That the war against the Trojans is in vain

4) Identify which thing happens near the end of Bk. I:

a) Agamemnon weeps b) Odysseus tells the story of how he married Penelope c)

Zeus and Hera have a fierce quarrel d) Achilleus is strongly tempted to slay

Agamemnon right then and there e) His horse falls, and Diomedes breaks a leg

5) When Zeus and Hera begin to quarrel, this god smooths things out:

a) Apollo b) Hephaistos c) Aphrodite d) Poseidon e) Thetis

And now, to work.

With Homer, just as with certain other works or writers–*The Inferno*, for example, or *Hamlet*–there was always more to do, see, and talk about than could be done in the number of class periods allotted for it. Seven meetings of seventy-five minutes each for the *Iliad*, for example, still required leaving things out. In that sense, our cup always ran over–a loss, but better than the cup's never quite being full.

Another logical anomaly–if you'll pardon the solecism–about these classes was that the pace of the discussion never kept up with the pace of the assigned reading–a pace that I strongly urged people to maintain by using the sticks and carrots of regular "reading quizzes." This plan of there being two "paces," one of reading and one of discussion, was both intentional and necessary. Setting out to tackle an exotic, complex, often difficult work like the *Iliad* called for laying a foundation of at least *some* facts and concepts helpful in getting a grip on the whole–not to mention taking some time for out-loud practice in reading the poetry. As a result, there were so many things to do just in starting out that we could easily spend whole meetings, maybe more, talking about Book I alone. Then we would suddenly spring forward to talk about Books III, IV, and VI in little more than a meeting and a half. So the reading-pace *had* to be faster than the discussion-pace.

Few things are less interesting than hearing other people discussing something you know nothing about–particularly when nobody is about to step aside from the excitement in order to fill you in.

For this reason, by day two everyone should have finished reading *all* of Book I. And by day three, *all* of Books III, IV, and VI. And so on.

This may be as good a time as any to say a word about abridgement, since you doubtless noticed that we just skipped Books II and V. I remember getting looks of horror from certain colleagues when they learned that I wasn't teaching the whole of the twenty-four book epic. I've never understood that kind of horror. If my ship docks in Barcelona harbor for twelve hours, I'm going to go ashore–though obviously I won't be able to see all of Barcelona. Does that mean I should stay on the ship and see *none* of the city? Hardly. Besides, not all parts of Barcelona are equal, and some can even be called boring, as with any city. Now, here comes a truth that may seem iconoclastic to some, though it's not–it's simply true. That truth is that the *Iliad*, some parts more than others, can be a pretty slow read. A parallel truth is that the *Iliad*, some parts more than others, can even be–well, can even be sort of boring. Samuel Johnson himself famously said much the same of another epic, Milton's *Paradise Lost*, commenting that it "is one of the books which the reader admires and puts down, and forgets to take up again. None ever wished it longer than it is."[17]

I'd much rather have beginners cut their teeth on the meatiest parts, and, if they become experts later on, then they can read the whole thing–or even if they *don't* become experts, but simply become grown adults with more time for it. Idolatry of the "great books" is a damnable trait, every bit as foolish as any other kind of idolatry. Many conservative writers–along the lines of Roger Kimball, in *Tenured Radicals* (1990)–seem to think that "great books" function as a kind of moral or ethical tonic, as if they actually contain something the way medicine contains something, an ingredient that, if you ingest it, will make you *better*–meaning, in the eyes of the conservatives, morally and ethically better.

I reject this idea entirely. In fact, I find it, beyond its being just plain wrong, actually quite repulsive. Good–or go ahead and say "great"–books, or any other creations in the huge family of the arts, have in them many good things, but those things are not magic and they certainly aren't, in themselves, anodynes of any sort for immorality or badness. A cruel and wretched tyrant can read Homer, Shakespeare, Milton, plus all the holy books on earth and still remain a cruel and wretched tyrant.

It's very likely that we'll return to this subject from time to time as we go along, but for now let's return to the *Iliad*. You'll know for yourself, now that you've finished reading Book One, that it is not in any way in "want of human interest."

How about Agamemnon, whom we might think of as the combined General MacArthur and General Eisenhower of the allied Greeks? Two questions: What kind of stuff is he made of? And what about his behavior: What kind of grades does he get for it?

Chryses has begged for the release of his daughter Chryseis, a release that "all of the rest of the Achaians cried out in favour" of. But the response from Agamemnon? Let's have a look:

> Then all the rest of the Achaians cried out in favour
> that the priest be respected and the shining ransom be taken;
> yet this pleased not the heart of Atreus' son Agamemnon,
> but harshly he drove him away with a strong order upon him:
> 'Never let me find you again, old sir, near our hollow
> ships, neither lingering now nor coming again hereafter,
> for fear your staff and the god's ribbons help you no longer.
> The girl I will not give back; sooner will old age come upon her
> in my own house, in Argos, far from her own land, going
> up and down by the loom and being in my bed as my companion.
> So go now, do not make me angry; so you will be safer.'
> So he spoke, and the old man in terror obeyed him
> And went silently away beside the murmuring sea beach. (I, 22-34)

What actor wouldn't love to deliver Agamemnon's lines here? As a figure, Agamemnon has enormity, stature, authority, all of these being traits both necessary and appropriate in a leader of the kind he is—and, on top of it all, he's also *mad as hell.*

Stand up in your living room, or study, or wherever you may be doing your reading, and try to find just the right way to deliver these hard, powerful words, every one of them one plain syllable only, but strung together with bolts of iron: "The girl I will not give back." Put some space between each syllable as you say it—but not too much space. Too little space will make the line go by too quickly, too much space, too slowly. Try it until you get it right.

You'll know when you've done it just right, because it will be terrifying. And it's all the more terrifying when you realize that Agamemnon doesn't—yet—even think of the state he's in as *being* an angry one. His threat to Chryses is clear, explicit, toweringly authoritative—and effective: "So go now, do not make me angry," he says. And now, think again about just exactly how you'd read the closing six syllables: "so you will be safer."

What he means, of course, is "in that way, you'll be safer. If you get me angry, your life will be worth nothing."

But how does he speak them, those six syllables, "so you will be safer"? Do they soften in their tone after the hard, imperious, cold, iron-like "So go now"? For that matter, is it possible that the middle six syllables ("do not make me angry") begin a transition into a softer tone, and that then the final six ("so you will be safer") conclude the transition, being the softest? Agamemnon is no sissy no matter how you cut it, and whether or not there's a softening in tone as the line of poetry goes from its start to its end, Chryses *remains* "in terror." Him aside, let's look at Agamemnon's psychology as it's hinted at by the line.

At his most imperious and least introspective, Agamemnon says "So go now." Three hard, rock-like syllables. But then—isn't it possible that an element of thoughtfulness enters in? Does Agamemnon *want* to get angry, after all? Certainly not. Isn't it perfectly likely that a memory of himself in a state of true anger has passed through his thoughts, reminding him of how wasteful, dangerous, even destructive it can be for him to fall into the grip of such rage rather than controlling and suppressing it? And–if such a thought really has passed through his mind, isn't it just as possible that his warning to Chryses–"so you will be safer"–is something almost along the lines of an offering or gift, a consideration for Chryses' well-being, possibly even containing a tiny touch of pathos or sympathy or pity–in any case, something *given* to Chryses by the great Agamemnon that wouldn't have *had* to be given?

We're going to see countless examples of this sort of thing–the poetic line that both follows and reveals the living psychological interior of a character–in *Oedipus*, *Hamlet*, Marlowe's *Dr. Faustus*, elsewhere. It's indisputably true that long stretches of the *Iliad*, like long stretches of *Paradise Lost*, can be tedious.[18] But there's also no doubt that Dr. Johnson was just as wrong in saying that "The want of human interest is *always* felt" (my emphasis) in *Paradise Lost* as he would have been had he said the same of the *Iliad*. It's not often that a person gets a chance to correct the great Dr. Johnson, but if we were to advise him simply to change that one adverb–from "always" to "often," say– the ground of his statement would become solid again.

Human interest runs at high tide in Book I of the *Iliad*. Without question, the price is a high one to pay for Agamemnon's saying "The girl I will not give back," for his decision brings nine days of plague as Apollo shoots his arrows first at "the mules and the circling hounds," then "against the men themselves, until "The corpse fires burned everywhere and did not stop burning" (I, 50-52).

Is Agamemnon showing what we might call "good leadership qualities" here? I don't much like that phrase, "leadership qualities," but it's necessary to ask the question anyway. And it's a question whose answer comes with high drama—when Achilleus also enters onto the stage.[19]

Achilleus' entrance, truth be told, is a highly creditable one, since he comes forth initially as a man moved by the waste of the plague-deaths everywhere all around. The text tells us that he's *actually* been impelled by divine will, in response to "a thing put into his mind by the goddess of the white arms, Hera / who had pity upon the Danaans[20] when she saw them dying" (I, 55-56). For the moment, however, let's forget about Hera and give credit to *Achilleus* as the one who has actually felt the pity (more on the goddess-versus-human subject very soon). If you do give Achilleus that credit, then you're in a position to evaluate *his* "leadership qualities" as they are or aren't revealed in his speech.

Here is the speech. Listen to it carefully as you read it, and judge how the words and actions in it portray the actual qualities of the man speaking the words and making the gestures. After you've read it, put down your book and on a sheet of paper write two or three sentences giving your evaluation of Achilleus the man. Well, I can't really make you do that, since we're neither in a real class nor a real classroom. What a good idea for an exercise it would be, though, if only we were!

Achilleus' speech is prefaced by the information that "Nine days up and down the host ranged the god's arrows, / but on the tenth Achilleus called the people to assembly" (I, 53-54).[21] Then Achilleus addresses Agamemnon:

> 'Son of Atreus, I believe now that straggling backwards
> we must make our way home if we can even escape death,
> if fighting now must crush the Achaians and the plague likewise.
> No, come, let us ask some holy man, some prophet,
> even an interpreter of dreams, since a dream also
> comes from Zeus, who can tell why Phoibos Apollo is so angry,

> if for the sake of some vow, some hecatomb[22] he blames us,
>
> if given the fragrant smoke of lambs, of he goats, somehow
>
> he can be made willing to beat the bane aside from us.' (I, 59-67)

What's your verdict? Is Achilleus being reasonable? Is he showing concern for the well-being of the whole? Is his proposal sensible?

I don't know what your written responses might say, but answering my own questions, at this point, I answer yes, yes, and yes. In only a minute, though, things may change.

Kalchas, "Thestor's son, far the best of the bird interpreters," speaks next, but he's too frightened to speak out what he really wants to say—namely that the plague's continuation is Agamemnon's fault for not giving Chryseis back to her father and priest of Apollo, Chryses. In short, Kalchas is afraid of the anger that we've already once seen Agamemnon successfully throttle back, warning Chryses, "do not make me angry." In what's about to happen now—and throughout the remainder of the poem—we've got to keep a certain distinction always in the forefront of our analysis. It's this one: Agamemnon is the leader of the allied Greek forces, the head without question, what we today would probably call the top military commander. Achilleus, like everyone else, is subordinate to the leader. But at the same time Achilleus is without any question whatsoever the greatest *warrior* among the assembled army, greater by far than Agamemnon.

With these facts in mind, read Achilleus' answer to Kalchas's request for protection from the anger that he knows might erupt from Agamemnon. Hold onto your hats. This is going to be fascinating:

> 'Speak, interpreting whatever you know, and fear nothing.
>
> In the name of Apollo beloved of Zeus to whom you, Kalchas,
>
> make your prayers when you interpret the gods' will to the Danaans,
>
> no man so long as I am alive above earth and see daylight

shall lay the weight of his hands on you beside the hollow ships,

not one of all the Danaans, even if you mean Agamemnon,

who now claims to be far the greatest of all the Achaians.' (I, 85-91)

Do you see the enormous trouble that's about to explode? It doesn't lie in Achilleus' guarantee of safety to Kalchas, since Achilleus, as we've said and agreed, is the best and greatest warrior of all. But the bomb ticking away lies elsewhere: It lies in Achilleus' fatal failure, or fatal *refusal*, to accept the true hierarchy within the Greek alliance. He actually has the notion, obviously not well thought through, that *he* ranks as high as Agamemnon does.

But he doesn't. No matter what, he doesn't. Does Achilleus know this? Yes. Does Achilleus accept it? No. And so come out those dreadful two lines, worthy of the super-deceiving intellect of Milton's Satan, the lines that explicitly taunt Agamemnon, and that do so before all the assembled and witnessing armies of the Achaians, all the assembled troops and battalions under Agamemnon's command.

No one will harm you, Achilleus says to Kalchas, "not one of all the Danaans, even if you mean Agamemnon, / who now claims to be far the greatest of all the Achaians."

Here's a job for you. Find the *single word* in those two lines that serve as the trip-wire that is about to unleash all the tragedy, woe, misery, and loss that are to come in the length of the poem that's to follow. When you've found that word, come on back to me. I'll be waiting for you right on the other side of the black dot.

●

Welcome back, and you did good work. But what's the significance of it, that one little word, "claims"?[23] What does it reveal about Achilleus? If we were in a classroom, I'd never answer this question, but I'd ask and ask until someone else answered it. If a student happened to have been in the military and to have had some familiarity with the hierarchic system there, that student might do some psychological detective work about that word "claims" and consider what charge, if there were to be one, Achilleus could be setting himself up to face. He's beginning to sound like a prime candidate, that is to say, for the very serious offense of insubordination.

Once your attention has been drawn to it, you can hardly stop hearing the sarcasm and snide tone in "claims to be far the greatest." You start hearing it even in E. V. Rieu's less biting "Agamemnon, who bears the title of our overlord." In short, Achilleus is revealing a hint of the *jealousy* in his character, the trait that is soon to prove calamitous.

In response, however, Agamemnon says and does nothing. Maybe he didn't notice it (what are the chances of *that*?). Maybe he didn't take it seriously (what are the chances of *that*?) On the other hand, maybe, just maybe, he did hear it, did notice it, did take it seriously—and suppressed any response to it, at least any immediate response. More than possibly, on the other hand, it's going to have a good part to do with the great anger that *is* soon to burst out from him. Chryses wasn't able to make Agamemnon angry. Not even Kalchas is going to make Agamemnon angry. Achilleus is the one who's going to make him angry.

He's already got a good start on it, with that side-swipe of "claims," even before Calchas announces that the real cause of the plague is nothing more nor less than Agamemnon's having "dishonoured" Apollo's priest Chryses by refusing to "give him back his daughter or accept the ransom."

> 'Therefore the archer sent griefs against us and will send them
> still, nor sooner thrust back the shameful plague from the Danaans
> until we give the glancing-eyed girl back to her father
> without price, without ransom, and lead also a blessed hecatomb
> to Chryse [sic]; thus we might propitiate and persuade him.' (I, 94-100)

And now watch out, because we're going to have some really strong poetry to read. To start with, it's only four lines, but ideally you ought to read those four aloud. Whether you do that or not, notice two things: First, notice where the punctuation falls (you're going to find only two pieces of it, not counting the period at the end), and, second, look for something that Lattimore has most shrewdly placed into his translation, one of the most commonplace of devices in century upon century's worth of later poetry, but a device unknown in Homer. See if you can catch it:

> He spoke thus and sat down again, and among them stood up
> Atreus' son the hero wide-ruling Agamemnon
> raging, the heart within filled black to the brim with anger
> from beneath, but his two eyes showed like fire in their blazing. (I, 101-104)

Isn't it wonderful, the punctuation? Lattimore's second line doesn't *end* with "raging," but the word is delayed to the start of the third line–where it's powerfully emphasized by the simple fact of the comma that holds that third line's movement. "Do not make me angry," Agamemnon said earlier. But now he's "raging." Try saying the word aloud, drawing out the vowel to your heart's content before going on with the rest of the line.

And the non-Homeric device that Lattimore so neatly sneaks in? Well, it's the rhyme he uses between "raging" and "blazing," though in such a way that the rhyming words are almost, but not quite, too far apart for the rhyme to be heard. Have another look and listen:

> raging, the heart within filled black to the brim with anger
> from beneath, but his two eyes showed like fire in their blazing.

Artful work! But there's more. The second comma holds back the line's movement just as the first comma did—and for an equally important purpose. The anger comes "from beneath," meaning of course from "the heart" and very center of the great warrior and leader. And what is the next word? A little strange, isn't it, that Lattimore chooses "but" instead of "and"? If the sense is "he burns inside and his eyes blaze," then the connective "and" is clearly the reasonable choice. But what if that *isn't* quite the idea? What if the idea is that Agamemnon's rage, cruelly powerful and coming "from beneath," doesn't show *except* in his eyes?[24]

In other words, what if the idea is that we're going to see Agamemnon control his great rage? It escapes, for now, but only from his eyes. Later, it won't escape at all.

There's a faint touch of the comic here as Agamemnon complains to Kalchas that he's always a "bad-news" prophet[25]—"'Seer of evil: never yet have you told me a good thing. / Always the evil things are dear to your heart to prophesy, / but nothing excellent have you said nor ever accomplished'" (I, 106-108). But there's nothing at all comic, whimsical, or slight in Agamemnon's next move: Showing nobility, showing self-control, *and* showing consideration for the entire allied army instead of only for himself, he agrees to give Chryseis back, however powerfully he wishes he didn't have to:

'Now once more you make divination to the Danaans, argue
forth your reason why he who strikes from afar afflicts them,
because I for the sake of the girl Chryseis would not take
the shining ransom; and indeed I wish greatly to have her
in my own house; since I like her better than Klytaimestra
my own wife, for in truth she is no way inferior,
neither in build nor stature nor wit, not in accomplishment.
Still I am willing to give her back, if such is the best way.
I myself desire that my people be safe, not perish.

Find me then some prize that shall be my own, lest I only
among the Argives go without, since that were unfitting;
you are all witnesses to this thing, that my prize goes elsewhere.'
(I, 109-119)

If we were to rate Agamemnon on a ten-point scale at this point in regard to his "leadership qualities," ten being top and one the bottom, I
know that I myself would be inclined to give him a ten. I've had plenty
of students, on the other hand, who were inclined to mark him down
a few points because of the word "unfitting," their argument being that
the word shows Agamemnon to be concerned more–or only–with
outside appearance rather than with humility and other matters of
true inner significance. But we're reading a story from an ancient world
of royalty and kingship, not a modern story from a world of republi-
can and democratic individualism. Humility *can* be a virtue in Homer's
world, but a king can't function as a king, can't *be* a king, without the
external appurtenances of that role–or without the external appurtenances of that *state of being*.

No one who remembers *King Lear*–of all Shakespeare's plays, the
one set in the most "ancient" time–can forget Lear's great lament
when Goneril and Regan continue stripping him of his retinue, asking why he needs fifty followers, or twenty-five, or ten, until Regan
says "What need one?"

And then follows the great, great speech of Lear's that begins with
"O, reason not the need." (II, iv, 263) It's not a matter of practicality
that's at stake, but it's a matter of *identity*, as Goneril and Regan perfectly well know: What they're doing is stripping their father not of his
belongings but of his kingship. They're stripping him not of things but
of his *meaning*. They're stripping him of his *being* as king.

So, with the help of this small historical adjustment, we can see that
no loss of points befalls Agamemnon for saying that he must have a

war prize, since not to have one "were unfitting."

But, just as in *Lear*–or in *Othello, Macbeth,* or *Hamlet*–there's also someone in the *Iliad* who's evil. The entire great question of good and evil in Homer is a vast, huge, vitally important one, and we'll come back to it in very great depth later on. For the moment, however, let's posit simply–and hypothetically, since it's not wholly or really true– that Achilleus is evil. We'll talk later about his character in its entirety, but for the moment, in order to get moving, let's think of him simply as the catalyst–like Iago in *Othello*–that brings about the woe, loss, sorrow, and "pains thousandfold" in the poem.

And what's wrong with him that makes him "evil" (the quotation marks are to show that we're using the word temporarily and for convenience)?

Well, let's go back to that imaginary or hypothetical court martial. Achilleus, in a word, really is insubordinate. It's perfectly true that as a warrior, he is superior to everyone else in the whole of the Argive army. As a warrior, that is, he is subordinate to no one. But in the matter of being *leader*, he both is and must be subordinate to his commander, Agamemnon. And there's something in the temperament and psychology of Achilleus that makes him unable to endure that truth. He just can't *stand* being subordinate to Agamemnon.

We'll have plenty more to say about Achilleus before we're done, but at this point how can any normal person not wonder why on god's green earth Achilleus didn't just let things be? Why didn't he just let Agamemnon's offer, and Agamemnon's plan, simply go forward? Why didn't he just let it go–the idea being that at some point Agamemnon would need to be provided with a prize?

After all, nothing in Agamemnon's speech pointed even remotely or indirectly, let alone directly, at the notion of Agamemnon taking *Achilleus'* prize, Briseis. Wouldn't the normal impulse or strategy for someone in Achilleus' position simply be to acknowledge what's been said, retire into the background, and maintain a low profile?

Now, part of what's involved here is that Homer is not and was not writing an original story. He could no more alter the central and essential elements of that story—which every single person in the audience of every rhapsode in every house of every nobleman already knew in every detail—than, say, Sophocles could alter the essential elements of his *Oedipus the King*—that is, that Oedipus killed his own father and married his own mother.

So it was out of the question that there *not* be a serious, divisive, and devastating quarrel between Agamemnon and Achilleus. This was the central element of the story that came down to Homer and that Homer now set out to commit to verse of his own kind.

But Homer is an extraordinarily sophisticated thinker, observer, and poet. As such, he's not about to let the story control *him* to any degree greater than absolutely necessary, but within its necessary confines he will, in a great number of ways, leave his various marks of control over *it*. If that hadn't been the case, if there hadn't been that kind of inter-action between Homer the poet and the material he received, if he had been *only* a passive recorder of the story as it already existed and was known—well, it's a near-certainty that we wouldn't be reading the *Iliad* now. The poem would never have been elevated to the heights of appreciation that it was and has been elevated to. It would never, for Greeks, say, of the sixth and fifth centuries, have become akin to scripture. And—from our own view most important—it would far less likely have survived and come down to us.

In any case, in reading what we call Homer, there's no question but that we're reading "inherited" stories fixed and known long before the poet's own life. So, while it's true that we're reading those previously "fixed" stories, it's equally true that we're also reading the work of Homer the poet, who added to the story near-countless means and ways of making it a greater and more amazing thing once it left his hand than it was when it *came* to him.

Homer, among other things, has interwoven into the story the presence of enormous elements of human *psychology* that's true, real, suggestive, detailed, and convincing. We'll soon see this aspect of Homer's art brilliantly–and wrenchingly–displayed in the portrayals of Andromache and Helen, in Book Six. Right now, though, we've got to look at the same sort of thing in the case of Achilleus.

•

We left off at the point where Agamemnon had finished saying something the equivalent of all right, then, for the good of everyone he'd agree to do it–he'd give Chryseis back to her father in order to end the Apollonian plague.

Do you think it might occur to a person to ask why the story doesn't just end there? Well, we know it *can't* end there–since that's not the way it came down to Homer. The tradition was that Achilleus and Agamemnon had an enormous quarrel, Achilleus became so angry that he withdrew from the fighting and sulked in his tent while the Achaians, lacking their greatest weapon of war–Achilleus himself– were threatened increasingly by the now-superior Trojan power that forced the Achaians at one point all the way back to their own wooden ships, threatening to set fire to every last one of them.

That's the story, but what's the motive for it? What's the catalyst? In other words, why doesn't Achilleus simply leave well enough alone in regard to the Chryseis problem, since Agamemnon, after all, has made no mention directly of Achilleus, nor has he in any way whatsoever pointed–at least not directly–toward Briseis or toward taking her *from* Achilleus. In fact, he's made no specific mention of *any*one, none of the other great warriors–not Odysseus, Aias, Elphenor, Menelaos, Sarpedon, Diomedes or any other. All he's done is say he wants there to be found "some prize that shall be my own, lest I only / among the Argives go without, since that were unfitting."

Nevertheless, in what would seem a complete absence of rational motive, Achilleus, instead of fading unnoticed into the background, loses not a second in pushing himself forward to the center of everyone's attention, not least Agamemnon's.

In the very next line but one after Agamemnon's difficult but generous concession, Achilleus begins:

> Then in answer again spoke brilliant swift-footed Achilleus:
> 'Son of Atreus, most lordly, greediest for gain of all men,
> how shall the great-hearted Achaians give you a prize now?
> There is no great store of things lying about that I know of.
> But what we took from the cities by storm has been distributed;
> it is unbecoming for the people to call back things once given.
> No, for the present give the girl back to the god; we Achaians
> thrice and four times over will repay you, if ever Zeus gives
> into our hands the strong-walled citadel of Troy to be plundered.'
> (I, 121-129)

What has Achilleus done? It's the equivalent of throwing a can of gasoline onto a bed of charcoal embers. He even throws Agamemnon's "unfitting" back at him with his own not-so-subtle taunt in the word "unbecoming." And the effect, hardly surprising, is that Agamemnon positively erupts into towering flames of rage:

> Then in answer again spoke powerful Agamemnon:
> 'Not that way, good fighter though you be, godlike Achilleus,'
> strive to cheat, for you will not deceive, you will not persuade me.
> What do you want? To keep your own prize and have me sit here
> lacking one? Are you ordering me to give this girl back?" (I, 130-134)

Try reading those three sentences–questions–out loud in order to follow the psychology of them the way we did earlier. They're important not only for the way they show Agamemnon's lightning-fast insight into what he now *knows* is a serious and rapidly worsening problem. But they're important also for the way they suggest Agamemnon's understanding of what command actually is *and* of his own readiness and suitability for it.

The *sequence* of Agamemnon's questions is important as well. It dramatizes his quickness of insight (as said), his procedural correctness, and his military accuracy–with the enormously important result of letting us see *exemplified* Agamemnon's obvious superiority, as a commander, to Achilleus. But the sequence does something else, too, equally important for our reading and understanding of the entire poem. Thanks to Agamemnon, that is, we finally approach an answer to the all-important question–what is it that's really wrong with Achilleus?

"What do you *want*?" Emphasizing the verb this way helps reveal the remarkable insight that Agamemnon has had: That is, the insight that Achilleus' inexplicable and unreasonable behavior suggests something worse–that there's something inexplicable and unreasonable inside of Achilleus, and that that something may be both unreachable and uncontrollable. In the same way it happened in Agamemnon's earlier "do not make me angry" speech, in the second step of *this* trio of questions something new comes into or passes through Agamemnon's mind, directing him to a new conclusion. All *we* are able to hear is a repetition of the situation as we already know it, "To keep your own prize and have me sit here / lacking one?" But then, just as in the earlier example, comes a new–and in this case piercingly insightful–understanding: "Are you *ordering* me to give this girl back?"

I've emphasized the verb again, and with good reason. This third question shows that Agamemnon has put his finger on exactly what the real trouble is. The trouble is that Achilleus really *is* insubordinate.

He's refusing to acknowledge the difference in leadership rank between himself and Agamemnon.

It's impossible to know whether in some part of his own mind Achilleus does understand that Agamemnon really is his military superior, commander, and king. It hardly matters, because the trouble with Achilleus is that in all *other* parts of himself, in his deepest warrior's heart, in the entirety of his huge spirit, in his uncontainable self-assurance and vanity, in the ineluctable elements within him that give him his towering courage and his unflagging and unparalleled powers in warfare–in every one of *those* parts of himself, of himself as a fighter, he really is Agamemnon's–and everyone else's–superior. Insofar as his self-definition is guided by these admittedly unparalleled parts of himself, the idea of Agamemnon *even so* remaining his superior –in leadership, in military rank–feels intolerable to him. Agamemnon remaining his boss drives Achilleus–over the edge? to a state of imbalance? nuts?

Look at the absurd way he brings everything crashing down around his own ears–even after Agamemnon deliberately and carefully leaves him numerous open doors and escape-hatches that he *could* use to escape being cornered.

Let's pick up where we left off and watch Agamemnon at his work of retaining the dignity and prerogative of command while at the same time offering careful diplomacy–only to have it rejected out of hand by the problem-man Achilleus.

"Either the great-hearted Achaians shall give me a new prize / chosen according to my desire to atone for the girl lost, / or else if they will not give me one I myself shall take her"–and now look very closely. Of *course* Agamemnon is angry at Achilleus, and that's why the first "girl" he mentions is Briseis, Achilleus' prize–"or else if they will not give me one I myself shall take her, / your own prize"–but then notice the lightning speed of Agamemnon's instinct to temper threat with diplomacy, deflecting the threat away from Achilleus and toward others—"or that of Aias, or that of Odysseus, / going myself in person and he whom I visit will be bitter." (I, 135-139)

Following this, Agamemnon's tour de force ends with his revealing himself not only to have overcome his *own* anger with complete success but also to have remained fully capable of reassuming all the details of command just as if nothing untoward had happened. We can continue this discussion later, he says. But right now we have work to do, and here's how we're going to do it.

> Still, these are things we shall deliberate again hereafter.
> Come, now, we must haul a black ship down to the bright sea,
> and assemble rowers enough for it, and put on board it
> the hecatomb, and the girl herself, Chryseis of the fair cheeks,
> and let there be one responsible man in charge of her,
> either Aias or Idomeneus or brilliant Odysseus,
> or you yourself, son of Peleus, most terrifying of all men,
> to reconcile by accomplishing sacrifice the archer.' (I, 140-147)

How eager Agamemnon is to offer grounds for peace to Achilleus! Not only does he suggest that Achilleus, "son of Peleus," might be suitable as the man responsible for handling the return of Chryseis, but he chooses to include the flattering epithet (more on epithets later) for Achilleus, "most terrifying of all men."

But does Agamemnon's diplomatic effort do the least bit of good? Inside Achilleus, no matter what his greatness as a warrior, there resides something awful: There's something in him of the spoiled brat, the thug, or the bully. There's something in him of the *punk*.

No amount of reaching out to him on Agamemnon's part is going to do any good now. Agamemnon's generosity and diplomacy are lost on the punk,[26] who responds to Agamemnon's courtesies and dignities with–well, with name-calling, slander, and gutter-talk:

> 'O wrapped in shamelessness, with your mind forever on profit,
> how shall any one of the Achaians readily obey you
> either to go on a journey or to fight men strong in battle? (I, 149-151)

Pardon me? That first line is the pot calling the kettle black. And the second and third are plainly a non sequitur. Let's go on:

> 'I for my part did not come here for the sake of the Trojan
> spearmen to fight against them, since to me they have done nothing.
> Never yet have they driven away my cattle or my horses,
> never in Phthia where the soil is rich and men grow great did they
> spoil my harvest, since indeed there is much that lies between us,
> the shadowy mountains and the echoing sea; but for your sake,
> o great shamelessness, we followed, to do you favour,
> you with the dog's eyes, to win your honour and Menelaos'
> from the Trojans.' (I, 152-160)

Could we possibly ask for *logic* from Achilleus? That he's now whining, and will whine again in a moment, diminishes him tremendously, as do his gutter epithets, "o great shamelessness" and "you with the dog's eyes." The Trojans have never harmed *him*, he says–and then admits that it's because he and they are separated by mountain and sea. Lucky for him. Menelaos wasn't so lucky.

Paranoia is also mixed in to the psychology of any quick-to-take-offense punk, and Achilleus is no exception. His next line is patently false on the one hand, while on the other it shows the self-pity that's so large a part of his particular brand of sullenness and paranoia:

> 'And now my prize you threaten in person to strip from me. . .' (I, 161)

"My prize"? Everyone knows that that's a falsehood, at worst, and a half truth, at best. Agamemnon said he would take "your own prize, *or* that of Aias, *or* that of Odysseus"–a fact conveniently forgotten by the same Achilleus who accuses *Agamemnon* of poor memory ("You forget all this or else you care nothing" [160]). But elsewhere Achilleus' memory could not be sharper when he clearly remembers, and echoes, Agamemnon's words "going myself *in person*."

Now comes more whining–Agamemnon always gets the best of *everything* (could it be because he's king?)–followed by the universal last resort of all small-minded and beyond-reach-of-reason-or-kindness punks. That last resort? Picking up your marbles and stomping off with them, never to play again.

> 'And now my prize you threaten in person to strip from me,
> for whom I laboured much, the gift of the sons of the Achaians.
> Never, when the Achaians sack some well-founded citadel
> of the Trojans, do I have a prize that is equal to your prize.
> Always the great part of the painful fighting is the work of
> my hands; but when the time comes to distribute the booty
> yours is far the greater reward, and I with some small thing
> yet dear to me go back to my ships when I am weary with fighting.
> Now I am returning to Phthia, since it is much better
> to go home again with my curved ships, and I am minded no longer
> to stay here dishonoured and pile up your wealth and your luxury.'
> (I, 161-171)

We have just enough time to look at Agamemnon's reply–and its result. To save some of that time, I'll italicize the crucially important phrases and lines. (If we were in a "real" situation, after all–assuming that classrooms *are* real–tone of voice and manner of delivery would do the job in a trice.)

Then answered him in turn the lord of men Agamemnon:
'Run away by all means if your heart drives you. I will not
entreat you to stay here for my sake. There are others with me
who will do me honour, and above all Zeus of the counsels.
To me you are the most hateful of all the kings whom the gods love.
Forever quarrelling is dear to your heart, and wars and battles;
and if you are very strong indeed, that is a god's gift.
Go home then with your own ships and your own companions,
be king over the Myrmidons. *I care nothing about you.*
I take no account of your anger. But here is my threat to you.
Even as Phoibos Apollo is taking away my Chryseis.
I shall convey her back in my own ship, with my own
followers; but I shall take the fair-cheeked Briseis,
your prize, I myself going to your shelter, *that you may learn well*
how much greater I am than you, and another man may shrink back
from likening himself to me and contending against me.' (I, 172-187)

A fair speech, and a just one? Yes. The speech of a commander? Yes.
A speech with anger in it, but anger controlled by the man feeling it?
Yes. A speech serving not only a military purpose but here a necessary
military purpose–that of maintaining order through chain of command? Yes.

If the entire quarrel as we've looked at it so far were a debate, would
Agamemnon have won it, or would Achilleus have won it? Answer:
Agamemnon, hands down.

And what, then, can we expect of Achilleus in response to this defeat? Let's have a look, then be done for the day.

So he spoke. And the anger came on Peleus' son, and within
his shaggy breast the heart was divided two ways, pondering
whether to draw from beside his thigh the sharp sword, driving

away all those who stood between and kill the son of Atreus,

or else to check the spleen within and keep down his anger.

(I, 188-192)

Good god! Is it conceivable? Is Achilleus actually going to *murder* the commander in chief of the Achaian armies? Just like that, then and there, right in front of all the assembled warriors?

Well, we're out of time. Quiz next class on Books III and IV.

Day Three

Assignment: *Iliad,* Books III and IV

Have you read your assignment? Here's quiz two:

1) In Bk. III, a truce is declared so that:

a) Agamemnon and Hektor can discuss terms for peace   b) Diomedes and Ajax can have a single duel   c) Helen can visit the Achaian camp   d) Paris and Menelaos can fight a single duel   e) Achilleus can visit the city of Troy as an ambassador

2) When Iris comes down to visit Helen early in Bk. III, Helen is:

a) weeping in her bedroom   b) weaving a great tapestry that shows the events of the war   c) making love with Alexandros   d) writing a poem   e) praying to Hera

3) Identify which is most directly important to the action in Bk. III:

a) a severed Achilles tendon   b) an evil omen from the gods   c) a broken chin strap   d) a ship's torn sails   e) a pair of golden sandals

4) Identify which thing happens at the end of Bk. III:

a) Paris gets his bleeding wounds bandaged   b) Paris and Helen go to bed and make love   c) Achilleus gets Briseis back from Agamemnon   d) Zeus and Hera have another quarrel   e) Odysseus insults Priam

5) In Bk. IV, Pandaros breaks the truce by shooting an arrow at Menelaos. The result is that:

a) Menelaos dies   b) Pandaros misses   c) Helen comes running onto the battlefield to embrace the wounded Menelaos   d) Pandaros misses Menelaos but kills Odysseus e) Menelaos is wounded, but only slightly, since Athene deflects the arrow so it won't hurt him badly

Well, Agamemnon is still alive, and he seems in good health, not having gotten murdered by a seething Achilleus. And what does that mean for us? It means that it's time to talk a little bit about the gods.

You remember that when we left Achilleus, he was on a razor's edge of indecision about whether to slay Agamemnon outright or "to check the spleen within and keep down his anger."

And we know what happened–although, on the other hand, maybe we *don't* know what happened.

Here's something for people to try–if they're willing. It would be very easy, if we were back in that "real" classroom, to make it a requirement, but here in *this* "real" situation, it's going to have to be voluntary. In the classroom, I'd ask everyone to take a minute–literally, just sixty seconds–to write on a piece of paper a *very* brief explanation of what actually happened in order to resolve the question of whether Achilleus would murder Agamemnon then and there–or whether he wouldn't.

I'll put another small black circle on the page. Meet me on the far side of it as soon as you've written down your answer.

●

Okay. And hello again. Now, here's my next question: Did you, by any chance, write down anything along the lines that Hera, "who loved both men equally," sent Athene "down," and Athene thereupon used her divine powers to prevent Achilleus from slaying Agamemnon?

There's nothing really *wrong* with that answer, or any generally equivalent answer—that is, "The gods intervened and resolved Achilleus' indecision," or "The gods intervened and caused Achilleus not to slay Agamemnon."

Nothing wrong, that is, except that if you *did* give an answer like either of those, and if you *also* choose to be, or want to be, a person who lives a life that's as consistent intellectually as it possibly can be—well, if those two things are both true, then the consequence is that you must also be a believer in and worshipper of the literal Hera, Athene, Apollo, Zeus, et al.

What I'm about to say next may seem impolite, bad-mannered, or even cruel. But if you *did* answer that "the gods did it" and if you *don't* pray every night or every morning to the gods of Greek antiquity—and if you don't do so for the very good reason that you don't believe in them—well, then, you're being one of three things, and maybe all: foolish, self-deceiving, or hypocritical.

If I've hurt your feelings, I apologize! I *do*! That is, I apologize for having stung you or for having been mean, if indeed I did or was or seemed to be. But I won't—can't—apologize for the *reason* I said what I did.

Here's why. What we're talking about is what level we hope or plan to read the *Iliad* on. As far as the gods are concerned, I myself choose to read it *not* on the literal level.

Some reasoning: To be divine, after all, is to be eternal, is it not? That gods don't die while mortals do is one of the central tenets and truths about each. That's why Achilleus' father, Peleus, being a mere mortal, will die, while the divine Thetis, Achilleus' *mother*, never will. Because he's only a mixture of the two—the same as Vergil's Aeneas, centuries later (Aeneas had Aphrodite for mother but the mortal Anchises for father)—Achilleus will die, like Peleus, and won't live forever, like Thetis.

So if gods are eternal and they existed *then*, where are they now? If they're really eternal, they've still *got* to be existing *now*.

A corollary matter. If a person does maintain that Hera and Athene "did it," in the case of "making" Achilleus' decision not to slay Agamemnon, then Hera and Athena must indeed be divine, with divine and magic-like powers, and therefore they must also be, logically, eternal. What that means, again, is that they must be still around. And what that means, again, is—that, well, you'd better get busy praying to them like gangbusters, maybe even arranging to offer them a hecatomb tonight before dinner—in short, you'd better get busy doing whatever it takes to be sure of remaining on their good side.

Back in my own generation, usually sometime around junior high, we were introduced to "Greek mythology" by means of hearing or reading many of the old stories in conventional re-tellings, though by no means were we introduced to all of them. We learned about the Judgment of Paris, sort of, but not about Leda and the Swan, that being the rape of mortal Leda by Zeus, who had taken the form of the great bird, a union wherefrom came both Helen *and* Clytemnestra.[27] We learned that Hermes was swift and Heracles strong—but not that Cronus, on the advice of his mother, cut off the genitals of his father and threw them into the sea, not to mention that "From the genital organs, as they gathered foam (*aphros*) in the sea, was born Aphrodite."[28]

In other words, we learned our mythology in simplified form, seldom in depth, and certainly not in the darkness to which it so often can and does lead—the darkness of human psychology. And I guess there's little wrong with those limitations for twelve- or thirteen-year-old kids. But habits stick, and it's always alarming to me to see readers *in adulthood* clinging with the passivity of movie-goers to literal interpretations of the gods and their actions in poems like the *Iliad* and the *Odyssey*, or in dramas like *Oedipus the King*.

Here's another question that's a favorite of mine at this point in a discussion of this sort. Is it too soon for another round black spot on the page, so we can meet on the other side of it after you write your answer?

I'm sure not. So, again, use as few or as many words as you like, so long as you take no more than a minute to do it, maybe even much less. The question is this: Suppose that by some trick of magic, every last one of the gods and goddesses was removed from the *Iliad*, was made to disappear entirely from the story, as if none of them had ever been. What effect would their absence have on the action and the events of the poem?

•

I wish I could read, or hear, your answers. To my way of thinking, one perfectly acceptable though undetailed answer would be, "Nothing." Another would be, "The atmosphere and coloring would be thinner, but the events wouldn't change." Or yet another would be, "Homer would have lots fewer stories-within-stories, much less colorful background, and many fewer story devices, but the essential and central events of the poem would be unchanged because the human beings in it would be unchanged."

I expect I'll never know what your own answer may have been, but on the other hand you could always write or email me and let me know.

But what do you think of the reasoning? More questions can help lead to answers. Which came first, lightning and thunder or Zeus? Which came first, ocean waves and storms, or Poseidon? Which came first, the earth, or Rhea?

In each and every case, the answer is obvious. Things happen first. And then stories grow up *about* those things.

And now we've got to move on to the next, and the more difficult, question—and that's the question of the extent to which there ever was *literal* belief in the stories. I suppose few would doubt that *very* long ago, long before the flowing-haired Achaians swept down from the north and pushed the earlier tribes off mainland Greece and across the Aegean Sea to Ionia (where it's thought that Homer lived), Ionia being present-day Turkey (where you can visit the site of ancient Troy itself,[29] with its wide, long, low plain–the plain of battle–leading down toward the edge of the sea where the Achaians' wooden ships were pulled up)–in any case, I suppose few would doubt that way, *way* back, there must certainly have been literal belief in the deities, however different those may have been in concept, shape, character, or form from the highly anthropomorphized versions that have come down to us–or, for that matter, that had come down to Homer and *his* era.

Who isn't able to imagine a shepherd in 2,000 B.C., cowering in a hillside cave during a crackling, fierce, wind-whipping thunderstorm who *wouldn't* believe literally that a Zeus-like god was waving his wand across the skies?

But in contrast to *that* early date, Homer is positively modern. I myself am unable to believe that Homer–not necessarily his characters, but *Homer*–saw the gods as other than inherited story-telling material, not as beings to be taken as literally "true." In Homer, for example, the gods don't even possess absolute powers of causation. The towering Zeus himself, as we'll see clearly in Books XX and XXII, lacks powers sufficient to let him even determine single-handedly the outcome of events. [30]

But let's return to Book I and Achilleus' struggle with himself whether to slay Agamemnon or not. We left him wondering whether he was going to kill Agamemnon then and there, or whether he was going "to check the spleen within and keep down his anger."

Here is the rescue-descent of Athene:

> Now as he weighed in mind and spirit these two courses
> and was drawing from its scabbard the great sword, Athene descended

from the sky. For Hera the goddess of the white arms sent her,

who loved both men equally in her heart and cared for them.

The goddess standing behind Peleus' son caught him by the fair hair,

Appearing to him only, for no man of the others saw her.

Achilleus in amazement turned about, and straightway

knew Pallas Athene and the terrible eyes shining.

He uttered winged words and addressed her: "Why have you come now,

o child of Zeus of the aegis, once more? Is it that you may see

the outrageousness of the son of Atreus Agamemnon?

Yet will I tell you this thing, and I think it shall be accomplished.

By such acts of arrogance he may even lose his own life.' (I, 193-205)

Quite a girl, isn't she, this Athene! She "descended / from the sky" and landed, I'm sure, lightly on her feet, managing to remain invisible to all but Achilleus–whom she rather sexily grabbed from behind "by the fair hair." Athletic, tricky, coquettish, and knock-out gorgeous on top of it all.

It's easy to make fun like this, but it's also, at least to my way of thinking, absolutely essential to do it–that is, *if* a person wants to read Homer in a way that's both as deep as possible and as *real*, a word that's found its way into the title I've given this section of our literary tour: *If*, that is, a person wants to read Homer in a way at all commensurate with a consciousness of the subtlety, profundity, sophistication, humanity, compassion, and poetic richness of Homer the poet and writer himself.

To me, it's inconceivable that a figure, like Homer, of such absolutely extraordinary humanism, intellectual sophistication, sense of history, and ability to see and understand every element of human nature, temperament, and character–to me it's inconceivable that a figure of this kind would also "believe"–literally–in the cast of hyper-anthropomorphized divinities that populate so much of the *Iliad*.

I'll go further. It's inconceivable to me that the poet Homer believed in any kind of superior being whatsoever.

That, I know, is a statement that'll take some talking about–and talking about it is going to have to wait a while, possibly all the way until the end of our discussion.

And maybe by then, in fact, the matter will be so obvious that it won't even need discussing.

Either way, one more point needs touching on before we analyze Athene's visit to Achilleus in detail: Namely, that it's also inconceivable to me, as it must be to everyone, that Homer the poet would ever choose or ever *could* choose to eliminate the presence of the gods from the *Iliad*. The gods come along with all the other elements of the story as an inherited part of the whole. Homer could no more leave the gods out and still please his listeners than he could change the end of the story, say, by having Hektor slay Achilleus instead of the other way around. That's not the way it *goes*.

By and large, changes in the story aren't allowed, a matter we'll also talk about more later. But just imagine the loss if the gods weren't "in" the *Iliad*. They're fun, they're colorful, they bring along with them endless great old stories that everyone wants to hear again or at least hear *mention* of again, and they're very often most, most sweet and charming as well as, sometimes, a real laugh riot. I'm reminded of Falstaff's lines in *Henry IV, Part One*, in the play-within-the-play, when the drunk Falstaff is pretending to be Prince Hal's father, Henry IV, and is urging Hal not to end his friendship with the aging and fat old knight, namely, Falstaff himself:

> No, my good lord; banish Peto, banish Bardolph, banish Poins: but
> for sweet Jack Falstaff, kind Jack Falstaff, true Jack Falstaff, valiant
> Jack Falstaff, and therefore more valiant, being, as he is, old Jack Fal-
> staff, banish not him thy Harry's company, banish not him thy

Harry's company: banish plump Jack, and banish all the world.
(II, iv, 450-456)

Banish the colorful, wonderful, amusing, and fascinating gods, and banish all the world.

•

And yet, if they're not real, if they're not literally "true," if they're not "believed" in–then what *are* they?

Well, they're us. They're human beings. Let's look into just how this can be so.

Nobody will miss the stand-out word when Achilleus sees Athene's "*terrible* eyes shining" any more than they'll fail to notice the same word in Book III when the elders sitting gathered with Priam on the wall of the city, seeing Helen approach, murmur to one another that "*Terrible* is the likeness of her face to immortal goddesses" (III, 158).

Lattimore is using the word in a much older way than we use it now. For us, "terrible" no longer means much more than "bad" or "awful," or "severe," as in "a terrible movie" or "a terrible headache." But Lattimore means, far more literally, that Athene's eyes were in fact capable of inspiring terror. E. V. Rieu makes a similar choice, in saying that Achilleus "recognized Pallas Athene at once–so terrible was the brilliance of her eyes" (p. 28).

Few women whom I know would be pleased if I were to say to them, "You look terrible." On the other hand, it would be different if I were to say, "You look so astonishingly wonderful that I'm in awe." That's closer to what Athene is like, and closer to the reason the old word "terrible" is used for her–because, even if she's *not* magic, she nevertheless is or represents a very, very powerful force or idea.

And what is that force or idea? We'll know much better what it is once we've gotten to know Athene better, but for now we certainly can say that it has to do not only with feminine beauty but with extraordinary intelligence, and also that it has to do with the significance and force of woman or womanhood, with the significance and force of power (and that's not a tautology[31]–more on this later), and with the significance and force of *wisdom.*

The idea or force that Athene, then, *is,* or that she represents, is itself a most powerful one–even though, as its representative, she is herself by no means all-powerful (and neither is Zeus or any other of the gods, as Homer makes evident again and again). Look at the doubt she herself expresses almost immediately, in her first words to Achilleus: "'I have come down to stay[32] your anger–but will you obey me?– / from the sky. . ." (I, 207-208). The tone of her whole speech is one of pleading, not commanding:

> '. . . the goddess of the white arms Hera sent me,
>
> who loves both of you equally in her heart and cares for you.
>
> Come then, do not take your sword in your hand, keep clear of fighting,
>
> though indeed with words you may abuse him, and it will be that way.
>
> And this also will I tell you and it will be a thing accomplished.
>
> Some day three times over such shining gifts shall be given you
>
> by reason of this outrage. Hold[33] your hand then, and obey us.' (I, 208-214)

Interesting indeed to hear this near-greatest of all the goddesses *imploring* Achilleus–less a suggestion of omnipotence than of real doubt and uncertainty. The question, then, is why such uncertainty? And Achilleus' response to Athene is equally interesting, raising a question of its own:

> Then in answer again spoke Achilleus of the swift feet:
>
> 'Goddess, it is necessary that I obey the word of you two,
>
> Angry though I am in my heart. So it will be better.
>
> If any man obeys the gods, they listen to him also.' (I, 215-218)

If we were in that "real" place, I could ask *you* to spot what the question is that Achilleus' answer raises. In fact, why don't you have a go at it even though we're in this "unreal" place? There may—no, there is—*more* than one question raised for us in those three lines, but *one* of them is triggered by a single word all by itself. Find that word, phrase the question in a few words, and I'll meet you again across the black dot.

•

Bingo! You've done it again: Why on earth is it "necessary" that Achilleus obey Hera and Athene? Clearly, neither one of the goddesses has any sort of absolute power that would or could make it imperative, as if by a magic hex or spell, that he obey them. So why does he do it? Well, he himself says that "it will be better" if he does. So now our next question becomes *why*? Why will it "be better" if he obeys? What on earth does he mean?

And then there's this line, the last of the four, to make the whole scene even more of a conundrum:

'If any man obeys the gods, they listen to him also.'

Oh, yeah, sure. Give us a break, Achilleus. It's not even *true*, what you're saying, if what you mean is something along the lines of tit for tat. Just think of poor Hektor, for example, your own virtual doppelgänger in the poem, the greatest warrior and hero of all among the Trojans. *Hektor* obeys the gods and is reverent toward them—and look what happens to him. He gets killed anyway—by *you*!

Of course, maybe Hektor just ran out of luck, the same as Achilleus, too, will eventually run out of luck. But then we have to ask what *luck* is, where *it* comes from, and who's in charge of *it*?

We can't say that "luck" is "fate" or that "fate" is "luck" without just going in circles.

So, as we leave Book I behind, let's allow fate and luck—and necessity, too–to take care of themselves for the time being and agree among ourselves as to what things about Homer and his world we *can* properly determine at this point.

Here's great, indisputable, over-riding truth number one: In Homer, there is life. Putting it more fully, in Homer there is *only* life. Life is all there is. More later–much more–on this crucial fact–or, if you insist, crucial idea.

Here's great, over-riding truth number two: In Homer, two things and *only* two things exist. The first of these two things is nature. The second is human beings. There are no gods–how could there be, if the only two things that exist are nature and human beings?

Here's great, over-riding truth number three: Human beings have minds, and with their minds they think, and with their minds they make up stories. If the stories are good ones, they may get told again and again. They may come to be taken as "true stories," a wonderful phrase that gives us one of the most mysterious and entertaining oxymorons[34] of all time. How, after all, can something be both "true" and also be a "story"? More–much more–on this enormous idea later.

That's quite a bit to draw from just one out of the twenty-four books of the poem, but of course I'm cheating a bit–I've read all twenty-four, and I've got more evidence than comes only from Book I to help support these three "great, over-riding truths." Much of the fun in reading the poem will lie in finding that evidence and applying it.

One last thing, though. We can't just leave poor Achilleus back there telling what seem in effect to be *lies*, can we, without figuring out *why* he's doing it?

You'll remember the two lies: that it's "necessary" that he obey Hera and Athene, and that "'If any man obeys the gods, they listen to him also.'"

I'm sure that by now you can see without any help from me that what Achilleus is really doing is–talking to himself. Another way of putting it is that he is *thinking*. Still another way of putting it is that he's talking to the Hera-like and the Athene-like elements that are part of his own mind, make-up, and temperament.

Remember how mean and judgmental I was earlier on, calling Achilleus an adult spoiled brat, a bully, even a punk? Well, guess what– I was wrong. Or at best, I wasn't telling the *whole* truth–and, as everyone knows or should know, a half truth is a falsehood.

No, Achilleus does have redeeming qualities–just wait for Book XXIV–and those qualities come from inside of him, as *all* human qualities come and *can* come only from inside the human being who has them, although of course many of these can be or may be learned qualities.

But who "obeyed" whom? Who "stayed" Achilleus' hand? Achilleus obeyed Achilleus, and Achilleus stayed the hand of Achilleus. Why did he think it was "necessary" to stay his own hand? Because he knew that it "[would] be better" that way–meaning that he knew killing Agamemnon would ruin everything and very likely everyone. So, for the good of all, he pushed down his anger "and thrust the great blade back into the scabbard" (220).

And thank god he did, a person might say–using a metaphor that's with us all, and one that was with Homer, too.

Day Four

Assignment: *Iliad,* Books VI, IX

Well, have you read it? Here's quiz three:

1) **Glaukos and Diomedes discover In Bk. VI that their families have shared ties of friendship in the past, though now the two men are fighting on opposite sides in the war. When they discover this tie, they agree to avoid one another in battle. They "exchange the promise of friendship." And they:**

a) trade horses   b) both decide to flee the terrible fighting   c) exchange suits of armor
d) drink a toast to the gods of hospitality   e) determine to keep their friendship absolutely secret

2) **When Hektor holds out his arms to his baby boy Astyanax, the baby:**

a) playfully tugs at Hektor's beard   b) laughs pleasantly   c) screams in fright   d) holds out his own arms to his father

3) **When Agamemnon lists the gifts he will give to Achilleus, including the return of Briseis, he says of her that:**

a) she is an unfaithful woman, like Helen   b) her beauty is awesome, like a goddess's

c) she has wept every night since being taken from Achilleus d) he has never entered her bed and made love with her e) she is a better tapestry weaver than any Achaian woman

4) When Odysseus, Phoinix, and Aias come to Achilleus' tent to extend Agamemnon's offer to him, they find Achilleus:

a) playing songs on a lyre as Patroklos listens b) playing chess with Patroklos c) pacing angrily in his tent d) sleeping after a meal e) weeping quietly

5) Phoinix, "the aged horseman," pleads at length with Achilleus to temper his anger and ends up staying overnight as a guest in Achilleus' tent. Phoinix's rapport with Achilleus is greater than most men's because:

a) Phoinix and Achilleus are half-brothers b) Phoinix and Achilleus each have one immortal parent c) Next to Achilleus, Phoinix is the greatest Achaian warrior d) Phoinix raised Achilleus from the time he was a small baby e) Phoinix is brother of Achilleus' father, Peleus

For lack of time, we leave Book II untouched. I urge you, though, to do two things. One is to read lines 283-332 of Book II, if only because we're going to see the contents of those lines revisited—in altered form—by Aeschylus, in *The Oresteia*, some three or four centuries from Homer-time. In these lines from Book II, here, you'll find Odysseus recalling the seemingly miraculous event that took place nine years earlier, at the port of Aulis on the east coast of the Peloponnesus, where the assembled armies of the Greeks waited for a fair wind to carry them northeastward across the Aegean Sea to Troy. This story of the snake that ate the eight young sparrows and then the mother sparrow herself, interpreted by Kalchas to mean that nine years would pass before an Achaian victory in Troy would occur in the tenth year, will come back in grand form when Aeschylus takes it up. It's quick to read in the *Iliad*, and it will be a very good thing to have under your belt a few centuries from now, when we read our next book, *The Oresteia*.

And the second thing I'd like you to do in Book II is at least *sam-*

ple a hundred or so lines, or maybe two hundred, from among the lines beginning with line 493–"I will tell the lords of the ships, and the ships [sic] numbers"–and continuing on to line 759. These are the 266 lines that contain the great "catalogue of the ships," a kind of telephone book of each and every group and tribe and entity–along with the commander of each–that assembled together to form what we call the Achaian, Greek, Danaan, or Argive army. This enormous catalogue, the first of its kind in literature, besides constituting absolutely wonderful poetry for the ear, will have enormous influence in later centuries, reappearing, or being echoed, even in John Milton's *Paradise Lost* more than a millennium later, in 1667 A.D. For its length, grandeur, detail, and the sense of pride it conveys, this grand Homeric passage is well worth a serious look and listen–even though there will *not* be a quiz on it.[35]

Now, on to Book III.

●

By now, you ought to be feeling more comfortable with your reading of the poem–partly because all the complicated exposition that's needed at the start to get the story up and running is over and done with, but also because you've caught the swing of this formal, long-lined verse. One thing you *mustn't* do is try to read it *fast*. It wasn't composed for quickness, but for slowness, with the aim of filling long fire-lit evenings, bringing to listeners, yet again, from a remote, distant, heroic past, the old stories that they already knew, very nearly by memory, but wanted to hear yet again. The purpose was to fill time by making it become slow, rich, wondrous, and enjoyable. Homer isn't a fast read and was never meant to be.

More on this subject later, when we talk specifically about the Homeric style–with its extreme repetitiousness, for example, and, among other things, its complete absence of suspense or even the illusion of suspense. Unlike most readers today, no one in antiquity listening to the Homeric epics had the least conceivable interest in such a thing as suspense. They already knew every turn and detail of the story anyway. What they wanted, sort of like a fine meal, was for it to *last*. A fine meal is good even if you've eaten one just like it before.

And there were no surprises in regard to the people in the story, either. The listeners already knew all of them by name, background, and origin, as well as knowing the chief characteristics, temperaments, achievements, and qualities of each. What they wanted was to hear—or "see"–them again, waiting patiently for what they knew was going to happen–the see-sawing of the war as Achilleus sits pouting in his tent, the slaying of Achilleus' best comrade, Patroklos, by Hektor, and the subsequent revenge-slaying of Hektor by Achilleus. And smaller things, too, like the incident right here in Book III, when Paris, given a golden opportunity to fight Menelaos–whose wife, Helen, Paris has stolen and brought with him across the sea from Argos to Troy–chooses not to fight against but to hide from in fear instead:

> But Alexandros[36] the godlike when he saw Menelaos
> showing among the champions, the heart was shaken within him;
> to avoid death he shrank into the host of his own companions.
> As a man who has come on a snake in the mountain valley
> suddenly steps back, and the shivers come over his body,
> and he draws back and away, cheeks seized with a green pallor;
> so in terror of Atreus' son godlike Alexandros
> lost himself again in the host of the haughty Trojans. (III, 30-37)

Interestingly, Paris is called "Alexandros the godlike" and "godlike Alexandros" even when he's behaving, it would seem, like a coward. But "Godlike" for Alexandros is what's called a "fixed epithet" in the oral-formulaic tradition of epic poetry as composed by Homer. You've doubtless noticed these fixed epithets all over the place, since they're one of the most noticeable traits of the poem's style. In Book II, just before the catalogue of the ships, is a wonderful example of the fixed epithet–with its companion, the fixed phrase–in all its splendor:

> Then after they had finished the work and got the feast ready
> they feasted, *nor was any man's hunger denied a fair portion.*
> But *when they had put away their desire for eating and drinking*
> the *Gerenian horseman Nestor* began speaking among them:
> '*Son of Atreus, most lordly and king of men, Agamemnon,*
> Let us talk no more of these things, nor for a long time
> set aside the action which the god puts into our hands now.
> Come then, let the heralds of the *bronze-armoured Achaians*
> make proclamation to the people and assemble them by the vessels,
> and let us together as we are go down *the wide host*
> *of the Achaians,* to stir more quickly the *fierce war god.*'
> He spoke, nor did the *lord of men Agamemnon* neglect him,
> but straightway commanded the *clear-voiced heralds* to summon
> by proclamation to battle the *flowing-haired Achaians,*
> and the heralds made their cry and the men were assembled swiftly.
> (II, 430-444)

I've italicized both the fixed epithets–"flowing-haired," for example, is "fixed" to "Achaians"–and also what I call the "fixed phrases." The first and second lines are almost completely formulaic, and they'll be almost as familiar to you as breathing by the time you finish reading the poem. I've always found a pleasure in them–the pleasure of the familiar, I suppose, a pleasure held also in very high esteem by Homer's listeners, as I've already suggested.

Since we've come upon the subject of style, let's stay with it for a minute or two–we can leave Alexandros back there where we left him for as long as we want to, waiting like a statue for his elder brother to give him a tongue-lashing that Hektor hopes will take Alexandros' hide off (though it won't, as we'll see soon).

Stopping the action this way, in order to give time to other matters, is something that Homer himself does again and again, as we'll see. Whatever may be going on in the story, even if it happens to be the very middle of one of the most dreadful of pitched battle scenes, Homer is perfectly happy to bring time to a stop as if with a click of the fingers. The action halts, the characters go into freeze-frame, and there they wait, motionlessly, as Homer provides–this is usually what it is–background having to do with family or personal history, whether of gods or mortals.

A short example appears in Book II, at the point where the Achaians are assembled to hear Agamemnon speak. In this case, the action stops to give way for a history of the scepter Agamemnon holds:

> Thus they were assembled
> and the place of their assembly was shaken, and the earth groaned
> as the people took their positions and there was tumult. Nine heralds
> shouting set about putting them in order, to make them cease their
> clamour and listen to the kings beloved of Zeus. The people
> took their seats in sober fashion and were marshaled in their places
> and gave over their clamouring. Powerful Agamemnon
> stood up holding the scepter Hephaistos had wrought him carefully.
> Hephaistos gave it to Zeus the king, the son of Kronos,
> and Zeus in turn gave it to the courier Argeïphontes,
> and lord Hermes gave it to Pelops, driver of horses,
> and Pelops again gave it to Atreus, the shepherd of the people.
> Atreus dying left it to Thyestes of the rich flocks,
> and Thyestes left it in turn to Agamemnon to carry
> and to be lord of many islands and over all Argos.
> Leaning upon this scepter he spoke and addressed the Argives:

'Fighting men and friends, o Danaans. . . ' (II, 94-110)

For an example of a *long* background history inside the space provided by a freeze-frame of the action, you can read in Book VI about the recognition between Diomedes, on the Achaian side, and Glaukos, on the Trojan side, that they are connected by the bonds and obligations of hospitality—a recognition that requires no fewer than 116 lines altogether, most of them given over to personal, familial, and historical background.

The episode occurs when the time for battle has come:

> Now Glaukos, sprung of Hippolochos, and the son of Tydeus came together
> in the space between the two armies, battle-bent. (VI, 119-120)

But no forward motion takes place until after the two warriors have declared their bond:

> '. . . Therefore I am your friend and host in the heart of Argos;
> you are mine in Lykia, when I come to your country.
> Let us avoid each other's spears, even in the close fighting.
> There are plenty of Trojans and famed companions in battle for me
> to kill, whom the god sends me, or those I run down with my swift feet,
> many Achaians for you to slaughter, if you can do it.' (VI, 224-229)

Only after these 116 lines of background is the action brought out of freeze-frame and allowed to resume forward movement: "Now as Hektor had come to the Skaian gates and the oak tree. . . " (VI, 237)

The Homeric style isn't one to win the hearts of those who may be especially fond of modern-day thrillers, mysteries, or action-movies. Needless to say, no one among Homer's audience had tastes of that sort, however familiar they are to us. In fact, so much did Homer's audience love the poem's slowness–the longer it lasted, the better–that a *third* characteristic of the style needs to be mentioned after the fixed epithets and formulaic phrases, and after the action-stopping background histories. And that's the device of *literal repetition*.

In Book II, a false dream that Zeus sends to Agamemnon takes up twelve lines (II, 23-34) and begins with "'Son of wise Atreus, breaker of horses, are you sleeping?'" Then soon after, when Agamemnon tells his assembled warriors about the dream, he begins with "'Son of wise Atreus, breaker of horses, are you sleeping?'" and continues to recite *verbatim* eleven of its lines (II, 60-70).

And back in Book I, you doubtless noticed the detailed description, after the return of Chryseis, of preparations for feasting:

> And when all had made prayer and flung down the scattering barley
> first they drew back the victims' heads and slaughtered them and skinned
>   them
> and cut away the meat from the thighs and wrapped them in fat,
> making a double fold, and laid shreds of flesh upon them.
> The old man burned these on a cleft stick and poured the gleaming
> wine over, while the young men with forks in their hands stood about him.
> But when they had burned the thigh pieces and tasted the vitals,
> they cut all the remainder into pieces and spitted them
> and roasted all carefully and took off the pieces.
> Then after they had finished the work and got the feast ready
> they feasted, nor was any man's hunger denied a fair portion. (I, 458-468)

In Book II, then–I know it wasn't assigned, but maybe you read it anyway–you may have been surprised to come upon very nearly the same, identical passage:

> Now when all had made prayer and flung down the scattering barley

first they drew back the victim's head, cut his throat and skinned him,

and cut away the meat from the thighs and wrapped them in fat,

making a double fold, and laid shreds of flesh above them.

Placing these on sticks cleft and peeled they burned them,

and spitted the vitals and held them over the flame of Hephaistos.

But when they had burned the thigh pieces and tasted the vitals

they cut all the remainder into pieces and spitted them

and roasted all carefully and took off the pieces.

Then after they had finished the work and got the feast ready

they feasted, nor was any man's hunger denied a fair portion. (II, 421-431)

Lattimore himself comments that in Homer "All repeats are founded on the principle that a thing once said in the right way should be said again in the *same* way when occasion demands" (Introduction, p. 38, emphasis in original). I think he's quite right. But I also think there's one other aspect of Lattimore's point that ought to be mentioned in regard to the repetitions. It's not a new point, but really a variant of what we've been saying all along about Homer's audience being in no hurry for the poem to end. Obviously, the repetitions are perfect opposites of time-saving devices, and for that reason they were desirable to Homer's listeners.

But there's also another thing. My own hands-down favorite of all repetitions in the poem is the extraordinary one in Book IX, when not only does Agamemnon, in the first place, recite the entire list of the splendid, gorgeous, shining, sparkling, beautiful gifts that he's willing to give Achilleus (IX, 122-158) if only Achilleus will agree to come back into the fighting and save the Achaians from certain defeat. What a list! But then, once Odysseus, Phoinix, and Aias reach the tent of Achilleus to tell *him* what gifts Agamemnon is willing to offer, Odysseus repeats the entire list of the proffered gifts. It's worth, more than worth, quoting again here.

Agamemnon

offers you worthy recompense if you change from your anger.

Come then, if you will, listen to me, while I count off for you

all the gifts in his shelter that Agamemnon has promised:

Seven unfired tripods; ten talents' weight of gold; twenty

shining cauldrons; and twelve horses, strong, race-competitors

who have won prizes in the speed of their feet. That man would not be

poor in possessions, to whom were given all these have won him,

nor be unpossessed of dearly honoured gold, were he given

all the prizes Agamemnon's horses won in their speed for him.

He will give you seven women of Lesbos, the work of whose hands

is blameless, whom when you yourself captured strong-founded Lesbos

he chose, and who in their beauty surpassed the races of women.

He will give you these, and with them shall go the one he took from you,

the daughter of Briseus. And to all this he will swear a great oath

that he never entered into her bed and never lay with her

as is natural for human people, between men and women.

All these gifts shall be yours at once; but again, if hereafter

the gods grant that we storm and sack the great city of Priam,

you may go to your ship and load it deep as you please with

gold and bronze, when we Achaians divide the war spoils,

and you may choose for yourself twenty of the Trojan women,

who are the loveliest of all after Helen of Argos.

And if we come back to Achaian Argos, pride of the tilled land,

you could be his son-in-law; he would honour you with Orestes,

his growing son, who is brought up there in abundant luxury.

Since, as he has three daughters there in his strong-built castle,

Chrysothemis and Laodike and Iphianassa,

you may lead away the one of these that you like, with no bride-price,

to the house of Peleus; and with the girl he will grant you as dowry

many gifts, such as no man ever gave with his daughter.

He will grant you seven citadels, strongly settled;

Kardamyle and Enope and Hire of the grasses,

Pherai the sacrosanct, and Antheia deep in the meadows,

With Aipeia the lovely, and Pedasos of the vineyards.

All these lie near the sea, at the bottom of sandy Pylos,

and men live among them rich in cattle and rich in sheepflocks,

who will honour you as if you were a god with gifts given

and fulfill your prospering decrees underneath your scepter.

All this he will bring to pass for you, if you change from your anger.

(IX, 260-299)

What's left to be added to Lattimore's observation that "a thing once said in the right way should be said again in the *same* way when occasion demands"? Well, only the consideration of how awesome, wonderful, desirable, splendid, and enviable such a list must seem to many—perhaps even most—of those in the audiences of the rhapsodes. Such splendor! Such riches! Such wealth! Such wonder! It's easy for modern readers to forget that Homer, whether he was active in the 7th or even in the 6th century BC, was using material that, in purely historical terms, was most likely drawn from a time between 1190 and 1180 BC.[37] That means the historical events of his Troy—not counting the legends and events permeating it that were rooted even more deeply in ancient myth—were as far in the past for him as, say, the early New England Puritan settlements are for us. That's a long time. In addition, the epics intentionally evoke a past that's thought of not just as ancient but also as heroic, a past larger, bigger, and grander than the present could ever be. And so it is that the characters, the deeds, the heroism in the *Iliad* are bigger than life and create wonder and awe. Not everyone in 850, or 750—or later—ate feasts every day, or even very often, of the kind as these great feasts described in the *Iliad*. No wonder that people loved hearing them described over again.

And not everyone in Homer's period—and later—maybe not *any*one, had gifts and wealth and riches and beautiful things in such quantity as Agamemnon did. Plenty of people go to see movies twice if they like them enough. Well, plenty of people in antiquity were more than happy to hear *these* kinds of passages twice—or more.

An additional note. Suppose you were a young rhapsode-to-be and you were setting about memorizing the *Iliad* for performance. You'd be happy, wouldn't you—since it would make memorization all the easier—for every formulaic passage, every fixed epithet, and every repetition that happened to come along?

But we've kept poor Alexandros waiting long enough, freeze-framed back there in Book III, where he "shrank into the host of his own companions." Let's go release him.

Or maybe he'd rather we didn't. After all, his brother, the great Hektor, saw him run scared from Menelaos and is ready with his tongue-lashing:

> 'Evil Paris, beautiful, woman-crazy, cajoling,
> better had you never been born, or killed unwedded.
> Truly I could have wished it so; it would be far better
> than to have you with us to our shame, for others to sneer at.
> Surely now the flowing-haired Achaians laugh at us,
> thinking you are our bravest champion, only because your
> looks are handsome, but there is no strength in your heart, no courage.
> (III, 39-45)

Alexandros couldn't possibly have been this cowardly back when he seized Helen from her husband, Hektor goes on, when he "carried away a fair woman / from a remote land, whose lord's kin were spearmen and fighters" (III, 48-49). And furthermore, nothing but devastating things, the entire war itself, have been the result of what

Alexandros did. A couple of emphases help suggest Hektor's razor-sharp tone of scorn:

> 'And now you would not stand up against warlike Menelaos?
>
> Thus you would learn of the man whose blossoming wife you have taken.
>
> The lyre would not help you then, nor the favours of Aphrodite,
>
> nor your locks, when you rolled in the dust, nor all your beauty.
>
> No, but the Trojans are cowards in truth, else long before this
>
> you had worn a mantle of flying stones for the wrong you did us."
>
> (III, 52-57)

That word "evil," in the first line of Hektor's scolding (l. 39), is something we're going to have to talk about, but let's do it later. Let's do it nearer the time when we get to Book XXIV, say, and hear–from *Achilleus!*–that "There are two urns that stand on the door-sill of Zeus. They are unlike / for the gifts they bestow: an urn of evils, an urn of blessings." (XXIV, 527-528)

For now, then, let "evil" go and have a look instead at how Alexandros responds to the scorn, vitriol, and disgust for him that his great warrior-brother has just dumped like a bucket of rocks over his head.

Try to imagine what would happen if you were charged with the job of writing the next scene. How would you go about even conceiving of Alexandros' response? Wouldn't you–or any of us–wouldn't we most likely imagine anger from Alexandros in return to Hektor's, the way we saw it in the Agamemnon-Achilleus quarrel in Book I, or maybe even a *fight* between these two Trojan brothers who are so completely different from one another in every way, one a fighter and the other a lover, one rugged and the other vain and pretty, one a leader and highly responsible, the other happier with lyre-playing and love-making?

Well, let's have a look and find out:

> Then in answer Alexandros the godlike spoke to him:
> 'Hektor, seeing you have scolded me rightly, not beyond measure–
> Still, your heart forever is weariless, like an axe-blade
> driven by a man's strength through the timber, one who, well skilled,
> hews a piece for a ship, driven on by the force of a man's strength:
> such is the heart in your breast, unshakable: yet do not
> bring up against me the sweet favours of golden Aphrodite.
> Never to be cast away are the gifts of the gods, magnificent,
> which they give of their own will, no man could have them for wanting them.'
> (III, 58-66)

Amazing, isn't it? I'm not sure we'll see exactly this sort of wholly non-aggressive response to a brutal scolding for close to three thousand years, not until Mrs. Ramsay, in *To the Lighthouse* (1927 AD), reacts to an especially vile verbal blow from *Mr.* Ramsay simply by "[bending] her head as if to let the pelt of jagged hail, the drench of dirty water, bespatter her unrebuked."

Unlike Achilleus, Alexandros is quite capable of hearing Hektor's hateful and angry slings–you should never have been born, we should have stoned you to death before now–without exploding into anger himself. Hektor never does let up, it's true, just as Alexandros says, he's always as hard as an "axe-blade" and as "driven on" as one. Still, Alexandros can admit calmly that nothing Hektor has said was "beyond measure." In other words, it fit the facts.

But then something even more interesting happens. If you think of those nine lines as constituting a small poem in themselves, you'll see that, again, it reveals two steps in the thinking or psychology of its speaker. And the second step begins with what can arguably be said to be the most powerful word in any language. Take a look for it, and then meet me again on the other side of the spot.

•

You're sensationally good at these bits of detective work–and, yes, there it is, the word "yet." Along with its sibling-word, "but," in whatever language it appears, "yet" may possibly be the most powerful of all words–for the simple reason that it can qualify *any* statement. There's Orwell's famous "All animals are equal but some are more equal than others," for example, although Orwell's example, it's true, makes use of an additional element of deceit in the solecism "more equal" (a wily phrase worthy of Satan, whom we'll see twisting words this way to beat the devil–sorry; couldn't help myself–when we get to *Paradise Lost* (in twenty-five centuries or so).

Another simple example of the power of the word "but," and one avoiding any false word-play, is this one: "I love Susannah in more ways than there are grains of sand on the beach, stars in the sky, or atoms of carbon in the universe–but I love Catherine more."

Now, we've already seen Alexandros acknowledge calmly that Hektor's fierce berating of him was "not beyond measure." And we've seen him lament that Hektor is indefatigable, always pushing, always working, never letting up. We can combine these two closely-related "steps" into the first part of Alexandros' psychological portrayal of himself in this passage. What, then, is the second step? Well, it begins, as expected, with the word "yet," and it constitutes a powerful psychological reversal: From "yet" on, it's now Alexandros who is castigating Hektor, exactly as Hektor shortly before this was powerfully castigating his younger brother.

Says Alexandros, "yet do not / bring up against me the sweet favours of golden Aphrodite"–meaning something like, "Don't pull your warrior-rank above my lover-rank, automatically assuming yours to be superior to mine."

Could this possibly be a strong position for Alexandros to argue from? Telling the huge, brawny, immense, formidable Hektor that he'd–well, that he'd better not pull rank on Alexandros just because he, Alexandros, happens to be handsome, vain, perhaps even what you'd call pretty, as well as immensely attractive to women, whose sexual companionship he most powerfully enjoys?

How strong a come-back could this possibly be against the second-greatest fighter in all of the Trojan War? Well, as it happens, it's a come-back that's strong enough. Or to put it another way–touching on an idea that we'll return to in much greater depth as we go further into Homer–Alexandros' position here is *just as strong* as Hektor's.

It may not be as impressive in delivery, but the underlying strengths of what Alexandros is saying are the equal of Hektor's. He is castigating Hektor, after all, for his behavior regarding a matter of the gods. He is castigating Hektor for nothing less than the sin of impiety.

But how much of a sin can *that* be, you may well ask, if we've already agreed that the gods don't exist? A point well taken, but let's look more closely, first at Alexandros' delivery, then at the question of "impiety."

Says Alexandros to Hektor, you are huge, formidable, and you have a heart that's "unshakeable," and "*yet do not / bring up against me* the sweet favors of golden Aphrodite."

It's another of those lines, like Agamemnon's powerful "The girl I will not give back," that deserves to be heard aloud just to get a feeling for the strength, firmness, and absoluteness of it. Read this one aloud, too, being sure to leave a fair amount of time (and space) between each word so as to let the full extent of Alexandros' earnestness, almost imperiousness, come through. Take your time.

●

Did it work? I'm sure it did, and that you got the full effect of how powerful Alexandros' negative imperative to Hektor really is: Do *not* do this.

Ever.

All right, Alexandros' delivery has much more strength that we might have noticed at first. Now, though, we've got to go back to our old question about the gods. What we agreed is that aren't any gods– that is, not the Walt Disney kind, flying through the air and doing every sort of magic trick imaginable, all with tap of sparkling wand or lick of lightning bolt.

No one I've known in my entire life–including Homer, I believe– has been a literal believer in the Walt Disney aspects of what we call "the Greek gods." But, as I suggested earlier, all the many stories of and about the divinities–maybe we can even call them "all those many 'true stories'"–didn't disappear, and still haven't disappeared, just because the gods stopped hopping around (if they ever did) and stopped being taken as literal beings.

And so when Alexandros tells Hektor that "Never to be cast away are the gifts of the gods, magnificent," he's being as serious as he can possibly be.

Whatever he may or may not think about the gods as literal beings, he means here that the "gifts," not the gods themselves, are what's "magnificent." Even more important than their magnificence is that they can't be gotten just for the wanting of them, or just for the asking. As he puts it, the gods "'give [these gifts] of their own will, no man could have them for wanting them.'"

No human attribute of greatness or strength in *any* aspect of life can be had merely for the wanting of it, and in that sense–like any great human talent–*each* outstanding human attribute is a gift. In the *Iliad*, the poetic and metaphoric vocabulary of the anthropomorphic divinities remains and is put to plentiful and abundant use. And yet very little truly makes sense in the poem, and very little would explain its great strength and millennia-long durability if it weren't clear that these "gifts" are the "gifts" of human attributes and abilities themselves, coming *from* human beings, and that if *these* are to be scorned, then *the very existence and best qualities of human life themselves are* to be scorned.

Don't castigate *me*, says Alexandros, for being so masculine, gorgeous, and appealing that women–like Helen–are helpless to resist me. That's as wrong as his own castigating of *Hektor* would be for *his* powers as the greatest Trojan warrior, or as castigating the Achaians' Odysseus for his superiority as the most ingenious strategist of all the Greeks, or Agamemnon for being their greatest leader of men, or Hektor and Alexandros' own aged father Priam for being the greatest leader among the Trojans.

The conclusion? The conclusion is: Human beings *are what they are*. Every aspect of greatness in them is equal to every *other* aspect of greatness in them.

There's more–much more–to be said about this last statement *and* about this entire subject as it pertains to Homer. But let's wait, once again, until we've read more and the time is right.

Alexandros shows another side of himself, in his case the more conventional because less splendid warrior side, by proposing a single duel between him and Menelaos, winner take all:

> 'Now though, if you wish me to fight it out and do battle,
> make the rest of the Trojans sit down, and all the Achaians,
> and set me in the middle with Menelaos the warlike
> to fight together for the sake of Helen and all her possessions.
> That one us of who wins and is proved stronger, let him
> take the possessions fairly and the woman, and lead her homeward.'
> (III, 67-70)

And now, with the stage set, we're about to experience one of the most wonderful sections in all the *Iliad*.

•

In it, another magical god drops down to visit. This time, it's the messenger Iris, to see Helen, who at the moment is "in her chamber" busy with the "weaving [of] a great web, / a red folding robe, and working into it the numerous struggles / of Trojans, breakers of horses, and bronze-armoured Achaians, / struggles that they endured for her sake at the hands of the war god" (III, 125-128).

Disguised as Helen's sister-in-law "Laodike, loveliest looking of all the daughters of Priam" (III, 124), Iris brings Helen the message that the duel between Menelaos and Alexandros is to take place and that "'You shall be called beloved wife of the man who wins you'" (III, 138). Helen ("letting fall a light tear" [III, 142]) follows Iris outdoors to "the place where the Skaian gates stood" (III. 145), the great gates into the city of Troy. As it happens, Priam himself is sitting there, on the wide top of the wall beside the gates, along with seven other distinguished old Trojans, "elders of the people" with wonderful names like Panthoös, Thymoites, and Oukalegon.

We're back now to the place in Book III we visited earlier in order to look at the word "terrible" as used regarding Helen's beauty. This time, though, we're going to look at much more than only a word. Priam and the other men, having been named, are then said to be, though old, "yet. . .excellent / speakers still, and clear, as cicadas who through the forest / settle on trees, to issue their delicate voice of singing" (III, 151-153).

And then:

> Such were they who sat on the tower, chief men among the Trojans.
> And these, as they saw Helen along the tower approaching,
> murmuring softly to each other uttered their winged words:
> 'Surely there is no blame on Trojans and strong-greaved[38] Achaians
> if for long time they suffer hardship for a woman like this one.
> Terrible is the likeness of her face to immortal goddesses.
> Still, though she be such, let her go away in the ships, lest

she be left behind, a grief to us and our children.' (III, 153-160)

More often than you might imagine, an idea or fact of enormous importance can be detected by a simple phrase, one gesture, even a single small word. Here is one of those times. We talked about the enormous significance that can lie in the word "but." Now it's time to talk about the curious suggestiveness of another tiny word—as it happens, another coordinating conjunction. Look carefully at the fourth line of the passage above. See if you can find the one three-letter word that, if you're thinking carefully and closely, might possibly seem an unusual or even not-quite-right choice. Then I'll see you, as usual, on the other side of the black spot.

•

Not as easy this time, but if you did get it, you deserve ten extra points—although where they'll be applied, I don't know. But the word is "and." Did you spot it? It's a curious thing. Almost everyone nowadays, if they follow, say, athletics at all, has a team they favor over another. And when something like World Series time comes around, or Super Bowl time, *then* it's quite uncommon for most sports-followers *not* to have a favored, or even *very* strongly favored, team. Now, I know that, in reality, sports and war are only distant analogs, though in both of them it's common for many, many people to think of one side as good and the other as bad, or, at the very least, one side as *preferred* over the other side.

But look at the line spoken by the seven Trojan elders murmuring among themselves: "'Surely there is no blame on Trojans *and* strong-greaved Achaians / if for long time they suffer hardship for a woman like this one.'"

How interesting. What's with this "and" that they use? Don't they think of the Achaians as the bad guys and the Trojans as the good guys? Wouldn't it be something we'd much more naturally expect if the old men were to say "Surely there is no blame on Trojans if for long time they suffer hardship for a woman like this one"? Why are the old Trojan leaders even concerned about what hardships the Achaians might suffer, feel, or be fraught with? Aren't they the enemies of the Trojans? Shouldn't the elders of Troy be concerned only with what sufferings and hardships the *Trojans* are subjected to—rather than thinking of the two opposing sides in this fierce and dreadful war as being connectable by the word "and," as though the sufferings of each side are of *equal* consideration in the minds of the old men?

Just exactly whose side are these elders on? For a diplomat or elder statesman under, say, Joseph Stalin in 1943 or 1944 to so much as hint that he felt concern for the suffering of the German armies would doubtless, were Stalin to hear about it, result in that diplomat, statesman, or general's sudden departure from the pleasures of life. But here, the old men are sitting *right next* to the king of Troy, Priam himself, and they seem to have not the remotest fear of any such danger.

Why not?

Well, that's another enormous question waiting for much more to be said about it. But Book VI is the place to do that in earnest, and so for the moment, instead of studying *this* question, let's visit again with Helen right here in Book III, and, after that, watch the outcome of the duel.

•

Even though they've used the word "and," and even though Helen is "terrible" in her "likeness. . . to immortal goddesses," the old men do still hope that she will "go away in the ships, lest / she be left behind, a grief to us and our children."

Here's another curiosity in comparison with what the case might be in our own day. The old men in effect are advocating what today could well be considered treasonable, along the lines of giving aid and comfort to the enemy, since, in order for Helen to "go away," it will be necessary for Menelaos the *Achaian* to defeat Alexandros the *Trojan* in the duel.

But, as I said, more on this later.

Right now, Priam and Helen require our attention. The old men murmured to each other, but Priam himself has no such constraint to keep his own voice low:

> So they spoke: but Priam aloud called out to Helen:
>
> 'Come over where I am, dear child, and sit down beside me,
>
> to look at your husband of time past, your friends and your people.
>
> I am not blaming you: to me the gods are blameworthy
>
> who drove upon me this sorrowful war against the Achaians.
>
> So you could tell me the name of this man who is so tremendous;
>
> who is this Achaian man of power and stature?
>
> Though in truth there are others taller by a head than he is,
>
> yet these eyes have never yet looked on a man so splendid
>
> nor so lordly as this: such a man might well be royal.' (III, 161-170)

It's obvious, as we've already seen, that in order to read Homer either well or sympathetically, a good number of what we think of as characteristics of "realism" are going to have to be given up.[39] The abrupt halts in forward-moving action in order to hollow out time-stopped spaces for inserting background histories is one kind of example. Here, though, is another kind, more "psychological," you might say. The poem takes place over a very short period of time[40] *in the ninth year* of a ten-year war. And yet, even at this late date, Priam asks Helen for the favor of telling him the identity of "this man who is so tremendous," "this Achaian man of power and stature." The man, of course, is Agamemnon, as Helen tells him. But we needn't be pardoned for doubting most seriously that King Priam, after *nine whole years* of warfare, still isn't sure which warrior is Agamemnon. Helen, too, points out Odysseus (leading to a background story spoken by Antenor (III, 203-224), and, after Odysseus, points out Aias[41] and then Idomeneus. According to our own measure of expectations of the powers of observation and memory in our military leaders, it's hilarious to hear Priam asking Helen for this extraordinarily late guided tour of who's who among the leaders in the Achaian army.

So, why is the episode there? Give a try to answering that, and I'll see you across the black spot.

•

What did you come up with? Did it have anything to do with the abundant presence and use of repetition in the poem? If so, good. But there's a little more to it in this case. True, the section has the familiar background histories in it as past encounters with the heroes are remembered by those now observing them as if for the first time. But in this case, as an excuse for allowing those histories into the narrative, Homer has to subordinate *to* those histories something that we ourselves would never allow to be subordinated in the same way in what we think of as realistic narrative. And that something is our insistent principle that memory of things must begin at the point of conscious exposure *to* those things–and not, say, for the sake of narrative convenience, only nine years later!

But so what? It's not "realistic" by our presumed standards. A military leader or head of state, for us, who still didn't know the leaders of an attacking army even nine years after the attack had begun–well, that's the stuff of *Dr. Strangelove* or *Saturday Night Live* for us, not of what, even in our intellectually depraved days, we still call "serious narrative."

But does it matter? No. Is it interesting? Yes, very much so. Does it show a difference between Homer's aesthetic world and ours? Double yes. Is our view of such matters superior to his? Triple, quadruple, quintuple, *no*. Our views are quite, quite different from his. But superior? *Never.*

Yet again, it's a subject that's as tremendous in importance as it is in interest, and one that we'll come back to later, more than once, and not only in regard to Homer.

But right now we have Helen to see to, commiserate with, and try to understand.

Before she begins providing Priam with the *Who's Who* of the Achaians out on the battle field below them, an extraordinary set of lines emerges from her. Quite likely these lines are triggered by Priam's most kind and sweet epithet of "dear child" in addressing to her, and his beckoning that she "Come over where I am . . . and sit down beside me" (III, 162). Listen to her reply:

> Helen, the shining among women, answered and spoke to him:
> 'Always to me, beloved father, you are feared and respected;
> and I wish bitter death had been what I wanted, when I came hither
> following your son, forsaking my chamber, my kinsmen,
> my grown child, and the loveliness of girls my own age.
> It did not happen that way: and now I am worn with weeping.
> This now I will tell you in answer to the question you asked me.
> That man is Atreus' son Agamemnon, widely powerful,
> at the same time a good king and a strong spearfighter,
> once my kinsman, slut that I am. Did this ever happen?' (III, 171-180)

Most beautiful woman in the world, illustrious figure of legend, who has been captured and celebrated in art of all kinds, who has been made immortal by Christopher Marlowe's Dr. Faustus, who, when he saw her with his own eyes, delivered his own unforgettable lines–

> Was this the face that launched a thousand ships
> And burnt the topless towers of Ilium?
> Sweet Helen, make me immortal with a kiss. (Dr. Faustus, V, I, 96-98)

–this same Helen, here, now, in Book III of the *Iliad*, sheds tears, laments the loss of her home and homeland, is sufficiently filled with self-blame to call herself a "slut," and depressed enough to ask disbelievingly how her life could conceivably have taken the turns that it has ("Did this ever happen?").

No "want of human interest" *here*! There's more psycho-drama ahead in regard to the great Helen, but, first, we turn to the duel. Lots are shaken, Alexandros gets first spear-throw, Menelaos second. Each throws a direct hit, but neither spear penetrates through shield to flesh. The two warriors close in on one another and Menelaos, striking against the helmet of Alexandros, breaks his sword three times, and then a fourth. The rest of this important and ever-memorable passage is worth quoting at some length:

> Groaning, the son of Atreus lifted his eyes to the wide sky:
> 'Father Zeus, no God beside is more baleful than you are.
> Here I thought to punish Alexandros for his wickedness;
> and now my sword is broken in my hands, and the spear flew vainly
> out of my hands on the throw before, and I have not hit him.'
> He spoke, and flashing forward laid hold of the horse-haired helmet
> and spun him [Paris] about, and dragged him away toward the strong-greaved
> Achaians, for the broidered strap under the softness of his throat strangled
>   Paris,
> fastened under his chin to hold on the horned helmet.
> Now he would have dragged him away and won glory forever
> had not Aphrodite daughter of Zeus watched sharply.
> She broke the chinstrap, made from the hide of a slaughtered bullock,
> and the helmet came away empty in the heavy hand of Atreides.[42]
> The hero whirled the helmet about and sent it flying
> among the strong-greaved Achaians, and his staunch companions retrieved it.
> He turned and made again for his man, determined to kill him

with the bronze spear. But Aphrodite caught up Paris
easily, since she was divine, and wrapped him in a thick mist
and set him down again in his own perfumed bedchamber. (III, 364-383)

Anyone who has read along with me this far knows perfectly well that in the *Iliad*, just as in our own lives, we've agreed that there are only two powers that influence or determine events–one of these being *human* effort, ability, or will; and the other being chance.[43] Even though the great episode of the duel is one of the passages in the poem most readily adaptable to, say, an illustrated work for children, with all its action and with its goddess's "magic tricks," *we* know that "There are no gods–how could there be, if the only two things that exist are nature and human beings?"[44]

The Aphrodite story is entertaining and pleasant. Homer would have been foolish to leave it out, and his audience would have been enraged at the omission. Any reader who really does pray to Aphrodite and worship in her temple may skip these next several sentences and pick up with us later. Any reader who *doesn't* do those things, however, and is therefore studying the *Iliad* as a work created from and by the human mind and human heart, is faced with the task–or the pleasure–of interpreting the Aphrodite passage's meaning on a purely human and psychological level–or, of course, on a level where events are governed by chance.

After all, the chin strap may actually just have broken–by chance–under the great strain being put on it. But if anyone keeps his equipment well polished and well cared-for, it's Alexandros. Still, it *could* have happened. On the other hand, obscured by the dust raised in thick clouds by the violent struggle on the battle-field, Alexandros himself could have "broken" the chin strap, and then, obscured by the same dust, and taking advantage of the moment when Menelaos was turned away in the act of throwing the helmet over to the throngs of the Achaians (and they, too, were distracted by watching the helmet come toward them)–Alexandros *may,* choosing to follow an option different from continuing the battle (especially considering his lack of a helmet), have run for his life, straight back to his own room.

Could have. Might have. Very likely *did.* One thing we do know is that Aphrodite didn't literally "[wrap] him in a thick mist / and set him down again in his own perfumed chamber." We also know that Paris is handsome as a dog, extremely alluring to women, extremely devoted to beauty *in* women, and extremely devoted to the enjoyment of his sexuality and that of his partners.

What are the very next lines in Book III following "and set him down again in his own perfumed bedchamber"? They are these, as Aphrodite wastes not a nano-second in continuing to devise her means of getting Paris and Helen into bed together again:

> She then went away to summon Helen, and found her
> on the high tower, with a cluster of Trojan women about her.
> She laid her hand upon the robe immortal, and shook it,
> and spoke to her, likening herself to an aged woman,
> a wool-dresser who when she was living in Lakedaimon
> made beautiful things out of wool, and loved her beyond all others.
> Likening herself to this woman Aphrodite spoke to her:
> 'Come with me: Alexandros sends for you to come home to him.
> He is in his chamber now, in the bed with its circled pattern,
> shining in his raiment and his own beauty; you would not think
> that he came from fighting against a man; you would think he was going
> rather to a dance, or rested and had been dancing lately.' (III, 383-394)

To get at the wonderful psychological richness that's being dramatized here, we'll have to quote a fair amount. And so here is Helen's angry response as she turns firmly against Aphrodite's command that she "Come with me."

A note of caution: While you're reading it, don't fall into the trap of "believing in" Aphrodite again. In the entire passage, Helen is alone–she *has* to be alone, after all, if, as we've agreed, the gods don't exist. Therefore she *can't* be arguing with Aphrodite. The fact is that Helen is arguing with *herself* throughout this great example of what came to be called "psychomachia."[45]

> So she spoke, and troubled the spirit in Helen's bosom.
> She, as she recognized the round, sweet throat of the goddess
> and her desirable breasts and her eyes that were full of shining,
> she wondered, and spoke a word and called her by name, thus:
> 'Strange divinity! Why are you still so stubborn to beguile me?
> Will you carry me further yet somewhere among cities
> fairly settled? In Phrygia or in lovely Maionia?
> Is there some mortal man there also who is dear to you?
> Is it because Menelaos has beaten great Alexandros
> and wishes, hateful even as I am, to carry me homeward,
> is it for this that you stand in your treachery now beside me?
> Go yourself and sit beside him, abandon the gods' way,
> turn your feet back never again to the path of Olympos
> but stay with him forever, and suffer for him, and look after him
> until he makes you his wedded wife, or makes you his slave girl.
> Not I. I am not going to him. It would be too shameful.
> I will not serve his bed, since the Trojan women hereafter
> would laugh at me, all, and my heart even now is confused with sorrows.'
> (III, 395-412)

Is Aphrodite really "treacherous"? Did she really "carry" Helen from Argos and all the way across the Aegean Sea to Troy, as Helen now fears she may be "carried" still farther, to "Phrygia or. . . lovely Maionia"?

Well, the answers are "Yes" and "Yes," *if* we understand "Aphrodite" to be Helen herself, or, more exactly, the aphroditic impulses, instincts, forces, and desires that make up a part of Helen, just as they make up a part of every human being, albeit more powerfully in some than in others. Helen's "Aphrodite" is what we might call her "libido."

And, using that "modern" word, we can ask our questions again. Is Helen's libido really "treacherous"? Did it really "carry" Helen from Argos and all the way across the Aegean Sea to Troy, as Helen now fears she may be "carried" still farther, to "Phrygia or... lovely Maionia"?

Sure. Many a version of the Helen of Troy story portrays it as an abduction story, with Paris, as guest of the Atreides in Argos, breaking *every* law of hospitality by seizing and, by force, taking Helen with him back home to Troy. Is that the way Homer sees the tale? There's certainly no evidence of it that I can find in the passages we're looking at here. Homer unquestionably gives the divinities highly visible roles in his story, but what *are* these figures? They're either 1) portrayals of psycho-emotional elements and forces that really do exist inside all human beings, or 2) they're portrayals of elements and forces that are parts of nature or that *are* nature—including, at least for now, time and chance.

Using the "gods" in their accustomed roles allowed Homer to move his story along in perfectly conventional ways that were absolutely familiar to—and loved by—his listeners, ways that wouldn't discomfit them in the least.

But just as, two and a half millennia from now, we're going to be seeing Shakespeare and Marlowe writing for two audiences simultaneously, one highly literate and one not literate at all, so we're seeing Homer, right now, composing for two audiences simultaneously, one of them deeply perceptive and *very* philosophically serious, and the other eager for entertainment and perfectly delighted and charmed by the color and variety, the heroism and sorrow, the magic, mystery, and wonder of the tales that fill up the *Iliad*.

If Homer had composed his poems only for that second audience, we wouldn't be reading them now. Why not? We wouldn't be reading them now because they never would have achieved a stature higher than that of, say, folk tale, or folk legend, or than that of mythology itself (as we call it, and also as we "learn" it, somewhere around, usually, the eighth grade).

But Homer understood perfectly and he saw profoundly that these many stories of the gods that came to him through popular (or religious, if you wish) tradition were in fact far, far more meaningful–and far, far more durable–than would occur to most of the people who heard and loved them. He saw clearly that the stories of the gods were more than anthropomorphized "ways" of "explaining" natural external phenomena like earthquakes or lightning, but that they were also anthropomorphized ways of explaining, seeing, and describing natural *internal* phenomena–phenomena, that is, *inside human beings themselves.*

It's obviously no accident that Freud had a deep and abiding interest in the myth and literature of antiquity and particularly Greek antiquity. Much from that antiquity can be said to pre-Freud Freud. And in the *Iliad* itself, or a very powerful case can be made for this assertion, we have the first extended piece of Western literature that has as its very basis and as its deepest subject and purpose the exploration of human psychology.

Once again, we'll have to wait until later to go further with this subject–to take a look, for example, at what conclusion Homer makes from and through his exploration. My apologies yet again for the delay. But in order to find out *what* Homer concludes, we've got to see *how* he concludes it, don't we? If I told you now what Homer concludes–well, what possible good would that do? You would just be taking it from me–and who's to say that you should take it from me? Until you've seen it for yourself, you'll have no way of knowing whether I'm giving you the straight goods or not.

Don't trust me, trust the book. Let the book do the talking–and the showing–as much as is humanly possible.

We must get back to poor Helen, to see how she gets through that awful[46] struggle with herself–if she does. But this is also a natural moment to say one more thing about Homer, or about the influence of Homer. We're going to see Vergil, seven or eight hundred years from now, imitating Homer by making use of enormous numbers of his literary inventions, methods, means, and devices. Then, in about twelve or thirteen hundred more years, we're going to see Dante doing very much the same thing. It's a long wait, but worth it. It will be an even longer wait, an additional three centuries plus change, before we'll see John Milton doing the same thing.

Homer is doubtless the most-imitated writer in world history. But don't let people fool you, the way they may have fooled you in one or another more or less boring classroom, by telling you that the reason he's the most imitated in world history is because he composed the first epic poem.

Not so. Yes, he did compose the first epic poem–although there's Gilgamesh to be considered, too.[47] But the reason the Homeric epic– in this case, the *Iliad*–got imitated and imitated and imitated isn't because it was an *epic*, but because it was the western world's first extended piece of psychological literature. It was the first extended piece of Western literature that was *about human psychology* (and, as we'll see, that was also about the ontological questions–what is the meaning of being alive, the meaning of existing–that are raised both by human consciousness *and* by human self-consciousness).

Still, as Agamemnon said, these are things we shall deliberate again hereafter. For now, we'd better return to poor Helen and *her* psychological torment.

"'Not I. I am not going to him.'"

Imagine the courage and strength it would take to say that to a *goddess*, actually to disobey her command! All right. Now, pluck Aphrodite right out of the scene and leave only Helen–entirely alone, no one there but herself. Imagine the courage and strength it would take to tell her*self* the same thing she told Aphrodite, the courage and strength to disobey not only so powerful a thing as your own libido, but things so powerful as your own *self-pity*, your own sorrow and loneliness that make you desperate for relief, along with yet other things, things so powerful as the vibrant and very real memories of pleasure, security, contentment, praise, and honor you've had and have enjoyed with the person whom, now, even though all of those things are urging you otherwise, *you're not going to go back to.*

The struggle is every bit as hard, bitter, intense, and seemingly unresolvable without Aphrodite in the scene as it is with her in it. And we've left out something even further, and even worse, that Helen has to struggle against in her determination not to go back. That something is fear.

All right, but what is it fear *of*? Homer knew what it was fear of–and, once again, he made use of Aphrodite as a literary device to let all of us in on the awfulness of it. And a desperate one it is, this terrible fear. Let's look at it.

Aphrodite is considerably less than pleased by Helen's refusal to obey her:

> Then in anger Aphrodite the shining spoke to her:
> 'Wretched girl, do not tease me lest in anger I forsake you
> and grow to hate you as much as now I terribly love you,
> lest I encompass you in hard hate, caught between both sides,
> Danaans and Trojans alike, and you wretchedly perish.'
> So she spoke, and Helen daughter of Zeus[48] was frightened

and went, shrouding herself about in the luminous spun robe,

silent, unseen by the Trojan women, and led by the goddess. (III, 413-420)

What has happened? What thought–delivered, if you wish, via "Aphrodite's" scolding words, or, on the other hand, delivered by Helen herself *to* Helen herself–what thought has made its way into Helen's mind, a thought powerful enough so that all of Helen's refusal, all of her contrariness, all of her strong and rigid denial–all of these disappear in a single fleeting instant, without so much as an additional *word* from her? What is it that has so badly "frightened" her that without a sound she "went, shrouding herself about in the luminous spun robe, / silent. . . "?

Think it over. Look into it. Try to come up with *some* explanation of what it is Helen has realized, what it is that has frightened her so badly, whether you think of it as having been her own realization or as a realization having been given her by Aphrodite. Either way, work on it as best you can. In a minute or two, I'll meet you across the usual spot.

•

What would it mean, what *could* it mean, if Aphrodite really were to "forsake" Helen? Ah, if only we were in a "real" place, instead of being stuck here on this flat and silent sheet of paper, me alone and you alone–then I could ask and ask and ask until you came up with the answer! How much better that would be, if it could be left for *you* to make the discovery.

But think through the question of what "the aphrodite" inside a human being really is. Yes, it's libido, it's sex drive, it's desire for sexual pleasure. But it's something else, something more, and–all-important–it's something that no one can have or get just for the wanting of it: "Never to be cast away are the gifts of the gods, magnificent, / which they give of their own will, no man could have them for wanting them."

Beauty. No one on earth can have it just for the wanting of it. And yet some do have it, and it seems thus a gift from a god. And Helen? The most beautiful woman in the world? She *really* has it.

And, Aphrodite–or *her* Aphrodite–is reminding her, just as Alexandros reminded Hektor, she'd *better respect it.* She'd better not "cast it away," or else she'll find herself in very, very, very serious trouble whereby she would be "caught between both sides, / Danaans and Trojans alike," left there helpless and alone to "wretchedly perish."

Two horrifying thoughts come into Helen's mind at once. One is the extraordinary danger she would be in were she suddenly to become no longer beautiful to Alexandros. What if she lost her beauty, whether literally, or whether only in Alexandros' eyes? If he stopped loving her, what would *become* of her? What would become of her without Alexandros' protection?

A genuinely terrifying thought, this thought that enters–or so it seems–Helen's mind. And then there's another one, and it may be even worse. This one is a thought of the way time passes, the way old age takes beauty away, and of the way death will follow.

Helen will get old. Perhaps–just perhaps–that thought passed through her mind, too, as she was being "scolded" by Aphrodite.

We're going to see–and be powerfully moved by–some truly, truly complex and vastly sympathetic women as we go on–Clytemnestra, for one, Athene, for another, Dido, The Wife of Bath, Ophelia, Cordelia, Joe Gargary's beloved Biddy. All of them have their origin here, in Book III of the *Iliad,* in Homer's psychological portrait of dear Helen, great Helen, beautiful Helen, introspective Helen, and tremendously *intelligent* Helen. But it won't be for another twenty-six or twenty-seven centuries that we'll see another such woman captured psychologically at a moment almost precisely parallel to Helen's moment here in Book III. That moment is going to be, again, in a paragraph from Virginia Woolf's *To the Lighthouse.* It will depict a moment when Mrs. Ramsay, age 50, mother of eight, is–as she virtually *always* is–thinking.

She'll be sitting at a window with her six-year-old son James, trying to remain still and also to keep James still in order that Lily Brisco, behind an easel on the lawn some distance outside the window, can work on her painting of the mother and child. In order to keep James pre-occupied, Mrs. Ramsay points out objects in the "illustrated catalogue of the Army and Navy Stores" that he can cut out with his scissors.

Here's the paragraph, and what a paragraph it is! Two-and-a-half millennia from now, we'll see it again:

> But here, as she turned the page, suddenly her search for the picture of a rake or a mowing-machine was interrupted. The gruff murmur [of the men on the side porch outdoors], irregularly broken by the taking out of pipes and the putting in of pipes which had kept on assuring her, though she could not hear what was said (as she sat in the window which opened on the terrace), that the men were happily talking; this sound, which had lasted now half an hour and had taken its place soothingly in the scale of sounds pressing on top of her, such as the tap of balls upon bats, the sharp, sudden bark now and then, "How's that? How's that?" of the children playing cricket, had ceased; so that the monotonous fall of the waves on the beach, which for the most part beat a measured and soothing tattoo to her thoughts and seemed consolingly to repeat over and over again as she sat with the children the words of some old cradle song, murmured by nature, "I am guarding you–I am your support," but at other times suddenly and unexpectedly, especially when her mind raised itself slightly from the task actually in hand, had no such kindly

> meaning, but like a ghostly roll of drums remorselessly beat
> the measure of life, made one think of the destruction of the
> island and its engulfment in the sea, and warned her whose
> day had slipped past in one quick doing after another that it
> was all ephemeral as a rainbow—this sound which had been
> obscured and concealed under the other sounds suddenly
> thundered hollow in her ears and made her look up with an
> impulse of terror.[49]

Quite something, isn't it—the recognition of time passing unstoppably and of death's approach, a recognition that strikes fear into Homer's Helen sometime in the sixth or seventh century BC and that then does the same to Virginia Woolf's Mrs. Ramsay one afternoon either in 1927, when the book was published, or in 1910 or so, when that scene is set.

The recognition of the inevitable approach of death, and of the nothingness to follow; the terror that accompanies this recognition; and then the decision to carry on with life in the *best way one possibly can*—these are great themes in two works that remain kindred ones, though they're separated by millennia.

Now, watch the flashing intelligence and emotion of Helen in this next passage. Watch the dramatic and extraordinarily sophisticated progression of feeling and thought.

Aphrodite has led the silent and the simultaneously angry and frightened Helen back to Alexandros:

> When they had come to Alexandros' splendidly wrought house,
> the rest of them, the handmaidens went speedily to their own work,
> but she, shining among women, went to the high-vaulted bedchamber.
> Aphrodite the sweetly laughing drew up an armchair,
> carrying it, she, a goddess, and set it before Alexandros,

and Helen, daughter of Zeus of the aegis, took her place there
turning her eyes away, and spoke to her lord in derision:
'So you came back from the fighting. Oh, how I wish you had died there
beaten down by the stronger man, who was once my husband.
There was a time before now you boasted that you were better
than warlike Menelaos, in spear and hand and your own strength.
Go forth now and challenge warlike Menelaos
once again to fight you in combat. But no: I advise you
rather to let it be, and fight no longer with fair-haired
Menelaos, strength against strength in single combat
recklessly. You might very well go down before his spear.' (III, 421-436)

Look at the immense change in Helen that takes place in the mere
nine lines of this short speech. At first she speaks to Alexandros "in derision," her voice sarcastic, harsh, maybe even venomous, and she actually says outright that she wishes he had died at the hands of
Menelaos "who was once my husband." Her mix of insolence and
anger carries her on as she urges that the duel be held again, right
now. Then comes the great word, "but," a signal of the inward change
in Helen. Her anger cools, her tone changes–she is crushed, thinking
how terribly endangered she would be without the protection of
Alexandros–and she urges him no, not to fight again. Read the last line
of her speech aloud–"You might very well go down before his spear"–
and see if you can find the right tone for it. It won't be an easy job. Is
this the Helen who is, still, "frightened"? Or is this the Helen genuinely
loving toward Alexandros? Should your delivery of the line hint that
Helen speaks from concern for *herself,* or should it hint that she speaks
from concern for *Alexandros?*

Unfair questions–don't you think?–because there can be no ei-
ther/or answers to them. And the fact that there can't be either-or
answers to them is all the more credit to the complexity of Homer's

portrayal of Helen's psychology, and all the more credit to the subtlety with which he saw, felt, and portrayed it. The mind of Helen moves with the poetry of her speech, and, in this way, in many of the pages of Homer lie the seeds of Shakespeare. Twenty-three or twenty-four centuries from now, in the age of Elizabeth I, we'll see those seeds sprout and grow.

Two more things before we move on.

Earlier in Book III, Helen said to Priam, as you'll remember, "I wish bitter death had been what I wanted, when I came hither / following your son." Isn't the implication clear, from these words, that Helen *chose* to come with Alexandros to Troy, and therefore also to come *away* from Argos? Isn't it apparent, for example, in the phrase "death had been what I wanted," meaning that, no, death *hadn't* been what she "wanted," but that coming with Alexandros had been what she "wanted." And isn't the implication of Helen's volition in the matter also apparent in her words "following your son," certainly different, say, from "being dragged by the hair in the iron fist of your son"?

As literary history moves on from Homer's day, the story of Paris and Helen, or the story of "Helen of Troy," will come to be known in myriad ways, with Helen as victim, Helen as villain, Paris as weakling, Paris as brute, and so on. In Virgil's *Aeneid*, for example, eight hundred or so years from now, we'll find Homer's dear and complex Helen transformed into a villainess on a scale of evil akin to that of Lady Macbeth.

But that's seven or eight hundred years off. As for the *Iliad*'s version of the Paris and Helen story, is *it* a good-guy/bad-guy melodrama? Who's the good party and who's the bad? Who's the victim, who the victimized?

Let's see if there's any hint in the passage, spoken by Alexandros, that follows Helen's previous speech:

'Lady, censure my heart no more in bitter reprovals.

This time Menelaos with Athene's help has beaten me;

another time I shall beat him. We have gods on our side also.

Come then, rather let us go to bed and turn to love-making.

Never before as now has passion enmeshed my senses,

not when I took you the first time from Lakedaimon the lovely

and caught you up and carried you away in seafaring vessels,

and lay with you in the bed of love on the island of Kranae,

not even then, as now, did I love you and sweet desire seize me.'

(III, 438-446)

Well, Alexandros' words are "took you," "caught you up," and "carried you away." Helen's are "what I wanted," "following your son," and "slut that I am." Hers are "But no: I advise you / rather to let it be, and fight no longer with fair-haired / Menelaos," and "You might very well go down before his spear."

Helen is clearly the more complex and fascinating character of the two. And isn't it perfectly possible that she both loves *and* despises "aphrodite," meaning *her* "aphrodite"? And isn't it equally possible that she both loves *and* despises Paris? And that–perhaps–the same is even true of her feelings toward Menelaos?

In Book VI, we will find a variant of this subject, or this theme, or this *portrayal* of inner psycho-emotional conflict, and of its great complexity. We'll see the same thing in other manifestations throughout the *Iliad*, and it's impossible for me not to think that, in reading this poem, we're reading the first work of narrative art whose creator, as I suggested earlier, saw and understood that human psychology was its *very reason for being*. The first who saw and understood that the interior life of human beings is what his narrative art was *about*–was the *fuel* of it, you could possibly say. In this sense, Homer was–and is–the first modern writer.

The motive force for Homer is not one of judgment but it *is* one of seeing and thereafter one of portrayal. Helen isn't "good." Helen isn't "bad." Helen *is*. Remaining even more faithfully true in suggesting the Homeric motive, you might say–a statement that Homer would understand immediately, just as he would understand the profundity that lies within its simplicity–"*Helen is Helen.*" She is caught between complex and conflicting feelings for the very good reason that complex and conflicting feelings exist inside her. That is what she is *made of.*

And because that is what she's made of, Helen is caught between those conflicting things inside herself, just exactly as every other living human being is caught between the conflicting things inside *them*selves. And so it is that by following Helen as we have done here, by following Homer's portrayal *of* her to us, we are brought to an extraordinarily important moment. We are brought to a moment that's only one very small step away from bringing us to an understanding of what it is that Homer, in the *Iliad*, and at the very deepest level, really saw, felt, perceived, understood, and *portrayed* about human beings. And it was this: It was the understanding that, just as Helen was caught between the conflicting things within herself, so was every human being on earth caught between the conflicting elements that existed inside *them*selves in the state they found themselves in, the state of conscious existence–the state of being inside life, *caught* inside life. For Homer, all human beings are in fact "caught" in the state of what we indeed do call life. How to deal with that imprisonment, what to do with or about that imprisonment, how or whether to escape that imprisonment–an escape that almost certainly is impossible–these are the great questions–ontological questions–that Homer routinely saw, routinely understood, routinely questioned, and routinely portrayed in his presentations of characters and events throughout the entirety of the *Iliad.* These questions *are* his great epic subject.

To repeat, his understanding that human psychology must be the foundation of narrative art *if* that narrative art is to be significant and enduring made Homer the first modern writer. And his understanding that the state of existing *inside* of life is an unchosen "imprisonment" that each human being must find or forge a way of dealing with, escaping from, or excelling at makes him the first existentialist.

The implications of these ideas are enormous, fascinating, and compelling.

In Homer, it's impossible not to conclude, as said earlier, that life is all there is. And, given that truth, the great question immediately arises, what must be done *with* life? What is to be done when one is caught *inside* the state of life?

The answer to that question may sound simplistic to our own ears now, but we'll soon find out how enormously complex and profoundly creative and affirming and enduring an answer it really is. The answer is this: What must be done with life is that *life must be lived*.

At the close of Book III, Helen and Paris, as we know, are making love. Meanwhile, Menelaos remains on the battlefield, searching in vain for Paris:

> So these two were laid in the carven bed. But Atreides
> ranged like a wild beast up and down the host, to discover
> whether he could find anywhere godlike Alexandros.
> Yet could none of the Trojans nor any renowned companion
> show Alexandros then to warlike Menelaos.
> These would not have hidden him for love, if any had seen him,
> since he was hated among them all as dark death is hated. (III, 448-454)

The point we'll end on isn't that Alexandros is hated, at least just now, or that he's hated by both sides. No, the point of greater importance is that the most hated thing for anyone and everyone in the Homeric world is *death*. And why is death so hated? Death is so hated for the very simple but absolute reason that death is the absence of *life*, the only thing there is.

(A note. As a bit of a reprieve, we'll hold the fourth quiz–on Books XIV and XVIII–until the start of Day Six.)

Day Five

Assignment: *Iliad*, Books XIV, XVIII

I'm sure that when we were talking about the central characteristics of the Homeric style a while ago, there must have been many who caught me out for my having made what seemed a horrible mistake. Of characteristics of the Homeric style, I mentioned the fixed epithet and formulaic phrase; the abrupt freeze-framing of action to make space in non-time for background histories; and I mentioned the use of literal repetition. But I said not a word about the most famous characteristic of them all–the Homeric simile.

Well, that was on purpose. Then wasn't the time for talking about the simile. Now is the time.

Almost anyone who has heard of Homer has also heard of the Homeric simile. Almost certainly, they'll also know that a simile differs from a metaphor in that the simile uses "like" or "as" to make a comparison between two things, whereas the metaphor does not. "My love is like a red, red rose" is a simile. My love isn't *literally* a rose, but in certain and varying ways she's *like* one.[50] In metaphor, the comparison is implicit, making no use of "like" or "as." There's metaphor in Homer, though it seldom gains the poet's attention the way simile does, and it is almost never elaborated in the complex ways the similes are elaborated. We saw Helen point out to Priam "gigantic Aias, wall of the Achaians," where Aias is not said to be *like* a wall, but instead actually to *be* a wall.[51] Some of the formulaic phrases are themselves metaphors—as in "addressed him in winged words,"[52] which for me is an especially beautiful one. Who knew exactly how sounds reached across space from one person to another? Well, no one could see them, but it must have been that they flew, like birds. Then, after the "like" disappeared, they *were* birds, and Agamemnon "spoke in winged words."

The classic simile in Homer is interesting for all sorts of reasons—and it's obviously very easy to find, not just because of its omnipresence but because of the perfectly clear signal-words at the points where it opens and closes.

Here's one that just happens to be before my eye, since I've just been browsing through Book IV, where Ideomeneus, starting at line 266, speaks in favor of moving rapidly against the Trojans because "the Trojans have broken / their oaths." Agamemnon is only too happy to begin the rally:

> So he spoke, and Atreides, cheerful at heart, went onward.
> On his way through the thronging men he came to the Aiantes.
> These were armed, and about them went a cloud of foot-soldiers.[53]
> As from his watching place a goatherd watches a cloud move
> on its way over the sea before the drive of the west wind;
> far away though he be he watches it, blacker than pitch is,
> moving across the sea and piling the storm before it,
> and as he sees it he shivers and drives his flocks to a cavern;

so about the two Aiantes moved the battalions,

close-compacted of strong and god-supported young fighters, black, and

jagged with spear and shield, to the terror of battle. (IV, 272-282)

And there's the simile, tucked neatly in between its opening word, "as," and its closing word, "so."

As everyone knows, legend has it that Homer was blind. Other legends have it, too, that he wasn't really just a single, real, individual poet, but that instead he was one of many poet-singers who, over time, handed down, through the oral-formulaic tradition, contributions to the assemblage of segments and stories that finally became the *Iliad*– a great poem that in the end, somehow, "Homer" got final credit for.

I have no idea whether an authorship question as ancient as the Homeric one can ever be answered,[54] but as for the legendary blindness, certain things can obviously be said. Foremost among them is that the poems are positively chock-full of things seen, observed, and then recorded through visual imagery–so that if Homer, or "Homer," really was blind, he couldn't have been so for the whole of his life. Consider just the simile: inside each and every one of them, even the one we just looked at, with its "west wind; / far away though he be he watches it, blacker than pitch is, / moving across the sea and piling the storm before it," there are things that, above all, have been *seen*, observed, and, even more important, *remembered*.

Every simile is structured in the same way, though at the same time each is unique insofar as the material contained within it is unique– showing us that the simile has an altogether different purpose than do the other stylistic devices of repetition, background histories, fixed epithets, and formulaic passages. Here, for example, is a simile identical in structure to the one of the shepherd watching the sea-storm coming inland, yet wholly different from the earlier simile in its content:[55]

So he spoke and led the way departing from the council,
and the rest rose to their feet, the sceptred kings, obeying
the shepherd of the people, and the army thronged behind them.
Like the swarms of clustering bees that issue forever
in fresh bursts from the hollow in the stone, and hang like
bunched grapes as they hover beneath the flowers in springtime
fluttering in swarms together this way and that way,
so the many nations of men from the ships and the shelters
along the front of the deep sea beach marched in order
by companies to the assembly, and Rumour walked blazing among them,
Zeus' messenger, to hasten them along. (II, 84-94)

•

For me, one of the most fascinating things about the similes is that they're like windows opening back into time. When the forward action—be it battle, debate, war council, or whatever—stops to allow space for a simile, the chances are awfully good that inside that simile is going to be something *not* brought down from the legendary ancient heroic age that the rest of the poem is brought from, but inside the simile, instead, is going to be something that the poet actually saw or heard or observed or experienced *during his own lifetime.* The shepherd huddling in the cave—Homer must have seen such a thing, or at the very least heard about it first hand. Or the swarming bees—certainly he must have seen those. Lattimore writes that "In simile, we are referred from the scene in the *Iliad* to a scene which is not part of the *Iliad*; sometimes to the supernatural, more often to the everyday world."

> Such passages [he continues] represent in part an escape from the heroic narrative of remote events which is the poet's assignment and the only medium we know of through which he could communicate his craft. It is perhaps such a liberation that wittingly or not vitalizes

the development with the simile (4. 452-456):

> *As when rivers in winter spate running down from the mountains*
> *throw together at the meeting of streams the weight of their water*
> *out of the great springs behind in the hollow stream-bed,*
> *and far away in the mountains the shepherd hears their thunder;*
> *such, from the coming together of men, was the shock and the shouting.*

Such similes are landscapes, direct from the experience of life, and this one is humanized by the tiny figure of the shepherd set against enormous nature.[56]

"Simile," Lattimore points out, "offers the most natural and frequently used, but not the only, escape from the heroic." He asks us to consider II, 86-90:

> *But at that time when the woodcutter makes ready his supper*
> *in the wooded glens of the mountains, when his arms and hands have grown weary*
> *from cutting down the tall trees, and his heart has had enough of it,*
> *and the longing for food and for sweet wine takes old of his senses;*
> *at that time the Danaans by their manhood broke the battalions.*

This is to indicate the time of day, but the time of day has been indicated as we end line 86. What follows is gratuitous. It has the *form* of the simile, as well as the content: unheroic but interesting woodcutter, a moment out of his life and feeling.

Of both the simile and of the "near-simile," like the woodcutter example just given, Lattimore makes this important conclusion: "I take such passages to be non-traditional and original. For as an essential characteristic of the formula is repeat, an essential of simile is uniqueness."[57]

In the similes we find windows, then, as I said before, that open up for us straight into the observed past, and inside the similes we find the actual details of what it was that the poet *saw with his own eyes*—or, of course, heard with his own ears or took in through any other of his senses.

Wonderful as they are even if our discussion of them were to stop right here, the truth is that the similes have more, *much* more, to reveal to us both about Homer the poet *and* about the world he was a part of.

But before we look more deeply into the similes, and therefore into Homer, let's turn to Book VI and the heart-wrenching things we'll find there. *That* experience, beyond the fact of its pulling us more deeply into Homer's world, will also help set the stage for our return to the simile and for the rest of this stroll that we're taking through the *Iliad*.

•

Homer—I'll say this here, although we'll return to it only later—has his share, *more* than his share, of enemies, and, in my own view, this enmity is based predominantly on ignorance, one aspect of this ignorance[58] being a *half*-knowledge—resulting in a part-reading, or a superficial, or even an *arti*ficial reading—of Homer, as opposed to a deep, observant, and complete one. That's why, I've called this essay "Homer for Real."

Book VI, with its splendid complexity and powerful characterizations, is central to the entire question of half-reading as opposed to whole-reading. The book opens in battle:

> So the grim encounter of Achaians and Trojans was left
> to itself, and the battle veered greatly now one way, now in another,
> over the plain as they guided their bronze spears at each other
> in the space between the waters of Xanthos and Simoeis. (VI, 1-4)

Name after name is cited, names both of the slayers and of the slain:

> Polypoites the stubborn in battle cut down Astyalos,
> while Odysseus slaughtered one from Perkote, Pidytes,
> with the bronze spear, and great Aretaon was killed by Teukros.
> Nestor's son Antilochos with the shining shaft killed
> Ableros; the lord of men, Agamemnon, brought death to Elatos,
> whose home had been on the shores of Satnioeis' lovely waters,
> sheer Pedasos. And Leitos the fighter caught Phylakos
> as he ran away; and Eurypylos made an end of Melanthios. (VI, 29-36)

And then, by the great misfortune of Adrestos' chariot's horses getting "entangled in a tamarisk growth" (VI, 39), the chariot-pole is broken and the horses, freed, race back toward Troy while "Adrestos was whirled beside the wheel from the chariot / headlong into the dust on his face; and the son of Atreus,/Menelaos, with the far-shadowed spear in his hand, stood over him." (VI, 40-44)

The scene then becomes one of complete familiarity to readers of the *Iliad*, as the taken man begs for his life, offering great treasure if only he be left alive:

> But Adrestos, catching him by the knees, supplicated:
> 'Take me alive, son of Atreus, and take appropriate ransom.
> In my rich father's house the treasures lie piled in abundance;
> bronze is there, and gold, and difficultly wrought iron,
> and my father would make you glad with abundant repayment
> were he to hear that I am alive by the ships of the Achaians.' (VI, 45-50)

Menelaos, moved by the supplication, is about to let Adrestos live–until Agamemnon shames him forcefully by words *and* actions that to many readers may indeed seem repellent. The passage is laden with riches, and worth quoting:

> So he spoke, and moved the spirit inside Menelaos.
> And now he was on the point of handing him to a henchman
> to lead back to the fast Achaian ships; but Agamemnon
> came on the run to join him and spoke his word of argument:
> 'Dear brother, o Menelaos, are you concerned so tenderly
> with these people? Did you in your house get the best of treatment
> from the Trojans? No, let not one of them go free of sudden
> death and our hands; not the young man child that the mother carries
> still in her body, not even he, but let all of Ilion's
> people perish, utterly blotted out and unmourned for.' (VI, 51-60)

Many will feel that the word "hero" is nothing if not out of place as a word proper for Agamemnon after just having heard him advocate killing even "the young man child that the mother carries / still in her body." That kind of killing, after all, is repugnant to most people–me included–who would be likely to call it immoral, murderous, criminal, and even–and here, at last, comes that word we used, miles back, for Achilleus–evil.

As for that word, though, I'm sure you'll remember that when we *did* call Achilleus evil, what we really called him was "evil," adding that "the quotation marks are to show that we're using the word temporarily and for convenience."[59]

All right, it's time now to put the word, quotation marks left behind, on our list of *other* words that we can properly or responsibly define only after we've had an honest try–whether we're successful or not doesn't matter–at reading Homer in completeness and for *real*.

So, on that list is the word "evil." Here come two more for the list, one of them being the already-mentioned "hero":

> The hero spoke like this, and bent the heart of his brother
> since he urged justice. Menelaos shoved with his hand Adrestos
> the warrior back from him, and powerful Agamemnon
> stabbed him in the side and, as he writhed over, Atreides,
> setting his heel upon the midriff, wrenched out the ash spear. (VI, 61-65)

It leaps right out at us, doesn't it–that word "justice." Many might consider "vengeance" a more appropriate–or accurate–choice. Perhaps it would be, and we can certainly put it on our list, even though I don't think it's terribly likely to help us in our attempt to read Homer wholly and for real. But there's no harm in having it on our list, just as we really must also have "justice" included. As far as the particularly grotesque manner of Agamemnon's killing of Adrestos is concerned– well, what kinds of adjectives are people likely to come up with to describe *it*? Long experience tells me that a few such adjectives are "barbaric," "brutal," "primitive," "violent," "uncivilized."

And *that* list of five adjectives offers us occasion for another spot-on-the-page quiz. We haven't, clearly, completed our aim of reading Homer complete and for real, but we *are* well embarked on it. So let's test your sense of what our project actually is, or of what you sense the direction of it to be so far. Take that list of five adjectives and decide–

on the basis of your reading up to now, and on the basis of what we've talked about so far—which of them you would accept as fair, accurate, unprejudiced words descriptive of Homer and his world. You might choose to keep only one, or you might choose to reject them all, keeping none. That is, choose anywhere between none of them and all five of them. The words, again, are "barbaric," "brutal," "primitive," "violent," "uncivilized." See you on the other side of the spot.

•

How did you come out? I wish we could do this in a "real" place, so we could ask one another what we think. But we can't. So. It's very clear, isn't it, that "brutal" has got to remain as a keeper? If what Agamemnon does to Adestros isn't brutal, well, I don't know what brutal is. Also, isn't it absolutely clear that what he does to Adrestos is also violent? How in god's name can you thrust a spear into a man's side, put your foot against his torso for a brace, and "wrench out" the spear without calling this procedure "violent"? You can't. So it's obvious that we've got to keep both "brutal" and "violent." But then begin the interesting questions.

Can we call Homer and his world "barbaric"? Yes—but only if we're equally willing to call our *own* world "barbaric." Is dropping mega-thousand-ton payloads of bombs from 30,000 feet down onto peasant villages and farmlands any less or more "barbaric" than Agamemnon's stabbing of Adrestos and his wrenching out of the spear afterwards? Anyone who might try to make the argument that the business from 30,000 feet is any less barbaric than Agamemnon's slaying of Adrestos is going to have mighty heavy sledding in a fair debate on the question. Now, how about "primitive"? Um, doesn't it seem that the identical arguments pertain here as did in the case of "barbaric"? We could consider, for example, the use of napalm, comparing it with Agamemnon's ash spear. Is the use of napalm,[60] the jellied gasoline that sticks to the skin of human beings and burns them through the flesh and muscle and right on down to the bone less "barbaric" than Agamemnon's use of his ash spear? Clearly, on the same basis as before, we must rule out "barbaric" as an adjective appropriate to Homer and his world *unless* we're *also* willing to accept it as an adjective appropriate to our *own* world.

And what does that leave us? "Barbaric" and "primitive" are ruled out, since *we're* also barbaric and primitive. So let's take a look at "uncivilized." Don't napalm and bombings from 30,000 feet pretty much take care of "uncivilized" just as they took care of "barbaric" and "primitive"? And we could, just for the sake of debating points, toss in nuclear weaponry. Was the dropping of nuclear bombs on Hiroshima and Nagasaki–for no other reason, as I understand it, than to intimidate the Russians as a kind of diplomatic bank account for the future–something that we could call "civilized" as opposed to Agamemnon's stabbing of Adrestos? No, obviously there's no win in *that* debate.

And so we're left with "brutal" and "violent." And with these two adjectives, I must confess, I myself feel content. It seems to me that these two adjectives do–*in part*–accurately describe certain highly important and commonly-seen aspects of Homer's world: Just as they *also* accurately describe certain highly important–whether in a positive or in a negative sense can be left aside for the moment–and commonly-seen aspects of our own world.

Therefore, I'll accept them and I'll argue that they *should* be accepted as descriptive of Homer's world just as they should be accepted as descriptive also of our world. But in each case, they should and can be accepted *only on the condition* that they're understood to be descriptive of *some* aspects both of Homer's world and *some* aspects of our own. Insofar as they may be taken as descriptive of *all* aspects either of Homer's world or of our world, they must both be thrown out with the morning trash as being worthless, of no value, and, furthermore, totally and entirely wrong and incorrect.

Either of them taken alone, or even both of them taken together, in the absence of qualification, would effectively make them into half-truths. And it's got to be absolutely clear among those of us embarked on this "Homer for real" project, that the half-truth is a falsehood and a lie if, as, and when it's allowed to stand, be taken, intended, or understood as a *whole truth.*

That said, let's look further into Book VI in search of Homer "complete and for real," and, after that, look again into the extraordinary riches and treasures of the poet's similes.[61]

•

It may be that the beauties and the complexities of Book VI are almost equal, but the *importance* of the book—at least for our own analysis here—is immeasurable.

Imagine that a person who had read Books I through V of the *Iliad,* or even a bit more, were asked this question, "Which side in the great conflict of the Trojan War does Homer seem to be in favor of?" What do you think such a person's answer would most likely be?

Well, for several decades I asked my students that question every semester. I tried to ask it in a neutral tone, as if it had just at that moment, almost idly, occurred to me as a minor but possibly interesting question to ask. When the question was asked in that way, and near this point in our discussion of the poem, the answer was almost invariably that Homer did indeed seem to favor the Achaians over the Trojans.

It's by no means a crazy or illogical answer, but a fairly natural one. After all, the poem opens with scenes in the Achaian camp, not the Trojan, and it opens with *troubles* in the Achaian camp, not least being the plague the Achaians suffer after the rejection of Chryses' plea and then their additional suffering after the Agamemnon and Achilleus quarrel. Also, as the quarrel develops, the grandeur and enormity—for better and for worse—of the characters both of Agamemnon and of Achilleus are imprinted powerfully in the consciousness of the reader.

Throughout the opening books of the poem, in short, the point of view is mainly from the Achaian side, and even when Book III takes the reader inside Troy, the conflict between Helen and Aphrodite holds center stage and generally does nothing to create sympathy for the Trojan side. And Alexandros—is it really conceivable he's a *coward?*—fascinating as he is, he doesn't create much along the lines of pro-Trojan feeling.

All very interesting. But here's the question: If Homer really does have pro-Achaian sympathies, why in the name of Zeus does he compose Book VI, a veritable tear-jerker of a book that creates near-overwhelming reader-sympathy for the poor, suffering, destined-to-lose *Trojan* side?

Let's look at some of Book VI first, then tangle with the question afterward.

After sending his mother, Hekabe, to beg (unsuccessfully) that Athene give her support to the Trojan side, Hektor visits, first, Alexandros and Helen, and, second, his own wife Andromache and their infant son Astyanax.

Hektor finds Alexandros and Helen in a domestic scene, Helen "directing the magnificent work down by her handmaidens" (VI, 34) and Alexandros, with characteristic vanity—*or* is it pride in the tools of the warrior?—"busy with his splendid armour, / the corselet and the shield, and turning in his hands the curved bow" (VI, 320-321).

Hektor admonishes Alexandros in words reminiscent, at first, of Helen's "Strange divinity" admonishment of Aphrodite in Book III:

But Hektor saw him, and in words of shame he rebuked him:
'Strange man! It is not fair to keep in your heart this coldness.
The people are dying around the city and around the steep wall
as they fight hard; and it is for you that this war with its clamour
has flared up about our city. You yourself would fight with another

> whom you saw anywhere hanging back from the hateful encounter.
> Up then, to keep our town from burning at once in the hot fire.' (VI, 325-331)

And again, just as he did in Book III, Alexandros acknowledges the correctness of his brother's castigation:

> Then in answer godlike Alexandros spoke to him:
> 'Hektor, seeing you have scolded me rightly, not beyond measure,
> therefore I will tell, and you in turn understand and listen.
> It was not so much in coldness and bitter will toward the Trojans
> that I sat in my room, but I wished to give myself over to sorrow.
> But just now with soft words my wife was winning me over
> and urging me into the fight, and that way seems to me also
> the better one. Victory passes back and forth between men.
> Come then, wait for me now while I put on my armour of battle,
> or go, and I will follow, and I think I can overtake you.' (VI, 332-340)

Interesting: When we last saw Helen and Alexandros together, Helen was *hardly* "winning me over / and urging me into the fight," but in fact was urging him not to go back into battle against Menelaos for the very good reason that Alexandros "might very well go down before his spear." Is this another Homeric nod? Well, who knows *what* Helen and Alexandros may have been doing or talking about in the time that's lapsed since we last saw them? Furthermore, the reader's–or auditor's–interest is piqued by the hint that more has gone on between the pair than reader or auditor may have been privy to. An analyst might say, putting the idea in other words, that in Homer there's often a psychological complexity and texture that go beyond what's explicitly revealed in the lines of the poem. Homer's characters go on thinking, behaving, and acting even when they're off-stage, a quality that–to me–seems extraordinarily modern. Those who, from the pseudo-empyrean heights of the 20th or 21st centuries, have the blindness or gall to look down upon Homer as "primitive" seem to me very far from the mark and worthy of the scorn, say, of a Jonathan Swift.

Hektor makes no answer to Alexandros' speech. Instead, Helen herself makes a speech very much worth our attention:

> He spoke, but Hektor of the shining helm gave him no answer,
> but Helen spoke to him in words of endearment: 'Brother
> by marriage to me, who am a nasty bitch evil-intriguing,
> how I wish that on that day when my mother first bore me
> the foul whirlwind of the storm had caught me away and swept me
> to the mountain, or into the wash of the sea deep-thundering
> where the waves would have swept me away before all these things had
>> happened.
> Yet since the gods had brought it about that these vile things must be,
> I wish I had been the wife of a better man than this is,
> one who knew modesty and all things of shame that men say.
> But this man's heart is no steadfast thing, nor yet will it be so
> ever hereafter; for that I think he shall take the consequence.
> But come now, come in and rest on this chair, my brother,
> since it is on your heart beyond all that the hard work has fallen
> for the sake of dishonoured me and the blind act of Alexandros,[62]
> us two, on whom Zeus set a vile destiny, so that hereafter
> we shall be made into things of song for the men of the future.' (VI, 342-358)

How fascinating it becomes, a speech like this of Helen's, the moment you read it as something written by a poet whose true subject is human psychology—and *not* by a poet whose true subject is the tale of life as it was long-ago pre-planned, pre-determined, influenced, and brought about by "gods." Just look at some of what Helen says. Again, she wishes she had died, this time at *birth* rather than, as she said before, at the time when she chose, rather than death, to "follow" Alexandros to Troy ("and I wish bitter death had been what I wanted, when I came hither following your son" [III, 171-173]). Either way, it's *Helen* who is wishing she had wanted other than she *did* want. She blames the gods, yes, but only in the usual god-boilerplate that's wholly unnecessary for the poem's *human* meaning, the only meaning that could conceivably have caused it to remain of continued interest for what's getting close to three thousand years. When Helen says "Yet since the gods had brought it about that these vile things must be, / I wish I had been the wife of a better man than this is," we can in completely good and free conscience place the "blame" for the making of such life-choices on *Helen*–and, yes, on circumstance–rather than solely on the "gods."[63]

In short, it's Helen's fault if she ran off with a guy whose "heart is no steadfast thing." And what about the old concept of turn-about's-fair-play? Is Helen herself a woman of whom it could honestly be said that the "heart is a steadfast thing"?

No matter how much she is suffering, the answer still has to be "no." And who can avoid noting that, when Helen, speaking of herself *as* herself, says that she's "a nasty bitch evil-intriguing," she attributes that fact or evaluation to the doing or action of no god whatsoever! This, in other words, is Helen herself talking about Helen, analyzing Helen, evaluating Helen, describing Helen, lamenting Helen.

The gods are gone (or were never there), but long live Helen! The gods are gone (or were never there), but long live self-examining, self-determining humanity! The gods are gone (or were never there), but long live the poet Homer!

Again, if the *Iliad* really were about the gods that are portrayed in it rather than about the human beings that are portrayed in it, in every likelihood the poem would be unknown to us today, or, even assuming that it may have survived, it would at best be a footnote known only to specialized scholars and historians of the Homeric period.

But, instead of falling to that fate, the poem has lived and lived, and continues to live, on and on. And even though elements of it, in its entirety, *can* be tedious to us so-called moderns, there are plenty of other aspects, sections, and passages of it, no matter what *our* flaws may be or *its* archaisms may be, that remain absolutely riveting.

Andromache and Hektor, for example. After leaving Helen and Alexandros, Hektor goes home to find that Andromache isn't there. Instead of staying home, after having "heard that / the Trojans were losing" (VI, 386-387), she's gone to the wall-tower (while "a nurse attending her carries the baby" [VI, 388]), to get an overview of the battlefield. Hektor learns all of this from one of the housekeepers.

> So the housekeeper spoke, and Hektor hastened from his home
> backward by the way he had come through the well-laid streets. So
> as he had come to the gates on his way through the great city,
> the Skaian gates, whereby he would issue into the plain, there
> at last his own generous wife came running to meet him,
> Andromache, the daughter of high-hearted Eëtion;
> Eëtion, who had dwelt underneath wooded Plakos,
> in Thebe below Plakos, lord over the Kilikian people.
> It was his daughter who was given to Hektor of the bronze helm.
> She came to him there, and beside her went an attendant carrying
> the boy in the fold of her bosom, a little child, only a baby,
> Hektor's son, the admired, beautiful as a star shining,
> whom Hektor called Skamandrios, but all of the others
> Astyanax–lord of the city; since Hektor alone saved Ilion. (VI-390-403)

Heart-rending already–"his generous wife," "a little child, only a baby," "beautiful as a star shining," "Astyanax–lord of the city; since Hektor alone saved Ilion"–all this is as nothing to the truly heart-breaking passages that follow:

> Hektor smiled in silence as he looked on his son, but she,
> Andromache, stood close beside him, letting her tears fall,
> and clung to his hand and called him by name and spoke to him: 'Dearest,
> your own great strength will be your death, and you have no pity
> on your little son, nor on me, ill-starred, who soon must be your widow;
> for presently the Achaians, gathering together,
> will set upon you and kill you; and for me it would be far better
> to sink into the earth when I have lost you, for there is no other
> consolation for me after you have gone to your destiny–
> only grief. . .' (VI, 404-413)

As we've seen before, there are times in the *Iliad* when nothing other than reading aloud can succeed in giving us "moderns" a taste or sense of the powerful–sometimes, as here, of the extraordinarily powerful–emotion that lies always half-hidden under the stiffened surface of the formulaic poetry. For us, the "high" style of the oral-formulaic acts often, even most of the time, as a sort of lid or cover over the real, detailed, eloquently delivered emotional qualities that for the ancients (since for them the "high" style was no barrier but, instead, a perfectly natural and familiar means of delivery) were always immediate, present, and vivid.

And so here's a task for you. There are another twenty-five lines or so of Andromache's long speech that I'm going to cite–in order to get its cumulative effect *and* in order to get to its truly most magnificent and heartbreaking climax. The task I propose–something I could never do in a "real" class, for lack of time–is that you read it aloud. As for the pace of reading, feel your way along–you'll know if you're going too fast, and you'll also know if you're going too slowly: Try for the speed of a voice speaking, not orating, for the speed of a voice

that's *talking,* not speechifying. As for the line-endings–the enjamb-
ment–ignore them entirely, but just go on to the next line without
break or pause of any kind *unless* the punctuation tells you to do otherwise. Comma, semi-colon, period–be guided by them, and, in their
absence, be guided solely and only by the words, as if there *were* no
lines, and, of course, by the words' *meanings.* Remember whose speech
this is, Andromache's, and what it is she's saying: That without Hektor, her life will be nothing, dust and ashes, "only grief."

Here you go. Have a crack at it:

> . . . and for me it would be far better
> to sink into the earth when I have lost you, for there is no other
> consolation for me after you have gone to your destiny–
> only grief; since I have no father, no honoured mother.
> It was brilliant Achilleus who slew my father Eëtion,
> when he stormed the strong-founded citadel of the Kilikians,
> Thebe of the towering gates. He killed Eëtion
> but did not strip his armour, for his heart respected the dead man,
> but burned the body in all its elaborate war-gear
> and piled a grave mound over it, and the nymphs of the mountains,
> daughters of Zeus of the aegis, planted elm trees about it.
> And they who were my seven brothers in the great house all went
> upon a single day down into the house of the death god,
> for swift-footed brilliant Achilleus slaughtered all of them
> as they were tending their white sheep and their lumbering oxen;
> and when he had led my mother, who was queen under wooded Plakos,
> here, along with all his other possessions, Achilleus
> released her again, accepting ransom beyond count, but Artemis
> of the showering arrows struck her down in the halls of her father.
> Hektor, thus you are father to me, and my honoured mother,
> you are my brother, and you it is who are my young husband.

> Please take pity upon me then, stay here on the rampart,
>
> that you may not leave your child an orphan, your wife a widow. . .
>
> (VI, 410-432)

An extraordinary passage, isn't it—and, above all, as everyone must agree, a passage in no way likely to create the *least bit* of sympathy for the Achaian side in the war. Andromache's long citation of the ravages done to her family—by Achilleus himself, greatest of the Achaian warriors—is positively overwhelming, and the pair of lines that provide its rhetorical climax absolutely beg for being read aloud, and can't help but wrench the heart of anyone hearing them: "Hektor, thus you are father to me, and my honoured mother, / you are my brother, and you it is who are my young husband."

What reader, after hearing an appeal for pity and mercy like that, could ever again—after reading Book VI—be tricked into answering in the affirmative the casually-posed question, "Don't you more or less feel that Homer's sympathies lie more with the Achaians than they do with the Trojans?"

The fact is this: Homer is impartial in his portrayal of the Trojan-Achaian struggle, and we'll be looking at evidence of this impartiality all the way to the end of this essay. And we'll also be pushing the question further by trying to find out why Homer *has* an attitude such as this and to what other extents—ontological extents, possibly, having to do with an entire world-view—his impartiality really goes.

We still need to look at Hektor's answer to Andromache's appeal, so we'll have to come back to Book VI, and *also* go back to Book IV to see how Pandarus breaks the truce that's been declared. But before doing those things, let's go ahead to Book XIV, the book that begins hilariously with Hera's seduction of Zeus[64] and then, in a typical Homeric contrast, ends with some of the most horrific and bloody of battle scenes. There's something in those scenes that very beautifully reveals Homer's not-taking of sides.

The action begins with Hektor casting his spear at Aias, "since he had turned straight against him" (XIV, 403), meaning that Aias had turned to face Hektor, offering him the widest target. But Hektor's throw, though accurate, "struck [right] there where over his chest were crossed the two straps, / one for the sword with the silver nails, and one for the great shield. / These guarded the tenderness of his skin" (XIV, 404-406).

In a move reminiscent of Alexandros' back in Book III, "Hektor, in anger / because his weapon had been loosed from his hand in a vain cast, / to avoid death shrank into the host of his own companions" (XIV, 406-408). But before Hektor is out of range, Aias picks up and throws a rock, hitting Hektor right in the chest and knocking him out. The Trojans "sloped the strong circles of their shields over him" (XIV, 428) while others drew him to the side of the field. It will take him a bit of time to recover:

> He got his wind again, and his eyes cleared,
> and he got up to lean on one knee and vomit a dark clot
> of blood, then lay back on the ground again, while over both eyes
> dark night misted. His strength was still broken by the stone's stroke.
> (XIV, 436-439)

Sensing an advantage in Hektor's being temporarily out of the fighting, "the Argives. . . remembered again their warcraft and turned on the Trojans" (XIV, 440-441). The resurgence of battle is worth quoting generously:

> There far before them all swift Aias son of Oïleus
> made an outrush, and stabbed with the sharp spear Satnios,
> Enops son, whom the perfect naiad nymph had borne once

> to Enops, as he tended his herds by Satnioeis river.
> The spear-famed son of Oïleus, coming close to this man,
> stabbed him in the flank so that he knocked him backward, and over him
> Trojans and Danaans closed together in strong encounter.
> Poulydamas of the shaken spear came up to stand by him,
> Panthoös' son, and struck in the right shoulder Prothoënor
> son of Areïlykos, and the powerful spear was driven
> through the shoulder, and he dropping in the dust clawed the ground in his
> fingers. (XIV, 442-452)

Following his killing of Prothoënor, Poulydamas indulges in the "vaunting" or bragging that is the traditional entitlement, or maybe even requirement, of the warriors at such moments of victory. As you read Poulydamas' vaunting, you might want to think back again on our old quintet of words from earlier on–"barbaric," "brutal," "primitive," "violent," "uncivilized." Remember, we kept only *two* of them as being justly descriptive of Homer and his world. Here's the same *kind* of test again, to determine which of our quintet of adjectives *fairly* apply:

> Poulydamas vaunted terribly over him, calling in a great voice:
> 'I think this javelin leaping from the heavy hand of Panthoös'
> high-hearted son was not thrown away in a vain cast. Rather
> some Argive caught it in his skin. I think he has got it
> for a stick to lean on as he trudges down into Death's house.' (XIV, 453-457)

"Some Argive" is the dead Prothoënor, his body lying there on the field in plain sight while Poulydamas imagines him, in the invisible underworld, hobbling down towards "Death's house" using the javelin for a cane.

We reasoned earlier that we can't demean another culture by naming it "primitive" if our own culture behaves no differently from *that* one, or behaves differently in no *essential* way. Here's a test for us again—a test of whether we can or will remain consistent with that earlier thinking. There's no question but that Poulydamas' vaunt is brutal and violent—and terrifying, too, as we've seen that word used before—but if anyone wants to take the path of calling it "barbaric," "primitive," or "uncivilized"—well, that person is going to have to go it alone, or at least without *my* company.

That's not to say I'm anything but wholly in sympathy with the Argives, of whom Homer tells us, after Poulydamas' vaunt:

> He spoke, and sorrow came over the Argives at his vaunting. . .(XIV. 458)

Keep that line in mind as we go on through more of the battle:

> He spoke, and sorrow came over the Argives at his vaunting,
> and beyond others he stirred the anger in wise Telamonian
> Aias, for the man had fallen closest to him, and at once
> he made a cast with the shining spear at returning Poulydamas.
> But Poulydamas himself avoided the dark death
> with a quick spring to one side, and Archelochos son of Antenor
> caught the spear, since the immortal gods had doomed his destruction.
> He hit him at the joining place of head and neck, at the last
> vertebra, and cut through both of the tendons, so that
> the man's head and mouth and nose hit the ground far sooner
> than did the front of his legs and knees as he fell. And Aias
> spoke aloud in answer to unfaulted Poulydamas:
> 'Think over this, Poulydamas, and answer me truly.
> Is not this man's death against Prothoënor's a worthwhile
> exchange? I think he is no mean[65] man, nor born of mean fathers,
> but is some brother of Antenor, breaker of horses,
> or his son; since he is close in blood by the look of him." (XIV, 458-474)

And then Homer gives us this line, in contrast to line 458, when the *Argives* felt "sorrow":

> He spoke, knowing well what he said, and sorrow fastened on the Trojans.
> (XIV, 475)

Sorrow first for the Argives, then sorrow for the Trojans—and you could probably predict which side will be the *next* to feel the sorrow and the fear:

> He spoke, knowing well what he said, and sorrow fastened on the Trojans.
> There Akamas, bestriding his brother, stabbed the Boiotian
> Promachos with the spear as he tried to drag off the body.
> Akamas vaunted terribly over him, calling in a great voice:
> 'You Argives, arrow-fighters, insatiate of menace. I think
> we shall not be the only ones to be given hard work
> and sorrow, but you too must sometimes die, as this man did.
> Think how Promachos sleeps among you, beaten down under
> my spear, so that punishment for my brother may not go
> long unpaid. Therefore a man prays he will leave behind him
> one close to him in his halls to avenge his downfall in battle.' (XIV, 475-485)

And the next line, just as might be expected, returns the sorrow to the Argives:

> He spoke, and sorrow came over the Argives at his vaunting. . . (XIV, 486)

Now, if the pattern holds, the *next* group to feel the great sorrow will be the Trojans, since it's their turn again to suffer fear. So. Let's see if it does hold.

Doing this, getting to where we can check the alternating pattern of sorrow, requires that we make our way through a passage of especially vivid slaughter, brutality, violence, and gore. Be brave. After all, the prize is great, the prize of discovering whether or not the pattern does hold—and, through *that* discovery, setting out on our way to discovering things about *Homer* perhaps entirely unexpected:

> He spoke, and sorrow came over the Argives at his vaunting,
> and beyond others he stirred the anger in wise Peneleos.
> He charged Akamas, who would not stand up against the onset
> of lord Peneleos. He then stabbed with the spear Ilioneus
> the son of Phorbas the rich in sheepflocks, whom beyond all men
> of the Trojans Hermes loves, and gave him possessions.
> Ilioneus was the only child his mother had borne him.
> This man Peneleos caught underneath the brow, at the bases
> of the eye, and pushed the eyeball out, and the spear went clean through
> the eye-socket and tendon of the neck, so that he went down
> backward, reaching out both hands, but Peneleos drawing
> his sharp sword hewed at the neck in the middle, and so dashed downward
> the head with helm upon it, while still on the point of the big spear
> the eyeball stuck. He, lifting it high like the head of a poppy,
> displayed it to the Trojans and spoke vaunting over it:
> 'Trojans, tell haughty Ilioneus' beloved father
> and mother, from me, that they can weep for him in their halls, since
> neither shall the wife of Promachos, Alegenor's
> son, take pride of delight in her dear lord's coming, on that day
> when we sons of the Achaians come home from Troy in our vessels.
> (XIV, 486-505)

And then come two more lines—and, yes, they *do* break the pattern, and they do it with an enormous, terrifying, pitiful, significance:

> So he spoke, and the shivers came over the limbs of all of them,

> and each man looked about him for a way to escape the sheer death.
>
> (XIV, 506-507)

This time, the sorrow and terror come to "all of them," to every man on the field, whichever side he may belong to.

At this point, too, we're only a few lines—and wondrously impressive ones—away from the end of Book XIV. I'm going to cite them, partly because I can't resist doing it. And then, from the very end of Book XIV, we'll come back to our two pattern-breaking lines, "So he spoke, and the shivers came over the limbs of all of them, / and each man looked about him for a way to escape the sheer death." There are two hugely important things to be noticed about those lines, and something of huge importance to be *said* about them. Each of those two hugely important things is indicated by a single word—that is, we'll be looking for two words in all. Maybe while you're reading the limitlessly grim closing lines of Book XIV—a powerful contrast in this book of the *Iliad* that *began* with comedy, trickery, a magical waistscarf, and an abracadabra golden-cloud perfectly suitable for lovemaking.

Now, here's the close of that same book:

> Tell me now, you Muses who have your homes on Olympos,
> who was first of the Achaians to win the bloody despoilment
> of men, when the glorious shaker of the earth bent the way of the battle?
> First Telamonian Aias cut down Hyrtios, he who
> was son to Gyrtios, and lord over the strong-hearted Mysians.
> Antilochos slaughtered Phalkes and Mermeros. Morys
> and Hippotion were killed by Meriones. Teukros cut down
> Periphetes and Prothoön. Next the son of Atreus,
> Menelaos, stabbed Hyperenor, shepherd of the people,
> in the flank, so the bronze head let gush out the entrails

through the torn side. His life came out through the wound of the spear-stab
in beating haste, and a mist of darkness closed over both eyes.
But Aias the fast-footed son of Oïleus caught and killed most,
since there was none like him in the speed of his feet to go after
men who ran, once Zeus had driven the terror upon them. (XIV, 508-522)

Before long, we'll take up the subject of the great contrasts that Homer
offers us again and again, both in things large (the comic opening of
Book XIV as opposed to the overwhelmingly gruesome close of it)
and in things small. But that won't be possible until we finish up our
work here–and, after that, go back for a visit to Book IV.

But did you find the two key words in the lines that broke Homer's
pattern of alternation between sorrow and fear first on one side, then
on the other, and so forth?

Sure you did. First, you doubtless caught the word "all," in the
phrase "all of them." On these two or three pages, where Homer al-
ternates from saying that the Trojans feel terror to saying that the
Achaians feel terror and then back to saying again that the Trojans
feel it–then suddenly breaks the pattern by combining the two armies
into one, saying that "*all of them*" feel terror–*right here* on these pages,
and *particularly* in that simple phrase, "all of them," we find our answer
once and for all to the question having to do with where Homer's
sympathies lie in the war.

If Homer were, or if Homer had been, "for" one side or the other,
the chances of the poem's having survived for as long as it has, and the
chances that we would have the interest in studying it that we do still
have–both of these sets of chances would in great likelihood be enormously diminished, possibly to the point of disappearance. Homer,
the West's first truly great writer on war, makes it clear again and again
and again that the story of this war–as it came down to him and as he
"saw" it both poetically and philosophically–was *not* a war between

good and bad, was not even a war between good and *less* good.

No, it was a war not between but *among* people, all of them equal with one another insofar as *all* were trapped inside the war just as they were trapped inside the the the cage of existence, inside the condition of *being alive.* Does any one of them understand in the deepest and, to use "our" word, most *real* sense what they're doing or *why* they're doing it? Set aside the story of Helen's abduction by Alexandros and–do you think this for even a nano-second?–would the "Trojan War" cease to exist, fall into non-being? Not on your life. Which do you think came first, the *war* or the legend of Paris and Helen? For that matter, who among *all* in the *Iliad* is in control of his or her destiny or fate? Who among them really *knows what to do*?

The answer is that none does, not really. All make an effort of some kind, most often (like Helen) doing so blindly or half-blindly, equally actor and victim, some with greater success of *some* measurable kind– like Agamemnon–some with less, like Paris or Achilleus, and *many* lost altogether to brutal death in the melee.

If we really do want to get to Homer for real, we're first going to have to go into Homer *deeply*–to the level where, I'm absolutely convinced, his own poetic and psycho-intellectual life took place. Matthew Arnold's famous line about Sophocles, that the tragedian was one "who saw life steadily, and saw it whole,"[66] is as estimation, regarding Homer, that we're going to add to, slightly but significantly, by saying that Homer saw life steadily, whole, *and deep.*

Consider the war. The real truth is that the war has and would have no *known* cause even if were a war being fought, say, for territory, minerals, or other sorts of wealth–it *still* would have no known cause, for why should those things need to be fought over in the first place?

Well, because that's the way things go. War is one of the things that people *do,* and Homer sees with absolute clarity that in this sense the war is a trap for those caught up in it, just as life itself is a trap for those caught up in *it*. It's evidence of Homer's towering genius, perception, sensitivity and insight, that he sees this truth about the war—perhaps all war—in the first place, that it's an entrapment of *all* those involved in it and encompassed by it. No *wonder* he doesn't take sides!

But it's even more of a testament to the great poet's power and depth of seeing that he understands just as clearly that this entrapment of human beings in and by the war is parallel, in every possible ontological way of understanding it, to the human being's equivalent entrapment simply *in the state of being alive*.

Such thoughts as these, I don't doubt, may seem intolerably gloomy to some. But if we really do—as I know *I* do—want to find, reach, and understand Homer in the greatest possible degree and for *real*, well, then we're going to have to go the whole way with him. *He* went the whole way, after all. If *we* don't follow, the fault will obviously be ours, not his.

Without Homer, I'm really not sure *what* we'd do. In my own view he's a far, far more valuable figure for humanity's true understanding of itself than, say, Plato, or even than Jesus Christ, and *certainly* more than the hateful and brutally life-destructive Saint Paul, who gave us the so-called "Jesus Christ" that we now have and now live with.[67] These figures, including Jesus after his retooling by Paul, all function as naysayers toward life and thus as destroyers of it, serving instead as purveyors of the notion of life *after* life. In return for this desecration of life they get little but fame, praise, worship, and idolatry. On the other hand, Homer, the real and genuine life-affirmer, real life-embracer, and real life-celebrant—what *he* gets, at least in response to the *Iliad*, are slurs and contumely for being a primitive and uncivilized lover of gore, violence, ruin, and war.

I guess you can tell pretty easily where my own sympathies lie. To me, it's *such* a great pity that for most people Homer is boring. And to me, it's *such* a great pity that those relatively few who *do* read him are indoctrinated (yes, I could say "taught") to read him literally rather than psychologically and symbolically, and to read him on a superficial and near-literal level—a level that can lead only to a paucity of understanding and experience—rather than to read him on the breathtakingly deep level that the poet *himself* goes to, the level that can give those who go there *with* him experiences and questions that will remain with them for life—and that may even give them a sense of what it feels like not simply to be alive but actually to be *civilized*.

How can *any* of us be civilized, after all, if we know nothing of the darkness that's the opposite of that state, the state of being "civilized"? It's this exact thing that Homer does in the *Iliad*, with extraordinary courage, bravery, fortitude, perception, and sensitivity—he looks straight into the heart of the darkest, most complex, most difficult, most seemingly hopeless, and often the most terrifying elements and aspects of life as we are all destined—by the simple fact of birth—to live, survive, and endure it. And yet—and what a huge "yet" this is—he never, ever, descends to the level of the tragic, but he descends solely and only to the level of the *true*.

This has been hard work, and it's taken a fair amount of pretty hard thinking. Let's take a breather at another black dot, and then, when we've recovered, talk a bit about tragedy.

•

People often, even glibly, call the *Iliad* a "tragedy." But they're completely wrong. It's not a tragedy, although, as we've already seen in plenty, it's perfectly fair and accurate to call it *tragic*. But a tragedy? According to the classic definition as provided by Aristotle in *The Poetics*, from around 330 BC,[68] there can't be a tragedy without there being a tragic hero—someone of high stature who, through the workings of some quality or characteristic *in his or her own nature or self*, is inevitably brought to a calamitous and destructive fall.

Now, in the *Iliad*, who might such a figure be? Why, they're all over the place. If we assume that the calamitous and destructive "fall" is the war itself, or that it's this state *of* warring that the *Iliad* describes, well, who has within him or her self some quality or characteristic that might arguably be responsible for the coming about of this vast war-suffering that the *Iliad* describes?

Well, certainly Achilleus, with his "wrath" that "put pains thousandfold upon the Achaians" and that makes at least this short part of the war's tenth year more horrible than it might otherwise have been. But there's also Agamemnon, whose own not-always successfully restrained flashes of anger may have prevented him from mollifying Achilleus. And there's Helen, who, if she hadn't "followed" Alexandros to Troy, wouldn't have allowed *that* weakness (if it was a weakness, since we know that it was also an enormous and goddess-like power within her) to trigger the entire war in pursuit of her. Or how about Paris, whose love of love-making not only got him involved with Helen but may have kept him from doing his part, militarily, for the Trojans. And then there's even Hektor, whose "own great strength will be your death," as we saw Andromache say to him. If even *he* hadn't been so great and so single-minded a warrior, then maybe a political reconciliation or truce have been worked out.

Every word of that paragraph is pure supposition. Every single comment about a character is an "if" or a "maybe." And, even more important, no single one of these characters dominates the *Iliad*, but all of them live and move on the broad canvas of this enormous work. The *Iliad* isn't centrally about any single one of them. There *isn't* any "central character," but there are characters—all of them—and all of them are *centered inside the inescapable condition of the war.*

Drama hasn't been invented yet, and the *Iliad* is less a drama than an enormous tapestry covered all over, top to bottom and edge to edge, *with* dramas. As for its central character, we have—well, we have humanity. And the hero of the work is—yes again—all humanity. This very breadth is what people tend to mean by "epic."

The invention of drama will be an enormous and fascinating event, and it will be a wonderful thing to watch and talk about. But we're not there yet. We're still here, with Homer. And Homer, in the *Iliad*, is poet not of a central dramatic character, but poet of the drama of all humanity.

Now, to begin finding out what this tapestry-poem is *really about*, let's go back to our earlier two lines from Book XIV:

> So he spoke, and the shivers came over the limbs of all of them,
> and each man looked about him for a way to escape the sheer death. (XIV, 506-507)

And what is the word this time, the second of the two radically significant and revelatory words in the lines?

You're right again, of course. The word "sheer," in the phrase "sheer death." And what does it mean? Put most simply, it means *absolute*. And death, therefore, is absolute. For Homer and for all in the world of Homer, as I've said already and as we'll see many more times before leaving the poem, life is all there is. Death is awful, dreaded, and "hateful" because the only conceivably correct definition of it is that it is the *absence* of life. The absence, that is, of the *one thing that people have*.

Not until Plato, who won't live and die for at least another two or three hundred years after Homer's time,[69] will any seriously-developed idea of an afterlife be invented, *nor*, until then, above all, will any seriously-developed idea be invented to the effect that something that comes *after* life is superior *to* life.[70]

There are many–I include myself among them–who think that this idea, that death is superior to life, may very possibly be the most destructive single idea ever to have come from and been developed by the human mind. As we'll see in our three-thousand-year (or almost) journey from Homer through Samuel Beckett, much of the literature we're going to come upon will be work that is pondering, wrestling with, attacking, or trying desperately to escape from exactly this idea, that there's something *better* than life.

But for now we're still with Homer, still with the *Iliad*, and still, therefore, in the company of a *life*-affirming, *life*-embracing, and *life*-celebrating poet who is writing in a *life*-affirming, *life*-embracing, and *life*-celebrating world.

Can you hear your fellow readers clucking their tongues in disbelief, horrified that a person like me could say what I've just said about "life"–*immediately* after reading about Ilioneus slaying Peneleos, then raising Peneleos' eyeball on the point of his spear, "lifting it high like the head of a poppy," or *immediately* after reading the closing lines of Book XIV, where Menelaos stabbed Hyperenor "in the flank, so the bronze head let gush out the entrails / through the torn side"?

People–perhaps most people–are likely to berate me for saying that Homer and his world are life-affirming when the poet describes awful things like that, and does it over and over and over again, *and* does it in such gory, we might even think in such admiring, perversely loving detail.

But what foolishness. What nonsense. The briefest moment of careful observation, of introspection, or of fair-minded as opposed to closed-minded thinking will reveal to any honest person that "our" world is every bit as gory and grim as Homer's, certainly so in warfare. Hiroshima isn't gory, grim, and violent? Bataan? Falluja? Gaza? The Gulag?

No, the difference isn't that one world is more gory, grim, and violent, but that one world is honest about it in a certain way and the other is not. We are awful hypocrites. Thanks to Plato, we actually think that some aspects of "life" really are superior to other aspects of it, that some ways of being really are superior to other ways of being–that, for example, lamb-like behavior in a Jesus is superior to the slaughter achieved by a lion-like Aias or a Menelaos.

First, to help us see through our own hypocrisies, please remember our five words, "barbaric," "brutal," "primitive," "violent," and "uncivilized." We agreed far back in this essay that the only two of those five words that honestly apply to the world of Homer were "brutal" and "violent," while "barbaric," "primitive," and "uncivilized" are patently *not* apropos.

So don't anybody go backing out on our agreement now, and begin libeling Homer for describing violence in his world, or for describing the brutality that also *was* a part of it.

Homer also describes plenty of other things in his world, plenty of things *other* than violence. And, most important of all—unlike us—he doesn't take one aspect of his world as being innately superior to another, just as he doesn't take one aspect of his world as being innately inferior to another.

If life is all there is, what is the one truly most reasonable, sensible, profitable, and productive thing for a person to do?

The answer is this: When life is all there is, the most reasonable, sensible, profitable, and productive thing for a person to do is to live life as well as is *humanly possible.*

We'll clarify, move deeper, look further into exactly what we mean by this. But we'd better take a short break first.

•

There. That's better. Now, having gathered back a bit of our strength, let's return for a moment to "sheer death" and see how it can shed light on the heart-breaking Hektor and Andromache scene back in Book VI. That is the scene, you remember, where Andromache implores Hektor not to return to battle, since she fears that "your own great strength will be your death," and that her doom will be equal to his if he dies in battle, since she will have no family left to protect her, Achilleus having slain them all:

> Hektor, thus .you are father to me, and my honoured mother,
> you are my brother, and you it is who are my young husband.
> Please take pity upon me then, stay here on the rampart,
> that you may not leave your child an orphan, your wife a widow. . .
> (IX, 429-432)

Now, we know a lot more about Hektor and about Hektor's world than we did last time we visited this scene. And some of what we know may make more understandable Hektor's response to Andromache after her heart-rending appeal.

> Then tall Hektor of the shining helm answered her: 'All these
> things are in my mind also, lady; yet I would feel deep shame
> before the Trojans, and the Trojan women with trailing garments,
> if like a coward I were to shrink aside from the fighting;
> and the spirit will not let me, since I have learned to be valiant
> and to fight always among the foremost ranks of the Trojans,
> winning for my own self great glory, and for my father. (VI, 440-447)

Literature is jam-packed with scenes of this kind–where a mate, spouse, or lover begs, wishes, implores of a loved one that a separation, perhaps forever, be avoided by someone's *not* returning to war, that it *not* be brought about by a return to battle. The supplication never works, however, because the demands of war trump *any* consideration of the individual.

Now, it's very important at this point that we not start talking about *war*–good god, first thing you know we'd be talking about nations and patriotism and tyranny and the rise of the nation state and all sorts of things in no way relevant to Homer, Hektor, Andromache, or–at *this* particular moment–to us.

If possible, it would be wonderful right now if every reader could inject novocain into every assumption, thought, half-thought, or bias toward war or against war that he or she has ever had, learned, or gathered unthinkingly into his or her life or mind.

One such bias or false assumption that people are very powerfully indoctrinated into embracing as a truth is the patent falsehood that wars have good sides and bad sides. *Some* wars, *very* rarely, do, but most wars don't. In any case, concerning the *Iliad*, we've already seen that justice can't possibly be done to Homer's poem unless readers see, acknowledge, and accept the poet's many signals, signs, and ways of showing that what he's writing about is war, *not* war between a right side and a wrong side.

We assume, in general, that there's blame in war, and that there's blame *for* war–and that that blame is one-sided. But a reading of the *Iliad* reveals–if the reading is a real, honest, and whole one–that that just isn't true, the one-sided blame requirement. I'm not saying that this is a good thing or a bad thing–all talk of good and bad is as of now officially tabled in this "classroom" until some considerable time from now–but I *am* saying that from Homer we can't help but learn some very clear-eyed definitions of war–far too clear-eyed to be tolerable to us very hypocritical moderns. From Homer we learn–good or bad, better or worse aside–that war must be defined as a thing that human beings *do*. Now, not for a split-second is this to say that war is the *only* thing that human beings do. *Everything* in the Homeric world–aside, that is, from events of nature–is the result of things that *human beings do*.

Think very carefully for a moment about what it would mean if you were really to live in a world like Homer's–a world where, as we've agreed, life is *all there is*.

This question will come back again a long time from now, in the mid-19th century, where we'll come upon poems like "Dover Beach" and "Loveliest of Trees" and, some decades later, novels like *To the*

Lighthouse. For Arnold, Housman, and Woolf, Charles Darwin had helped bring back the old Homeric question: *What do you do if you live in a world where life is all there is?*

In the world of Arnold and Housman (and of Virginia Woolf's parents), conventional religious belief in any kind of superior "life-after-death" had been wiped away in a single bold stroke by Darwinian biology [71] and a couple of other empirical sciences. [72]

Just what was a person to do in the sudden taking away, the sudden non-existence of *anything whatsoever* beyond life?

Well, the greatest number of people, as human beings tend to do, most probably simply chose not to believe the truth, but to go on just as before, believing not in Darwinian theory but in god and heaven instead, like always. These, the greatest number, can be represented by ostriches, their heads in the sand.

Others, less willing to deceive themselves and to pretend to believe in a truth that's no longer there, might, instead, succumb to despair or even suicide. If for a long and well-comforted time a person has been a believer in the after-life and all its rewards, and if suddenly it's shown that there *is* no afterlife and that there *are* no rewards, then there must logically also be—well, no *god*, and therefore also no *external* source of meaning and purpose in life whatsoever. For such a person, it would be as though, with a snap of the fingers, meaning had been drained out of the world. In the absence of meaning, in the absence of any future *beyond* life, why live? And so, pistol, poison, noose, bottle—the choices are many.

Far down the road from here, when we do get to the works of Arnold, Housman, and Woolf, we'll find that those authors are interested not in imitating the ostriches, and not in adding their own lot to the suicide statistics, but in pursuing a third response and third course of action, one altogether different from the other two—and one that would be seen by *everyone* in the world of Homer as the only course of action that made any sense in the first place. Here is what these would do: They would set out to make the very best that could *humanly* be made out of the quintessentially meaningless state of life itself.[73]

In Homer, *that* was the ideal. In a world where life is all there is, the ideal was to do nothing less than to live life *as well as possible* and to make of it as much as could be made. Anything–*any*thing–else would be failure.

•

All right. The purpose of life, then, is life, and the purpose of living within the state of life is to do so as *well* as possible. With this thought in mind, let's go back to Hektor, in Book VI, and the lengthy reply he gives to the desperate pleadings of poor Andromache–an answer that gives us some idea of the enormity of courage, sacrifice, and loss required of those in the Homeric world in their aim to live life as *well* as humanly possible.[74]

Hektor's answer begins more or less conventionally, as he says that he would be ashamed if he were to avoid the fighting:

> 'All these
> Things are in my mind also, lady; yet I would feel deep shame
> before the Trojans, and the Trojan women with trailing garments,
> if like a coward I were to shrink aside from the fighting.' (VI, 440-443)

As he goes on–

> 'and the spirit will not let me, since I have learned to be valiant
> and to fight always among the foremost ranks of the Trojans
> winning for my own self great glory, and for my father.' (VI, 444-446)

–a mix of words and ideas tumbles out upon us. Hektor says the "the spirit will not let" him shrink from the fighting, implying yet again that some divinity has him in its power. In our reading of the *Iliad*, however, the gods are long since out of the picture as controllers of *anything*—and, *voilà*, Hektor shows that he's in agreement with us by saying that the reason "the spirit will not let me" is because

> 'I have learned to be valiant
> and to fight always among the foremost ranks of the Trojans
> winning for my own self great glory, and for my father.' (VI, 444-446)

So right there, in between "the spirit will not let me" and "since I have learned," we're given another glimpse of the difference between the real *Iliad*—the one about human beings who are caught inside the state and condition of life, that is, and what you might call the "junior high" *Iliad*, a poem about life, people, and events all under the control of the gods.

There's an entirely different meaning between Hektor's saying (if he *had* said it in these exact words) "the spirit will not let me *and* I have learned to be valiant," on the one hand, and what he really does say, on the other: "the spirit will not let me, *since* I have learned to be valiant."

In the first case, the determination precedes and brings about the obedient result. In the second case, what *Hektor himself* has decided to do determines the limit and nature of what *is* to be done and *can* be done.[75] The spirit that won't let him is his *own*.

As always in the *Iliad*, human perception and volition lead. And then, tumbling along after, albeit often with great color and charm, follow the divinities' various and variously rendered versions of already accomplished things.

Hektor's next words play on this motif:

> 'For I know this thing well in my heart, and my mind knows it:

> there will come a day when sacred Ilion shall perish,
>
> and Priam, and the people of Priam of the strong ash spear.' (VI, 447-449)

Again, with all due respect, may we be pardoned for asking just how Hektor knows this? We could hypothesize that he means it in the sense that the same thing could be said of *all* cities and *all* peoples—that none will last forever. But that's a concept so broad that it's outside the bounds of the story and lacks relevance to it. What can explain his knowledge? Well, what can explain it, indeed, except that he was given an advance look at the script—just as all of Homer's listeners were, too?

We can quickly get onto murky ground, in the *Iliad*, by turning to the question of foreknowledge—I'm sure you remember the moment in Book I when even Athena claimed not to know the future well enough to know whether or not Achilleus would obey her.[76] In this present, and larger, case, Hektor himself seems convinced that Troy will be crushed—"'I know this thing well in my heart, and my mind knows it'"—even though there's no real *dramatic* justification for his certainty (who told him? how did he hear it? why is he saying it *now*?).

But let it go. In truth, the question of foreknowledge is just as unimportant as is the question of foreordination. The supposedly fore-ordained life of Achilleus, for example—that if he lives without honor he will die old, but that if he lives *with* honor he will die young—hardly matters, either, does it? Homer shows little interest in it, and the truth is that Achilleus will live as long as he lives, and he will live in precisely the way that he does live, and he will die when and as he does. The legend will arise afterward. No, fortune-telling is no more "real" or "true" in Homer's world than it is in ours. Then as now, life and its events occur first, prophecy comes tagging along after. The foreordinations, the prophecies, the manipulations of events by the gods—these, all of them, are the gingerbread ornaments and frosting-on-the-cake rosettes that came into being, in every single case, *after* whatever fact, occurrence, or event took place—we then being lured afterward into believing that said fact, occurrence, or event was *caused* by the frou-frou, rosette, or the sparkling wand.

They can be great fun, the frou-frous, tricks, and tales,[77] and you'd have to be a curmudgeon to deny it. But, still, far, far more important than the prophecies, tales, and tricks themselves, the great question always remains—and that's the question of *what serves what*—do the people serve the gods, or do the gods serve the people?

And the answer, of course, is not only obvious, but it is also essential to a fruitful understanding of the entire story of Western literature as it follows Homer and as we are going to follow that story.

Kids can have a riot with the baubles and bells, the tales of magic, teleportation, and super-hero doings provided by the gods. And good for them. The trouble is, we're not kids any more—although you might be surprised at *how hard* it can be to get readers to change their childish ways of seeing, receiving, internalizing, and reading the *Iliad*.[78]

My own guess is that the main reason people say they find Homer "primitive" is that they themselves are looking at him in a primitive way and from primitive assumptions. I'm fully aware that "primitive" is one of the words we've ruled out of our present discussion—and rightly—so let's drop the dichotomy of primitive-civilized and replace it with another, one that hits maybe even closer to home for Americans—the dichotomy of "childish versus adult."

The minute a person subordinates the humans to the gods in the *Iliad*, that person is reading the poem childishly. In order to read the poem in an adult way, the divinities must, to a one, be subordinated to the humans.

For kids, excitement is watching the gorgeous Athene "come down" from heaven to grab the strongest warrior of them all by the back hairs and give him a pull. For adults, fascination is watching this same woman–on a sort of maternal embassy–express the fear that she won't be able to draw this huge alpha-male gorilla back from the edge of self-destruction.

For kids, excitement is watching Magic Aphrodite break Alexandros' chinstrap in the nick of time and "in a thick mist" waft him off the battlefield and back to "his own perfumed bedchamber." For adults, fascination is in pondering what it can possibly mean for the nature of things in Homer's world that a chief warrior like Paris can not only prefer making love to making war and *not* be punished for it, but can run from the field of battle without being punished for *that*.

For kids, excitement is watching Aphrodite issue her marching orders to Helen, making her jump like a lackey. For adults, fascination is listening to Helen's near-Shakespearean interior monologue, where, in contemplating her own beauty, her own sexual desire, and her own fear of growing old, her thoughts and feelings range from high anger to deep grief, finally settling in to resignation and, from there, to fear and self-pity sufficient to disguise themselves as actual love for Alexandros–or maybe even to *become* love for Alexandros.

All of that–every bit of it, all of the human complexity, all of the captivating struggle of a real person wrestling with the terms that have been *offered her by life*[79]–all of that disappears with the snap of a finger the instant you make Helen subordinate to Aphrodite rather than keeping–the real way, the grown-up way–Aphrodite *descriptive* of Helen.

Once you begin looking at the poem in this "adult" way, it becomes understandable how it came about that drama would end up emerging from Homer. We've already agreed that even though the *Iliad* is tragic, it still isn't a *tragedy*. And we're correct in that agreement.

On the other hand, we don't have to agree that the poem isn't a *drama*. Certainly, it's "dramatic." And, just as certainly, many of the dramatic sections in it–though far from all; what we're about to observe isn't so true of the battle scenes—are clear and fully formed episodes of *psychological* drama.

Who's the dramatic hero? There are lots of them—and that's the reason, you'll remember, the *Iliad* can never be tragedy. But it seems to me that it can still be—and that it *is*—drama, albeit not in the sense of the great Fifth Century tragedians. But drama.

Let's go back to one of Homer's dramatic heroes and take a look. The hero I've got in mind is poor Hektor, still waiting patiently back where we left him, midway through his farewell speech to Andromache—truly his farewell speech, since he'll never again return to her alive.

We can credit Hektor's deep warrior-knowledge for giving him his sense of certainty that Troy is doomed. No goddess whispers in his ear, no bird-reader interprets the battlefield for him, but long experience, keen observation, and immense knowledge of tactic, advantage, and disadvantage—we can credit these for Hektor's certainty that Troy is doomed. And, though bearing this heavy certainty, he doesn't sugarcoat so much as a particle of it. He doesn't flinch from looking straight at the most horrific and awful results that will be brought into being by defeat—not even glancing away from the prospect of Andromache's enslavement and ruin, the kind of thing we saw Helen so terrified of in Book III.

Says Hektor:

> 'But it is not so much the pain to come of the Trojans
> that troubles me, not even of Priam the king nor Hekaba,
> not the thought of my brothers who in their numbers and valour
> shall drop in the dust under the hands of men who hate them,
> as troubles me the thought of you, when some bronze-armoured
> Achaian leads you off, taking away your day of liberty,
> in tears; and in Argos you must work at the loom of another,

and carry water from the spring Messes or Hyperemia,

all unwilling, but strong will be the necessity upon you;

and some day seeing you shedding tears a man will say of you:

"This is the wife of Hektor, who was ever the bravest fighter

of the Trojans, breakers of horses, in the days when they fought about Ilion."

So will one speak of you; and for you it will be yet a fresh grief,

to be widowed of such a man who could fight off the day of your slavery.

But may I be dead and the piled earth hide me under before I

hear you crying and know by this that they drag you captive.' (VI, 450-465)

Hektor, then, as one of the epic's great dramatic heroes, stands here at the edge of the moment when one of the central events of the huge drama is about to be put into action. However stiff the speech may sound, and perhaps be, there's in it at the same time a faint touch of pathos and a touch, probably equally faint, of *dramatic* feeling. The passage is still formulaic in its tone, but at the same time there's a *seed* in it of something that will emerge openly in three hundred years or so—"dramatic irony," the element that will make stage plays seem and feel *like* stage plays.[80] Dramatic irony comes about when, for one example, the audience knows more than a central character does, as, in this case, *we* know that Hektor *will* be slain by Achilleus, *and* we know that Troy *will* be conquered, while Hektor only profoundly suspects it.

That's not much of a difference in degree-of-knowing for the purpose of creating dramatic irony, and Homer's interest in it, in any case, is negligible, maybe even non-existent. Its appearance here in the Hektor/Andromache episode is, I suspect, as much accidental as anything. For that matter, as far as the great Homer is concerned, with his absolute indifference to creating *any* narrative quality even remotely connected to suspense, it would hardly matter if every single character knew every single thing that was going to happen throughout the entire poem, since even if they did know what was going to happen, they wouldn't behave any differently from the way they do now. Even if everyone knew what the outcome was going to be, that outcome would remain unchanged in the least detail.

Why on earth is *that*? How on earth can that *be*?

Well, there are two answers. The first simple, the second complex.

The first is that the entire story, top to bottom and inside out, came down to Homer in finished form (except for the similes–more on them soon). The story is the story, the roles are the roles, the characters are the characters, the events are the events, and that's that. Nobody in Homer's audience even *wants* innovation or change or any element of the unexpected whatsoever–they've assembled as an audience in order to hear and see once again what they've all heard and seen or at least known about before. They have not come in order to be surprised or to be held in doubt or to be made to feel suspense, the very *last* sensation they'd have thought of as being desirable–if they'd thought of it at all. In fact, suspense hasn't been invented yet–though Aeschylus, a kid still minus-three-hundred years of age, is working on it.

For the moment, on to the second reason why the entire drama would remain unchanged even if every character did know the exact outcome of all that's taking place. In a sense, after all, they already *do* know. The audience knows, Homer knows, and so how on earth could the *characters* not know, since they, too, have been through the same old thing so many times already themselves? It's possible, in fact, that the only really significant "suspension of disbelief"[81] among Homer's audience is their accepting the convention that, as they hear the great old epic told yet again, the events in it are *taken* nevertheless as befalling the characters for the very first time ever.

And this fact, in turn, can help lead us to an understanding of what the subject of the great old epic really is, what its conflict really is, and what its audiences *took from it* decade after decade after decade. If we can gain a sense of what they took from it over all those centuries–

well, we'll be better positioned to make our way to understanding what the great old poem is *really about.*

A last glance at Hektor's farewell to Andromache, and then onward to the *Iliad* as a whole.

In spite of his sense of looming defeat, Hektor prays for the future greatness of his son Astyanax:

> 'Zeus, and you other immortals, grant that this boy, who is my son,
>
> may be as I am, pre-eminent among the Trojans,
>
> great in strength, as am I, and rule strongly over Ilion;
>
> and some day let them say of him: "He is better by far than his father",
>
> as he comes in from the fighting; and let him kill his enemy
>
> and bring home the blooded spoils, and delight the heart of his mother.' (VI,
>
> 476-482)

And then, his decision final that it's time to return to battle, Hektor tries to comfort Andromache, and in so doing makes mention of "fate." It's lucky for us that he does, since the very subject itself–of "fate"–offers us a necessary key for entry into the poem. Thanks to Hektor, we're now almost in position to get a good strong grasp of the whole of the poem, its real subject, its purpose, and legacy.

> So speaking he set his child again in the arms of his beloved
>
> wife, who took him back again to her fragrant bosom
>
> smiling in her tears; and her husband saw, and took pity upon her,
>
> and stroked her with his hand, and called her by name and spoke to her:
>
> 'Poor Andromache! Why does your heart sorrow so much for me?
>
> No man is going to hurl me to Hades, unless it is fated,
>
> but as for fate, I think that no man yet has escaped it
>
> once it has taken its first form, neither brave man nor coward.
>
> Go therefore back to our house, and take up your own work,

> the loom and the distaff, and see to it that your handmaidens
> ply their work also; but the men must see to the fighting,
> all men who are the people of Ilion, but I beyond others.' (VI, 482-493)

It sounds almost like double-talk, doesn't it. First, Hektor begs Andromache not to worry about him, since "No man is going to hurl me to Hades" on his re-entry into the battle. And then comes the malicious little qualifier trotting along behind: "unless it is fated."

In other words, a man won't die–*unless* it's his time to die.

That is, fate won't get a man–*unless* it's fated that fate will get him. And, in what's maybe the *most* radical of these already-radical implied definitions and their corollaries, there's this:

> but as for fate, I think that no man yet has escaped it
> once it has taken its first form, neither brave man nor coward.

And what's so radical about it? Well, let's consider. The farther we go forward with Homer, the farther we read into the *Iliad*, then all the more things do we see fall away to be left behind–all the various props and crutches and ornaments and pre-existing ideas and structures that at the start seemed to give form and shape and direction and purpose to the life we were seeing portrayed in the poem.

There were the purpose- and comfort-giving gods, for example, but we soon discovered that *they* have nothing whatsoever to contribute to the Homeric world other than tradition and color and lots and lots of very sneaky narrative shortcuts. But as for anything substantive? Anything *value*-making? No, they're like decorations at a party. They may make the party nice, but they don't *make* the party.

And then there was death–now, *there* was something worth living for, if you'll pardon the deliberate Post-Platonic usage. But we learned fast enough that death is not *something* but, instead, it's *nothing*, and certainly therefore it can't be anything to live for. Death is absolute, death is the worst thing, death is "sheer death" (XIV, 507), death is the absence of life, and death is the most despised thing there is. One of my own favorite lines in the whole poem comes in Book IX, when Phoinix, Aias, and Odysseus approach Achilleus in order to list the innumerable gifts Agamemnon will give him if only he promise to return to the fighting. Achilleus, understandably on guard against the possibility of a trick or a verbal trap, says this after Odysseus has given the recitation of the gifts:

> Then in answer to him spoke Achilleus of the swift feet:
> 'Son of Laertes and seed of Zeus, resourceful Odysseus:
> without consideration for you I must make my answer,
> the way I think, and the way it will be accomplished, that you may not
> come one after another, and sit by me, and speak softly.
> For as I detest the doorways of Death, I detest that man, who
> hides one thing in the depths of his heart, and speaks forth another.'
> (IX, 307-313)

So neither the gods nor death can be relied on to bring about meaning, or to create meaning, or to inject meaning into life. But certainly there must at *least* remain that great staple, that Meaning-Generator that we all remember from our first introductions to Homer (if we were lucky enough to have had such things) all the way back in junior high school, under the tutelage of the most idealistic and well-intended of teachers–who told us a thousand times if they told us once that what the Homeric heroes lived for was the great and high value of achieving *honor*, or, as Richmond Lattimore would have it, *honour*. But–well, er, um, *do* they? Best is to look and see for ourselves. And a way to do that is by going back to those two lines in Hektor's farewell to Andromache and to ask again what was especially radical about

them. Here they are. See if you can spot the radical quintet of puta-
tively harmless words:

> but as for fate, I think that no man yet has escaped it
> once it has taken its first form, neither brave man nor coward.

As I'm sure you did, without the least bit of trouble, those five little
words jumping right up at you like terriers ready to nip: *"neither brave
man nor coward."*

This is what I sometimes call a "whoosh" moment–others might
call it an "omigod" moment, or a "wind out of my sails" moment. Anyway, it's the kind of moment *insisting* that serious attention be paid to
the matter at hand–and, often as not, insisting that serious reassess-
ment be made of whatever prior thought or assumption a person may
have been holding about that matter at hand.

After all, what happens now to that last single source of meaning-
generation, the notion that what provided meaning in and for the lives
of the Homeric heroes was "living for the great and high value of
achieving *honor*"? If a person doesn't or can't or won't die unless it's
"fated" so, and if these same terms apply equally to "brave man and
coward," what possible incentive remains toward the achieving of
honor?

It begins to sound–doesn't it?–as though life in the Homeric world
becomes, really, nothing more than a crap shoot. You don't and can't
die until fate dictates, but who dictates fate? Answer: *Nobody.*[82] It
comes more and more clear–from Helen, from Andromache, from
Hektor, from the terrified fighters on the field, each "[looking] about
him for a way to escape the sheer death"–that *no* overseeing principle or power governs, directs, or shapes this world; that *nothing* gives
guarantee of reward to those alive *within* this world; that death offers
nothing except the absence of the one thing that matters to anyone,

namely, life itself; and that, if we were allowed to jump forward two-and-a-half millennia or so (and who says we're not), to the year 1867 and Matthew Arnold's famous poem, "Dover Beach," we might find in Arnold's lines about the spiritual emptiness of mid-Victorian England a near-perfect expression of what we're seeing and discovering more and more to be true about Homer's unguided world, about the unsupported world of the *Iliad*.

Standing at the window one mid-19th Century evening and looking out across the English Channel, a man says to the woman beside him:

> Ah, love, let us be true
> To one another! for the world, which seems
> To lie before us like a land of dreams,
> So various, so beautiful, so new,
> Hath really neither joy, nor love, nor light,
> Nor certitude, nor peace, nor help for pain;
> And we are here as on a darkling plain
> Swept with confused alarms of struggle and flight,
> Where ignorant armies clash by night.

With meaning, purpose, or support coming from *no* extra-human or external source whatsoever, either above or below, the only remaining place to turn for those missing elements–purpose and meaning in life–is to the human mind itself and the human heart that's inseparably attached to it. Arnold's line urges "Ah, love, let us be true / To one another," since no *other* source of meaning, no other source capable of providing the *meaning* of existence, is available in or from the world other than the meaning that comes from or is created *by* human beings themselves.[83]

We're getting very close now to the heart of Homer and of the world he lived in, saw, and preserved for us in his poetry.

We can now, for example, define "fate" or "destiny," those two synonymous terms. Here's our Homeric definition: Fate is *what happens*. Destiny, too, is *what happens*.

And what *causes* things to happen in Homer's world (as in ours)? What *causes* fate? There are two answers. First, what causes things to happen, or what causes fate, is *nature*. And, second, what causes things to happen, or what causes fate, is human action, human choice.

The only source of meaning, then, and the only source of *creating* meaning, is through human action. If you wish, you could use the phrase "human decision" instead.

When we get to Beckett's *Waiting for Godot*, in the 1940s AD, we'll take a peek Beckett's contemporary, Jean Paul Sartre, suggesting this very same thing when he says that "we are now on the plane where there are only men."[84] Homer knew that to be true also, and knew it well, all the way back in the 7th or 6th century BC. To my own way of thinking, this Homeric knowledge–or this Homeric way of *seeing*–is the single most durable and the single most important idea-fact, or fact-idea, in all of Western art. Speaking only of Western literature out of all the arts, I would argue that this idea-fact has managed by one way or another to survive–most of the time at very great peril–all the way from its Homeric origins down to "the pupil age of this present twelve o'clock at midnight."[85] The story of Western literature from Homer through Samuel Beckett is, among many other things, the story of this fact-idea or idea-fact disappearing, re-appearing, surviving in extraordinary and unexpected places, only to be lost again–and yet, I pray, at last found once more.

There are hundreds of ways to study literature. Over the past forty years or so, my own main way–both as reader and as writer–has come to consist of following this particular idea-fact through literary history from Homer to now. To me, it's a project of extraordinary, even limitless, interest. I'm willing, in fact, to go so far as to say that if we–now, today, in the twenty-first century–are able to find literary means to re-capture, re-recognize, and re-achieve Homer's ancient fact-idea– the fact-idea that we ourselves are all we've got, and that we ourselves are all we've got to *rely* on–*then* we may possibly be able to survive *as* a people, as an assemblage of peoples, or even as a species.

If, however, we're not able to re-achieve, or re-capture that fact-idea–then I suspect it much more probable that we are doomed.

•

And so there's a lot of work and exploration ahead. Before getting to it, though, we've got to finish talking about Homer's fact-idea as we find it in and receive it from the *Iliad*. And *then* we have to talk about the simile.

Lest anyone think, as I can imagine they might, that Hektor alone, enormous figure though he be, is too narrow a pedestal in and of himself to base our "new" definition of fate on, let me turn to none other than Achilleus to find a broadening of the foundation.

And that takes us back to Book IX, where Achilleus warned Phoinix, Aias, and Odysseus that they must speak honestly,

> For as I detest the doorways of Death, I detest that man, who
> hides one thing in the depths of his heart, and speaks forth another.'
> (IX, 307-313)

Now let's continue with the next nine lines of that speech:

> But I will speak to you the way it seems best to me: neither
> do I think the son of Atreus, Agamemnon, will persuade me,
> nor the rest of the Danaans, since there was no gratitude given
> for fighting incessantly forever against your enemies.
> Fate is the same for the man who holds back, the same if he fights hard.
> We are all held in a single honour, the brave with the weaklings.

A man dies still if he has done nothing, as one who has done much.
Nothing is won for me, now that my heart has gone through its afflictions
in forever setting my life on the hazard of battle. (IX, 314-322)

In light of the subjects we've been talking about, these are unquestionably amazing words. Achilleus himself says not only that fate and death are identical, but he says that they're the same thing for *everyone*: "We are all held in a single honour, / the brave with the weaklings." That word "honour" positively leaps up off the page at you—the word that my beloved junior high school teachers led me to believe was the *key word* to an understanding of the entirety of Homer! And yet here the very idea of honour is casually tossed aside onto the garbage dump by no less a towering figure than Achilleus, and not just tossed aside but also clearly subordinated to the one thing that so obviously outranks it—that one thing being *death*.

It's hard to see—isn't it?—how the question could be more obvious: Why go to all the trouble of seeking honor, spending entire lifetimes of pain and hardship—when in the end it will make no conceivable difference whatsoever? Achilleus himself says it: "A man dies still if he has done nothing, as one who has done much."

Now, we know perfectly well that in spite of all these insurmountably important things that Achilleus—echoing Hektor—says, he's *also* still a man of enormous pride and great anger, *and* he remains angry for the very reason that his honor has been hurt:

All the other prizes of honour he gave the great men and the princes
and held fast by them, but from me alone of all the Achaians
he has taken and keeps the bride of my heart. Let him lie beside her
and be happy. Yet why must the Argives fight with the Trojans?
And why was it the son of Atreus assembled and led here
these people? Was it not for the sake of lovely-haired Helen?

> Are the sons of Atreus alone among mortal men the ones
> who love their wives? Since any who is a good man, and careful,
> loves her who is his own and cares for her, even as I now
> loved this one from my heart, though it was my spear that won her.
> Now that he has deceived me and taken from my hands my prize of honor,
> let him try me no more. I know him well. He will not persuade me.
> (IX, 334-345)

Yes, *there's* our old Achilleus, just as we remember him from back in Book I, quick to anger, quick to take offense–even where offense *may* not have been intended–and unlikely ever to back down once he's been stung with dishonor–real or perceived–in ways such as this.
All true. "Honour." Very important indeed, and ever a part of daily life among the Homeric heroes. And yet not a *word* of what we said in the paragraph before this one, or what we've said so far in *this* one, undercuts or weakens the greater subject that both Hektor and Achilleus have introduced to us and that we have been talking about most seriously. Hektor himself, back in Book VI, said he would be ashamed before the Trojan women were he to hold back from the fighting. Now Achilleus *does* hold back from the fighting, but for the same reason, although inversely–that he's *been* shamed. No, there's no question whatsoever that pride, dignity, reputation, and honor are of enormous importance in the lives of the great Homeric characters.

But that doesn't mean that those things are of absolute importance. Achilleus is willing to let the Achaian side in the war lose to the Trojan side rather than swallow his pride and "give in" to Agamemnon's disrespect–real or perceived–toward him. But we've got to be very, very careful in the *Iliad*, as in all literary reading, to read what *is* revealed to us by the lines of poetry and not to make the mistake of reading *more* than what is revealed to us by them.

Achilleus, his mind made up, says of Agamemnon, in a line redolent of Shakespeare-to-come, "let him try me no more. I know him well. He will not persuade me."

Speaking of the achievements in style that we'll later call Shakespearean, how can anyone *not* feel compelled to read aloud these extraordinary lines crafted for us by Richmond Lattimore from the poem's hexameters:

> 'He cheated me and he did me hurt. Let him not beguile me
> with words again. This is enough for him. Let him of his own will
> be damned, since Zeus of the counsels has taken his wits away from him.
> I hate his gifts. I hold him light as the strip of a splinter.
> Not if he gave me ten times as much, and twenty times over
> as he possesses now, not if more should come to him from elsewhere,
> or gave all that is brought in to Orchomenos, all that is brought in
> to Thebes of the hundred gates, where through each of the gates two hundred
> fighting men come forth to war with horses and chariots;
> not if he gave me gifts as many as the sand or the dust is,
> not even so would Agamemnon have his way with my spirit
> until he had made good to me all this heartrending insolence. (IX, 375-387)

For all its grandeur and passion, the passage can hardly keep a modern reader or listener from asking, "What is Achilleus *doing* in giving up all this? Is he *crazy*? What can he be *thinking*?"

And, indeed, what *is* he thinking? Yes, he's thinking about his burning rage at Agamemnon. But he's thinking about something else, too—something more important than all the riches in all the world. Look:

> For not
> worth the value of my life are all the possessions they fable
> were won for Ilion, that strong-founded citadel, in the old days
> when there was peace, before the coming of the sons of the Achaians;

> not all that the stone doorsill of the Archer holds fast within it
> of Phoibos Apollo in Pytho of the rocks. Of possessions
> cattle and fat sheep are things to be had for the lifting,
> but a man's life cannot come back again, it cannot be lifted
> nor captured again by force, once it has crossed the teeth's barrier.[86]
> (IX, 400-409)

And there it is—not only what Achilleus seems really to be thinking about, but also what the entirety of the *Iliad* is really about. That is, again, it's about the ontologically plain and profound fact that in the Homeric world, there is *nothing but life*.

These corollaries follow: First, that waste of life is waste of *everything*; and, second, that failure to live life *as well as humanly possible* is waste of a parallel and equally important kind.

Achilleus is an enormous problem in the *Iliad*, since, from almost the very beginning, he performs poorly and negatively within the terms of each of these two corollaries. He is less hero than example of failed hero. He wastes life in great quantity *and* he lacks the strength to cause himself to live life as well as possible, an achievement, were he able to bring himself to accomplish it, that would bring an end also to a straight-out *waste* of life—and also of *lives*, those of the fighters being lost in the unnecessarily intensified war.

Agamemnon from the beginning has shamed Achilleus in a way that Achilleus hasn't even been perceptive of—by demonstrating himself, all the way back in Book I, the superior commander *and* the man superior in his ability to rein in, hold back, and control the forces of violent anger that exist inside himself just as they do inside Achilleus. And in Book IX, Agamemnon shows these traits of living as well as possible all over again. The wise Nestor castigates Agamemnon, speaking of his own disturbed thoughts:

'ever since that day, illustrious, when you went from the shelter
of angered Achilleus, taking by force the girl Briseis
against the will of the rest of us, since I for my part
urged you strongly not to, but you, giving way to your proud heart's
anger, dishonoured a great man, one whom the immortals
honour, since you have taken his prize and keep it. But let us
even now think how we can make this good and persuade him
with words of supplication and with the gifts of friendship.' (IX, 106-113)

Nestor is right, no one has the least doubt. But the more important matter is that Agamemnon again shows the strength and inner resources that, the first time around, enabled him to quell his own anger. Here, now, those same strengths allow him to admit his prior error and failure, to swallow his own pride, and to acknowledge the responsibility he bears in having brought about the calamity that now surrounds them all:

Then in turn the lord of men Agamemnon spoke to him:
'Aged sir, this was no lie when you spoke of my madness.
I was mad, I myself will not deny it. Worth many
fighters is that man whom Zeus in his heart loves, as now
he has honoured this man and beaten down the Achaian people.
But since I was mad, in the persuasion of my heart's evil,
I am willing to make all good and give back gifts in abundance.' (IX, 114-120)[87]

As for Achilleus, the greater fighter but by far the lesser man, it won't be until all the way back into Book XIX that he will at last acknowledge the better course of putting aside his anger toward Agamemnon–though it mustn't be forgotten that by *this* time there are other major influences on his decision, among them the fact that the Trojans have advanced their fight all the way to the Achaian ships *and*

that Achilleus' beloved friend and comrade Patroclus, fighting in
Achilleus' own armor, has been slain by Hektor:

> But now, when all the Achaians were in one body together,
> Achilleus of the swift feet stood up before them and spoke to them:
> 'Son of Atreus, was this after all the better way for
> both, for you and me, that we, for all our hearts' sorrow,
> quarreled together for the sake of a girl in soul-perishing hatred?
> I wish Artemis had killed her beside the ships with an arrow
> on that day when I destroyed Lyrnessos and took her.
> For thus not all these too many Achaians would have bitten
> the dust,[88] by enemy hands, when I was away in my anger.
> This way was better for the Trojans and Hektor; yet I think
> the Achaians will too long remember this quarrel between us.
> Still, we will let all this be a thing of the past, thought it hurts us,
> and beat down by constraint the anger that rises inside us.
> Now I am making an end of my anger. It does not become me
> unrelentingly to rage on.' (XIX, 54-68)

To give credit where credit is due, on the other hand, we really must
note that Phoinix, Aias, and Odysseus *are* able to make *some* progress,
during Book IX, in their simply humanitarian implorings that
Achilleus soften his glacial anger. Phoinix, the childless old man who
raised Achilleus as his own offspring, urges, from the very heart,
"'Then, Achilleus, beat down your great anger. It is not / yours to have
a pitiless heart'" (IX, 496-497). Perhaps most effective is the eloquent
plea of Aias, "'Now make gracious the spirit within you. / Respect
your own house; see, we are under the same roof with you, / from the
multitude of the Danaans, we who desire beyond all / others to have
your honour and love, out of all the Achaians'" (IX, 639-642). Ira
Bloomgarden, the friend and colleague I mentioned in the introduc-

tion to this volume, finds himself especially moved by Aias' line "'see, we are under the same roof with you,'" finding in it the equivalent of Aias asking Achilleus, "What about *us*? You're hurting *us*, too." And it's true that Aias alone does in fact get a little bit of compromise out of his angry fellow-warrior. Achilleus tells Aias and Odysseus to take *this* message back to Agamemnon:

> that I shall not think again of the bloody fighting
> until such time as the son of wise Priam, Hektor the brilliant,
> comes all the way to the ships of the Myrmidons, and their shelters,
> slaughtering the Argives, and shall darken with fire our vessels. (IX, 650-653)

And yet even so, after the embassy–except for Phoinix, who stays in camp overnight with Achilleus and Patroclus–returns to the Achaian camp, Diomedes speaks out to Agamemnon:

> 'Son of Atreus, most lordly and king of men, Agamemnon,
> I wish you had not supplicated the blameless son of Peleus
> with innumerable gifts offered. He is a proud man without this,
> and now you have driven him far deeper into his pride.' (IX, 697-700)

And what listener or reader doesn't tend to agree with him? Or with Odysseus, who, earlier, while still at Achilleus' tent, advises Phoinix and Aias that they call off the embassy and return to camp,

> '. . . seeing that Achilleus
> has made savage the proud-hearted spirit within his body.
> He is hard, and does not remember that friends' affection
> wherein we honoured him by the ships, far beyond all others.
> Pitiless.' (IX, 628-632)

The embassy's appeal to compassion, brotherhood, or humanity in the grotesquely rigid and self-centered Achilleus results only in the concession that we've already noted. Indeed, "Pitiless." Soon, we will hear no less than Apollo himself remark that Achilleus "'has destroyed pity'" (XXIV, 44).

•

Still, it's time now, at least for the moment, to leave the petulant and show-stealing Achilleus and return to the real–that is, return to the *whole*–stage of the actual and complete world of the epic as we find it in the *Iliad*. Achilleus is a difficult figure to get around, or to put aside, or to get out from *behind*, almost as if he's some giant sitting right in front of you in a theater, blocking your view of everything on stage (even though "everything on stage" continues to go on).

An interesting, though almost purely academic, question is whether, in the absence of the story of Achilleus' anger, the *Iliad* would ever have come into existence at all.

Well, almost certainly it would not have. Achilleus' terrible behavior is unquestionably the germ of the story ("Sing, goddess, the anger of Peleus' son Achilleus / and its devastation, which put pains thousandfold upon the Achaians. . ."). And yet, after spending the years and years with the *Iliad* that I have spent, there's no doubt in me whatsoever but that the story of Achilleus was *not* what interested the poet most, neither in the material as it came down to him nor in any reflections it had on the world he himself lived in.

Instead of calling Achilleus the "germ" of the story–a seed that would grow into a great plant–I think it would be more accurate to think of Achilleus and the Achilleus story in the metaphor of the oyster: The Achilleus story is the imperfection, the bit of sand, dirt, or stone, the *irritant* around which the pearl, layer by expanding and translucent layer, becomes gathered, formed, and whole.

If I'm right that, in the world as Homer sees and understands it, life is the medium within which people find themselves caught, and if I'm right that, for Homer, the *one* meaningful and creative[89] thing human beings can do is live that life as well as humanly possible—well, if I'm right about those two things, Achilleus, the central figure in the story, is sure a rotten example.

He does so poorly at living life as well as humanly possible, in fact, that even after rejoining the Achaian forces (not necessarily for the right reasons) and at last slaying Hektor, he has a relapse into the same kind of sullen, blinded, "mad,"[90] intransigent, wretched, thuggish, punk behavior as he showed in Book I—this time in his abusing and disgracing and horse-dragging the slain Hektor's body for *twelve entire days* without apparent diminishment either in his righteousness or his rage.

At last, even Apollo himself grows angry at his fellow gods[91] for failing to exert *some* sort of retardant influence on Achilleus' behavior, for their failing to give *some* sort of comfort to the family and kinsmen of Hektor, *some* extending toward them of decency and pity and plain human dignity:

> 'No, you gods; your desire is to help this cursed Achilleus
> within whose breast there are no feelings of justice, nor can
> his mind be bent, but his purposes are fierce, like a lion
> who when he has given way to his own great strength and his haughty
> spirit, goes among the flocks of men, to devour them.
> So Achilleus has destroyed pity, and there is not in him
> any shame; which does much harm to men but profits them also.
> For a man must some day lose one who was even closer
> than this; a brother from the same womb, or a son. And yet
> he weeps for him, and sorrows for him, and then it is over,
> for the Destinies put in mortal men the heart of endurance.
> But this man, now he has torn the heart of life from great Hektor,

> Ties him to his horses and drags him around his beloved companion's
> Tomb; and nothing is gained thereby for his good, or his honour.
> Great as he is, let him take care not to make us angry;
> For see, he does dishonour to the dumb earth in his fury.' (XXIV, 39-54)

Achilleus has become a monster, an unleashed and conscienceless force of destruction, a thoughtless, ravening power that goes about doing "'dishonour [even] to the dumb earth in his fury.'"

This is about as far from our hypothesized Homeric ideal of "living life as well as is humanly possible" as a model of behavior could be.

Either this–this awful story of the wretched and ruinous Achilleus–is *not* what the *Iliad* is really about[92]–or we'll be forced to throw out altogether our hypothesis about the Homeric ideal.

To accept that the Achilleus story constitutes the heart of the *Iliad* would necessitate conceding that the *Iliad*, at *its* heart, is also, after all, and contrary to my earlier insistences, primitive and barbaric.

But if that *were* true, believe me, we wouldn't find ourselves reading the poem today–and certainly not with the interest that we bring to it and that it offers us back in return. It seems to me a clear fact, therefore, that the poem must be *about* something else, must itself *be* something else–something quite different entirely.

What *is* that other thing?

Well, we haven't yet looked closely at the similes. *They* will help us find out.

Day Six

Assignment: Books XXI, XXII

Well, now you've had extra time to read. Here's quiz four:

1) In Bk. XIV, Hera tricks Zeus. Two other gods help her. These are:

a) Ares and Poseidon   b) Hephaistos and Hermes   c) Thetis and Aphrodite   d) Athena and Rumor   e) Aphrodite and Sleep

2) Identify the one that plays a part in the love-making of Zeus and Hera:

a) a new suit of armor   b) a length of magic wire   c) a golden cloud   d) a bolt of lightning   e) an earthquake

3) In Bk. XVIII, Achilleus sends the Trojans into disarray by:

a) throwing huge boulders at the Trojans   b) starting a great fire that forces the Trojans back   c) offering a single duel with Hektor   d) standing by the ditch near the Achaian ships and shouting loudly three times   e) organizing the other commanders to mount an immediate, concerted offensive

4) Identify which one asks Hephaistos to forge new amour for Achilleus:

a) Aphrodite   b) Hera   c) Agamemnon   d) Thetis   e) Helen

5) The first part of the new armor Hephaistos forges is the

a) helmet   b) corselet   c) shield   d) leg-armor   e) spear

Let's imagine that we really *are* in a room together—you know, a class-room—and I ask you to come up, by a kind of free association, with a random list of things, ideas, attitudes, perhaps even objects that might pop into your mind, or be lingering in your mind, now that you're fresh from reading all ten of the assigned books of the *Iliad*—or maybe more than just those ten.

Would it be unlikely that, if I were to ask, a list like the following might accumulate, and might be copied—by me—up on the black-board?

Violence, Brutality, Kindness, Slaying, Nurturing, Stabbing, Mothering, Beauty, Ugliness, Eyeball on spear-tip, Gentleness, Killing, Art, War, Bit-ing the Dust, Babies, Force, Passivity & turning other cheek, Cruelty, Softness, Assault, Bleeding, Terror, Bestiality, Spear points, Craftsman-ship, Guts spilled, Sheep-herding, Gushing blood, Storms approaching

In full disclosure, I can vouch for the fact, having seen it happen over many years in the classroom, that lists just about like this one would typically emerge and be copied by me onto the blackboard. Some-thing more convenient now is that I can ask the computer to alpha-betize the list, like this:

1. An Eyeball Stuck on a Spear-tip

2. Art

3. Assault

4. Babies

5. Beauty

6. Bestiality

7. Biting the Dust

8. Bleeding

9. Brutality

10. Craftsmanship

11. Cruelty

12. Force

13. Gentleness

14. Gushing blood

15. Guts spilled

16. Killing

17. Kindness

18. Mothering

19. Nurturing

20. Passivity

21. Sheep herding

22. Slaying

23. Softness

23. Spear points

25. Stabbing

26. Storms approaching

27. Terror

28. Ugliness

29. Violence

30. War

Now, let's propose an experiment. The computer says that there are thirty items on the list, and so, for convenience, let's imagine a class with thirty students.[93] Let's imagine these students dividing up the list into tens, so that the first person will take items 1-10, the second items 11-20, the third items 21-30, the fourth items 1-10, and so on, until everyone has ten items.

Then, equipped with clipboards, the students might be asked to do a kind of survey. Either in the neighborhood of the college or in the neighborhood where they lived, they could ask ten passers-by a very simple question about each of the ten items on the clipboard. The question would be, "Do you tend to have a more positive or a more negative attitude or response to. . . ?"

A clipboard could be set up something like this one, with its hash marks showing how one student's ten passers-by might have responded

The same sort of attempt to suggest our own contemporary attitudes toward things violent and gory, on the one hand, and toward things soft, fuzzy, and sweet, on the other, could be suggested by a person's simply drawing a horizontal line on the blackboard and then asking people to place each of our thirty words or phrases above the line,

GENERALLY POSITIVE		GENERALLY NEGATIVE	
1. Eyeball on speartip		1. Eyeball on speartip	#### ####
2. Art	#### ####	2. Art	
3. Assault		3. Assault	#### ####
4. Babies	#### ####	4. Babies	
5. Beauty	#### ####	5. Beauty	
6. Bestiality		6. Bestiality	#### ####
7. Biting the Dust	///	7. Biting the Dust	#### //
8. Bleeding	//	8. Bleeding	#### ///
9. Brutality		9. Brutality	#### ####
10. Craftsmanship	####	10. Craftsmanship	####

below the line, or—in cases of uncertainty or mixed feelings—more or less on a level *with* the line.

Why a horizontal line? Well, as we'll see when we get there, Plato tried—successfully, I'm afraid—to re-invent the world in such a way that the direction "up" is considered superior to the direction "down," just as anything "spiritual" or "non-physical" is considered superior to anything "material" or "fleshly" or "bodily."

The same, thanks to Plato and his followers, goes for beauty and ugliness. "Beautiful" things are associated generally[94] with the "immaterial" or the "pure" and are seen as superior to "ugly" things, which are to be associated with the "low," the "bodily," even with the putrid, diseased, or fecal.

All that said, here's the kind of pattern that, in general, results from the horizontal-line-on-the-blackboard experiment:

Passivity		
Gentleness	Kindness	
Beauty	Mothering	
Babies	Nurturing	
Art	Softness	
Craftsmanship	Biting the dust	
Sheep herding	Storms approaching	
Eyeball on speartip	Killing	
Assault	Slaying	
Force	Stabbing	
Bestiality	Ugliness	
Force	Violence	
Ugliness	War	

And now what? Well, now we want to consider how *Homer* might have responded to one of the students with a clipboard, had he been a passer-by in New York City sometime in the late twentieth century, and how *he* might have responded to the experiment with the horizontal line and thirty items.

So let's go back to Book IV, where Pandarus breaks the truce–and does it by attempting a very long bow-and-arrow shot at Menelaos.

•

The passage describing Pandarus' preparation for his shot is a good one, full of detail, and worth citing:

> Pandaros strung his bow and put it in position, bracing it
>
> against the ground, and his brave friends held their shields in front of him
>
> for fear the warlike sons of the Achaians might rise up and rush him

> before he had struck warlike Menelaos, the son of Atreus.
> He stripped away the lid of the quiver, and took out an arrow
> feathered, and never shot before, transmitter of dark pain.
> Swiftly he arranged the bitter arrow along the bowstring,
> and made his prayer to Apollo the light-born, the glorious archer,
> that he would accomplish a grand sacrifice of lambs first born
> when he came home again to the city of sacred Zeleia.
> He drew, holding at once the grooves and the ox-hide bowstring
> and brought the string against his nipple, iron to the bowstave.
> But when he had pulled the great weapon till it made a circle,
> the bow groaned, and the string sang high, and the arrow, sharp-pointed,
> leapt away, furious, to fly through the throng before it. (IV, 112-126)[95]

As you know–and as all Homer's listeners knew–Pandarus strikes his target, but not mortally.

Now watch closely, with our blackboard and clipboard experiments in mind. Here comes the first simile we've examined in an effort to find out how Homer would have responded in *either* of our experiments:

> Still the blessed gods immortal did not forget you,
> Menelaos, and first among them Zeus' daughter, the spoiler,
> who standing in front of you fended aside the tearing arrow.
> She brushed it away from his skin as lightly as when a mother
> brushes a fly away from her child who is lying in sweet sleep,
> steering herself the arrow's course straight to where the golden
> belt buckles joined and the halves of his corselet were fitted together.
> (IV, 127-133)

And *now* let's talk about juxtaposition–the placing of things immediately together–in this case juxtaposing radically dissimilar elements inside a single simile. Everybody will remember the simile we looked at earlier, also in Book IV, about the goatherd and the approaching storm:

> As from his watching place a goatherd watches a cloud move
> on its way over the sea before the drive of the west wind;
> far away though he be he watches it, blacker than pitch is,
> moving across the sea and piling the storm before it,
> and as he sees it he shivers and drives his flocks to a cavern;
> so about the two Aiantes moved the battalions. . . (IV, 275-280)

In that simile, the movement of the storm and the behavior of the Aiantes are in almost every way similar–both are large-scale, both have to do with gathering of force or power, and both would be frightening or at least imposing to an onlooker such as the goatherd.

But then look at the simile of Athene brushing away the arrow from its straight course:

> She brushed it away from his skin as lightly as when a mother
> brushes a fly away from her child who is lying in sweet sleep. . .

In this case, things seem to be constituted very nearly of opposites. The arrow is a death-dealing thing, a lethal weapon, whereas the mother is a life preserving, in fact, a life-creating, thing; the arrow is sharp, hard, penetrating, and ruthless, whereas the mother is gentle, tender, protective, and soft; the arrow swoops at great speed, whereas the mother scarcely moves a hand, just enough to brush "a fly away" as if from the face of her child.

How could two things be more *un*like? And what does the *un*likeness of them mean for readers of Homer?

Now, I know that someone might object at this point, saying that even though the opposites seem to be there, we're still not looking inside a real and complete simile. True enough–Homer is using Athene quite literally here as a narrative device, and though *he's* the one who makes up the mother-conceit, he still doesn't put it inside a completed simile structure.

So let's read on and find a more formally correct example–a path that will lead us through the wonderful detail of the arrow's end-course:

> The bitter arrow was driven against the joining of the war belt
> and passed clean through the war belt elaborately woven;
> into the elaborately wrought corselet the shaft was driven
> and the guard which he wore to protect his skin and keep the spears off,
> which guarded him best, yet the arrow plunged even through this also
> and with the very tip of its point it grazed the man's skin
> and straightway from the cut there gushed a cloud of dark blood. (IV, 134-140)

And so Menelaos bleeds profusely. And, *while* he bleeds profusely, we get our perfect simile:

> As when some Maionian woman or Karian with purple
> colours ivory, to make it a cheek piece for horses;
> it lies away in an inner room, and many a rider
> longs to have it, but it is laid up to be a king's treasure,
> two things, to be the beauty of the horse, the pride of the horseman:
> so, Menelaos, your shapely thighs were stained with the colour
> of blood, and your legs also and the ankles beneath them. (IV, 141-147)

If you go back to our clipboard and blackboard experiments, you'll find that both "bleeding" and "gushing blood" are ranked as essentially negative–while *here*, Homer himself seems to have not even the faintest hint of negativity or, say, revulsion. Of course he knows (as even we do, by now) that Menelaos isn't going to die and isn't even in truly great danger. Still, which does it seem to you that Homer is more interested in here? Is he more interested in the blood flowing down Menelaos' "shapely thighs," or is he more interested in the craftsmanship of the "Maionian woman or Karian [woman]" as she transforms the ivory cheek piece from plain ivory-color to purple?

The answer has got to be that he's interested in them equally–doesn't it?

Now, "craftsmanship" didn't do spectacularly well on our experiments, but that's only because, late in the twentieth century and early in the twenty-first, we tend to have lost our closeness to it and, for that matter, our closeness to what it is and what it means. We have "crafts fairs," it's true, but they do as much to show how *small* a part "craft" plays in the lives of most of us as they do to show how *much* it does.

And then, too, look at how "art" came out on the clipboard and blackboard experiments–top of the heap.

And so let me suggest for now, and for our understanding of Homer, that we just forget about the difference between "art" and "craft." In short, that we just go ahead and think of them as one and the same thing.

All right?

All right. A done deal. Art and craft are one and the same thing.

And yet, well, ahem, I do wonder whether I shouldn't warn you about something before we shake hands on this deal, just in case you may find yourselves getting into something you're not really quite prepared for. After all, I'm here because I want to be your guide through a reading of the *Iliad*, and I don't want to be taken as someone in the role, say, of a business trickster who gets people to sign on the dotted line before they understand what it is they're really signing. There goes your house. Ah *ha*! There goes your car. Ah *ha*!

I'm sure everyone remembers those lines near the end of Book XIV, when both Achaians and Trojans become equally terrified, "and the shivers came over the limbs of all of them, / and each man looked about him for a way to escape the sheer death" (XIV, 506-507). But possibly not everyone remembers the line that came shortly before that, when Hektor got hit by the stone that Telamonian Aias threw, knocking the wind out of Hektor for a bit. Here's that line, or those *two* lines:

> But the Argives, when they saw Hektor withdrawing from them,
> remembered once again their warcraft and turned on the Trojans.
> (XIV, 440-441)

And the same word is used again, right here in Book IV, where we've just seen Menelaos bleeding profusely from Pandaros' arrow:

> The Achaians again put on their armor, and remembered their warcraft.
> (IV, 222)

That word—or phrase, or phrases similar in meaning to it—recurs with great frequency throughout the *Iliad*, and, if we stick by our agreement, the word "warcraft" actually means "war art." That's okay, I suppose, so long as you don't think about how *positively* the concept of "art" came out in our experiments. I mean, if "art" ranks way high up there among the "positives," what about this new concept, "*war* art"? Are we going to say that only *some* kinds of art—"scenery art," say, or "seascape art"—are going to be allowed "up" there, while other kinds, like "war art," are going to be kept down below?

Well, kiddo, you pays your money and you gets your—however the musty old thing goes. A deal's a deal.

Still, it looks as though, thanks to Homer, we're getting very, very close–that is, if we're going to keep ourselves honest–to having to make some adjustments on our clipboards and our blackboard. If "art" is going to be up there on the top side, isn't it beginning to look as though "war"–or "war art"–is, logically, going to have to follow? And there goes the neighborhood. First thing you know, "violence" and "brutality" and "assault" and "slaying"–the whole horrendous bundle of ugliness and trouble–are going to be up there on the top side, too!

Frightening, isn't it. Or maybe it's not frightening at all, but bracing. Either way, it's Homer. Let's take a five-minute break, then get back to work–and see what's *really* awaiting us.

•

I said a minute ago, about "warcraft," that it's a word or phrase that "recurs with great frequency throughout the *Iliad*." I think it's important, before we go further, to point out another word, phrase, or sentiment that recurs with equal frequency and visibility throughout the poem. This other idea is expressed in phrases like "the hateful conflict" (IV, 240), or the "sorrow of warfare" (III, 112) or "the terrible fighting" (XVIII, 172) or "sorrowful war" (III, 132) or "the grind of the war god" (XVIII, 134) or even "the hateful division of Ares" (XVIII, 209).

Why do I mention this motif, and the plenitude of its repetition? Well, I mention it because I have no desire whatsoever to be made a victim, as Homer himself has routinely and wrongly been made, of false imputations to the effect that I "like" war, or that I am "for" war, or, above all, that I "celebrate" war–all of these stupid imputations being ones that have indeed been made against Homer himself.

But, no, there's not the least shred of truth or validity whatsoever to any of these false imputations. In fact, the very notion itself–of "liking" war, or being "in favor" of it or of "celebrating" it–this very notion has nothing whatsoever to do with anything that we're talking about in this study of Homer.

Here's what we're talking about, this and this only: Whether "war" must remain below the horizontal line on our blackboard experiment (where it was placed by every single respondent), or whether, like "art" (which was placed above the line by every single respondent), war should logically find its place somewhere, like "art," *above* the line.

And so, to work. Like Book XIV, in those parts of it following the seduction of Zeus by Hera, Book IV, in those parts of it following the truce-breaking by Pandarus, is taken over by description of some exceedingly vivid and gory passages of battle. "Conventional" similes provide a lead-in–"As when along the thundering beach the surf of the sea strikes" (IV, 422) and "as sheep in a man of possessions' steading / stand in their myriads waiting to be drained of their white milk" (IV, 433-434)–to the announcement that

> Ares drove these on, and the Achaians grey-eyed Athene,[96]
> and Terror drove them, and Fear, and Hate whose wrath is relentless,
> she who is only a little thing at the first, but thereafter
> grows until she strides on the earth with her head striking heaven.
> She then hurled down bitterness equally between both sides
> as she walked through the onslaught making men's pain heavier.
> (IV, 339-445)

Again as in Book XIV, the pain, fear, and agony are strewn equally across both sides as "the screaming and the shouts of triumph rose up together / of men killing and men killed, and the ground ran blood" (IV, 450-451). Antilochus kills the Trojan Echepolos ("the bronze spearpoint fixed in his forehead and drove inward / through the bone; and a mist of darkness clouded both eyes / and he fell as a tower falls in the strong encounter" (IV, 460-462), and then, as Elephenor tries to drag the body away in order "to strip the armour from him" (465), he himself becomes victim to "high-hearted Agenor," who, "marking / the ribs that showed bare under the shield as he bent over,

/ stabbed with the bronze-pointed spear and unstrung his sinews. / So the spirit left him and over his body was fought out / weary work by Trojans and Achaians. . ." (467-471).

And then, amid the tumult and carnage, a curious thing happens that reminds us of the Maionian woman's cheek piece or of the mother brushing the fly away from her sleeping baby's face earlier in this same book. It's worth quoting in full:

> There Telamonian Aias struck down the son of Anthemion
>
> Simoeisios in his stripling's beauty, whom once his mother
>
> descending from Ida bore beside the banks of Simoeis
>
> when she had followed her father and mother to tend the sheepflocks.
>
> Therefore they called him Simoeisios; but he could not
>
> render again the care of his dear parents; he was short-lived,
>
> beaten down beneath the spear of high-hearted Aias,
>
> who struck him as he first came forward beside the nipple
>
> of the right breast, and the bronze spearhead drove clean through
>
> the shoulder.
>
> He dropped then to the ground in the dust, like some black poplar,
>
> which in the land low-lying about a great marsh grows
>
> smooth trimmed yet with branches growing at the uttermost tree-top:
>
> one whom a man, a maker of chariots, fells with the shining
>
> iron, to bend it into a wheel for a fine-wrought chariot,
>
> and the tree lies hardening by the banks of a river.
>
> Such was Anthemion's son Simoeisios, whom illustrious
>
> Aias killed. (IV, 473-489)

Here again, and developed this time even more fully than in the case of the ivory cheek piece, violence by war functions as the outside "container" of a simile that in turn is filled up on the inside with discursive material having to do not with death or violence but with art, craft, and the *creation* of a fine artifact of one kind or another. Homer in each case allows himself the leisure to dwell for considerable passages of time on the artifact–in the case of the cheek piece on the long period of time that it waits for a proper owner, and in the case of the black poplar the long time that it lies aging until it's fit for bending by the wheelwright. I can't help but ask: Would any writer whose *primary* interest lay in "celebrating" or "admiring" or even "lingering over" the gore, bloodshed, ruthlessness, or presumable "heroism" of war, warcraft, or warfare–would such a writer feel as natural as Homer obviously does in his most curious way of *integrating* that subject with the other subjects of art, craft, and artifacts?

I think it's time to begin bending toward a conclusion, or, to put it another way, to begin bending toward a gathering up of our themes in a way that will best illustrate or reveal what this little book has hoped to show all along–how to read Homer in a way that's real, fair, accountable, and whole. Book IV, like Book XIV and others, makes a powerful case–as we agreed early on–that violence, brutality, and bloody gore are indisputably and undeniably very much a part of Homer, of Homer's world, and of the world of the *Iliad*.

But, at the same time, neither those two books nor any others in the poem make any convincing case that the *whole* of Homer, of his world, or of the world of the *Iliad* is constituted of or preoccupied by violence, brutality, and bloody gore–*nor* any convincing case that Homer's purpose is to "celebrate" those aspects of life or behavior over any or all others. Finally, neither do the books of the *Iliad* make any convincing case that focusing on those things alone will possibly allow a reader to come away with any kind of real, clear, or complete understanding of Homer, his world, or of the poem itself.

And so let's turn to Book XVIII, with its unique, immense, and extraordinary portrayal of the forging of a new shield for Achilles–and with its unique, immense, and extraordinary portrayal, by Homer, of the *entire world* as he saw and conceived it.

•

By the time we reach Book XVIII, much has changed. Patroklos, wearing Achilleus' armor, has fought Hektor and died, an event resulting in Achilleus' vow that he himself will now re-enter the fighting and slay Hektor–a decision that brings the lament from his weeping mother, Thetis, that she "must lose you soon, my child, by what you are saying, / since it is decreed your death must come soon after Hektor's (XVIII, 95-96).

In other words, as the poem is read by a non-worshipper of the ancients' divinities–albeit a non-worshipper happy for the many poetic delights "they" offer–what has happened has happened, and what is going to happen is going to happen. The story moves on, as does the war, and as do the events in it.

Before turning to our main business–getting an idea of how Homer *sees* his world–it may be, since we're now mentioning events, a reasonable moment to take a look at a *psychological* event. This psychological event takes place–or has now taken place–in the mind of the troubled and extremely troublesome Achilleus himself.

We need no "fate" or "destiny," no agency of "foreordination," to explain how it might be that Achilleus' view of things may well have changed–his psycho-emotional outlook, his *fear*–now that he has lost Patroklos, now that he himself is about to re-enter the fighting, and now that that fighting, newly charged by the insertion into it of a very specific new element of revenge, is likely to be more pitched and dangerous than ever.

Any young fighter in such a case is likely to be pressed upon by extraordinarily urgent, complex, and perhaps even personality-changing feelings. In Achilleus, speaking here to his mother, the inner changes are not only dramatic but, in their way, almost pitiably moving:

Now, since I am not going back to the beloved land of my fathers,

since I was no light of safety to Patroklos, nor to my other

companions, who in their numbers went down before glorious Hektor,

but sit here beside my ships, a useless weight on the good land,

I, who am such as no other of the bronze-armoured Achaians

in battle, though there are others also better in council–

why, I wish that strife would vanish away from among gods and mortals,

and gall, which makes a man grow angry for all his great mind,

that gall of anger that swarms like smoke inside of a man's heart

and becomes a thing sweeter to him by far than the dripping of honey.

So it was here that the lord of men Agamemnon angered me.

Still, we will let all this be a thing of the past, and for all our

sorrow beat down by force the anger deeply within us.

Now I shall go, to overtake that killer of a dear life,

Hektor; then I will accept my own death, at whatever

time Zeus wishes to bring it about, and the other immortals. (XVIII, 101-116)

Something he himself was incapable of doing back in Book I he now wishes *everyone* would do–banish gall, bitterness, resentment, and even banish *strife* from both self and world. Capable now both of introspection and of self-criticism, he admits that he allowed his ego's outrage at having been disrespected become to him "a thing sweeter... by far than the dripping of honey." Has he grown? Has he deepened? So it would seem. *Now*, after all the damage that he has caused to be done, he can do what Agamemnon was able to do all the way back at the beginning and admit that "Still, we will let all this be a thing of the past, and for all our / sorrow beat down by force the anger deeply within us."

And yet few things in Homer, as we've seen long before now and are about to see further, fail to seem contradictory if not in one way, then in another. And so it is that scarcely a hundred lines farther on, we find Achilleus addressing his dead friend Patroklos this way:

'Thus it is destiny for us both to stain the same soil

here in Troy; since I shall never come home, and my father,

Peleus the aged rider, will not welcome me in his great house,

nor Thetis my mother, but in this place the earth will receive me.

But seeing that it is I, Patroklos, who follow you underground,[97]

I will not bury you till I bring to this place the armour

and the head of Hektor, since he was your great-hearted murderer.[98]

Before your burning pyre I shall behead twelve glorious

children of the Trojans, for my anger over your slaying.

Until then, you shall lie where you are in front of my curved ships

and beside you women of Troy and deep-girdled Dardanian women

shall sorrow for you night and day and shed tears for you, those whom

you and I worked hard to capture by force and the long spear

in days when we were storming the rich cities of mortals.' (XVIII, 329-342)

And so doesn't it seem that we are free—or that we are impelled—to ask the simple question as to whether Achilleus has in fact changed or has in fact *not* changed? Don't we have him here, wishing one moment that gall and vengeance would disappear from the earth, and then the next moment announcing that he'll behead not only Hektor but a round dozen of Troy's best young men—for what? vengeance? spite? self-driven *rage* of the sort we heard him only a moment ago saying he was now fully capable of controlling and suppressing?

But enough. It's not time now for still more contradictions, but time for us, instead, to find a way beyond them, to sail into the open water—wherever it is—that will let us see the *Iliad* and see it both real and whole, the place that will allow us to see it as Homer sees it, however that's to be done.

And then there's still the question of those *dogs*, too. Do you remember the dog debate, from all the way back on our first day—whether wild dogs are "delicate" when they eat, or whether they are "foul" and "mangling"?

I say let's go to the shield. The shield will help us not only with Achilleus, but it will help us with the dogs, too.

•

The story is that Thetis is owed a favor by Hephaistos, the limping smithy of the gods,[99] and so she goes to him to ask that he forge a new suit of armor for Achilleus, since Hektor stripped Achilleus' own armor from the body of Patroklos at the time he slew him.

Hephaistos listens to Thetis' appeal, and then he goes immediately to work. As it happens, he begins not with greaves or breast-plate or other parts of the armor, but instead by forging the great shield–and in doing so creates not only one of the most extraordinary passages in all of literature, but very possibly also the key we've been looking for all along that will let us find our way into the open Homeric waters we've been searching for.

We'll talk[100] as we go. But at the outset, let it be said–as everyone will quickly see–that Hephaistos sets out, in creating the shield, to create nothing less than the entire world, or even, one might suggest, the entire *cosmos* as it was imagined by Homer and his contemporaries– or as it was imagined by all of them but also *realized* by Homer. Hephaistos' subject, in other words–like Homer's own subject in the *Iliad*–is the whole world, is *everything*:

> First of all he forged a shield that was huge and heavy,
> elaborating it about, and threw around it a shining
> triple rim that glittered, and the shield strap was cast of silver.
> There were five folds composing the shield itself, and upon it
> he elaborated many things in his skill and craftsmanship.
>
> He made the earth upon it, and the sky, and the sea's water,
> and the tireless sun, and the moon waxing into her fullness,

and on it all the constellations that festoon the heavens,
the Pleiades and the Hyades and the strength of Orion
and the Bear, whom men give also the name of the Wagon,
who turns about in a fixed place and looks at Orion
and she alone is never plunged in the wash of Ocean.

On it he wrought in all their beauty two cities of mortal
men. And there were marriages in one, and festivals.
They were leading the brides along the city from their maiden chambers
under the flaring of torches, and the loud bride song was arising.
The young men followed the circles of the dance, and among them
the flutes and lyres kept up their clamour as in the meantime
the women standing each at the door of her court admired them.
The people were assembled in the market place, where a quarrel
had arisen, and two men were disputing over the blood price
for a man who had been killed. One man promised full restitution
in a public statement, but the other refused and would accept nothing.
Both then made for an arbitrator, to have a decision;
And people were speaking up on either side, to help both men.
But the heralds kept the people in hand, as meanwhile the elders
were in session on benches of polished stone in the sacred circle
and held in their hands the staves of the heralds who lift their voices.
The two men rushed before these, and took turns speaking their cases,
and between them lay on the ground two talents of gold, to be given
to that judge who in this case spoke the straightest opinion.
But around the other city were lying two forces of armed men
shining in their war gear. . . (XVIII, 478-510)

And at this point, let's break in—partly to talk about the glories both
of Hephaistos' creation *and* of the poetry that Homer immortalizes it
in, and partly to talk about an enormous danger: An innocuous-look-

ing but in fact ruinously destructive reader-trap that, if we let ourselves fall into it, will prevent us from *ever* seeing Homer whole.

So: The poetry first, doesn't that seem the better choice?

And there it is, the complete and entire world emerging before us– the heavens above, and the sky, then the stars, the sun, the seas. So delicate, so detailed, so charmed is this verse that day turns to night ("They were leading the brides along the city from their maiden chambers / under the flaring of torches") with our scarcely noticing, and so charmed is it that not only do the figures *move* ("They were leading the brides" and "The young men followed the circles of the dance") but the very *sounds* of celebration rise up to our ears without our even noticing–"and among them / the flutes and lyres kept up their clamour as in the meantime / the women standing each at the door of her court admired them." Even the textures of things are offered to our touch, as in "the elders / were in session on benches of polished stone in the sacred circle. . . "

Lovely, lovely stuff, and we've scarcely even begun tasting its pleasures. But, even so, we need to break off. If we're going to keep ourselves from falling into it, we need to consider, very carefully, the pitfall.

This reader-trap has been well prepared, a deep pit covered over with a cross-hatching of twigs and small branches, these scattered with grass and brush so as to look as much as possible like solid ground. But it's not. If you walk straight ahead, down you'll crash right into the pit, a pit deep enough that you'll never again make your way up and out. Everything you see for the rest of your life–well, for the rest of your *Homeric* life–will be circumscribed and confined by the walls of that pit, while all you'll be able to see of the entire rest of the world will be the rectangular patch of sky directly above when you look up.

The only warning signs–the signs will themselves also be a trick–

are the word "But" and the phrase that follows closely after, "the other city," both in line 509. Now, for anyone who knows his or her way around Homer's world, these "signs" are easy to see for what they are–just some words–and that fortunate person can simply step lightly to one side or the other and then, safe and sound, continue on his or her journey into and through the complex, extraordinary, rich, incomparable–and *Homeric*–world of the *Iliad*.

I used two of those terms deliberately–"incomparable" and "Homeric"–because those words, as it turns out, have an important and hugely meaningful relationship in regard to reading the *Iliad* successfully. I could put it another way: Reading Homer *backwards* is an undertaking doomed inevitably to failure–and yet that's the way, backwards, that most people try to read him.

An example. Some time ago, I stumbled on a book, by Robert Grudin, with the very long title *American Vulgar: The Politics of Manipulation Versus the Culture of Awareness*[101] and found myself reading, in Grudin's seventh chapter, the work of someone who at line 509 of Book XVIII had fallen straight through the cross-hatched branches and twigs and right down to the bottom of the reader-pit.

From there, with that patch of sky his only view of the real world, Grudin went about his task of explaining to his own readers what Homer "means."

Grudin's seventh chapter, "Homer and the Birth of Consciousness," is sub-titled "Vulgarity and Evil: From Bush to Homer."

That word in the subtitle, "evil," goes a long way toward explaining why Grudin fell into the pit instead of knowing enough to walk around it. When he saw the word "but" and then the words "other city," and when he began reading about the "other city," he came immediately to the conclusion that Homer, in contrasting the two cities, was doing nothing less and nothing other than pointing out the differences between good and evil and, implicitly, arguing that good is better than evil.

What a debilitating mistake. How much it makes me wish that Grudin had been with us from the start of this little book, when we looked and looked for "evil" in Agamemnon, Helen, Alexandros, Hektor, even Achilleus himself (though I did myself once call him "evil," but for rhetorical reasons)[102] and couldn't find it in them. And now, in the "second city," where is this "evil" supposed to come from? It doesn't come from *Homer*, I know. And that can mean only one thing: This "evil" is coming from the future. It's not being supplied by Homer, but *it's being supplied by Grudin*. And that's what I mean by reading Homer backwards.

Let's have a look at the second city for ourselves:

> But around the other city were lying two forces of armed men
>
> shining in their war gear. For one side counsel was divided
>
> whether to storm and sack, or share between both sides the property
>
> and all the possessions the lovely citadel held hard within it.
>
> But the city's people were not giving way, and armed for an ambush.
>
> Their beloved wives and their little children stood on the rampart
>
> to hold it, and with them the men with age upon them, but meanwhile
>
> the others went out. And Ares led them, and Pallas Athene.
>
> These were gold, both, and golden raiment upon them, and they were
>
> beautiful and huge in their armour, being divinities,
>
> and conspicuous from afar, but the people around them were smaller.
>
> These when they were come to the place that was set for their ambush,
>
> in a river, where there was a watering place for all animals,
>
> there they sat down in place shrouding themselves in the bright bronze.
>
> But apart from these were sitting two men to watch for the rest of them
>
> and waiting until they could see the sheep and the shambling cattle,
>
> who appeared presently, and two herdsmen went along with them
>
> playing happily on pipes, and took no thought of the treachery.

Those others saw them, and made a rush, and quickly thereafter

Cut off on both sides the herds of cattle and the beautiful

flocks of shining sheep, and killed the shepherds upon them.

But the other army, as soon as they heard the uproar arising

from the cattle, as they sat in their councils, suddenly mounted

behind their light-foot horses, and went after, and soon overtook them.

These stood their ground and fought a battle by the banks of the river,

And they were making casts at each other with their spears bronze-headed;

and Hate was there with Confusion among them, and Death the destructive;

she was holding a live man with a new wound, and another

one unhurt, and dragged a dead man by the feet through the carnage.

The clothing upon her shoulders showed strong red with the man's blood.

All closed together like living men and fought with each other

and dragged away from each other the corpses of those who had fallen.

(XVIII, 509-540)

Do you remember, much earlier in this book, our collection of five adjectives and the choices we made as to which of them were fairly and justly applicable to Homer and the *Iliad?* Well, the adjectives were "barbaric," "brutal," "primitive," "violent," and "uncivilized" Our agreement, in case you've forgotten, was that only two–"brutal" and "violent"–were just and apt modifiers of Homer *and* of the world he portrays in the *Iliad*, while "barbaric," "primitive," and "uncivilized" had to be abandoned for their inaccuracy in light of the evidence–including the damning evidence that they applied equally to *our* own present age.

And now, in spite of all our own effort and hard work to be accurate, here comes Grudin popping in not only with "primitive" and "tribal" but, to top it all off, "evil." Grudin assumes the first city to be *really* good (even though there's been a murder in it, something he ignores) and the *other* city to be really *bad*–in fact, he sees the second city as reflective of the world of Agamemnon, Hektor, Helen, and Achilleus in the time of the Greek-Trojan war. You'll see what he thinks of *it*:

> Clearly, the second city represents the world of *The Iliad*, a chaotic struggle typified by deception, competitive heroics, gods in strife, and the absence of civic order. The first city, however, opens like a new window into a saner world. It displays a civility based on wisely ordained institutions and a commitment to reason (no gods necessary here). [In the first city,] Homer is looking into a mental landscape that is wholly lacking in the Troy story or in the primitive tribalism that the [Troy] story depicts. He is looking into the morally challenged world of *The Odyssey* and towards the dawn of modern politics. His description of Achilles' shield is an assertion of social consciousness..[103]

How are we to deal with a "reader" of Homer like Grudin? Where even to start? Apparently, for one thing, he remains a worshipper of and believer in the gods, since he understands the *Iliad* as being about "gods in strife." If he's really a Zeus-ist or a Hera-ite or an Aphroditist, it would be interesting (and only fair) for him to let us in on the wording of some of his *prayers* to those divinities, and to let us know a bit about what kinds of religious rituals and observations he uses in his actual worship.

Where was Grudin when we had our own long discussion about the gods and our analyses of them? Playing hooky, I guess. And now, gods schmods, he feels free to tell us all kinds of mega whoppers about all sorts of other things–like the one about the first city being more "sane" than the second one (murder is *sane*, then? and war, as in the second city, is *in*sane?),[104] or the big fib that the subject matter of the *Iliad* is "tribal primitivism" and has nothing equally to do with modern human psychology or even with the biggest of all Homeric sub-jects–the subject of death versus the very medium of life itself into which the Homeric characters are born, and out of which–heading for "hateful death"–they are understandably not eager to go.

Something is tremendously amiss here. In a certain way we're lucky, though, in having Grudin available as an example of one of those who can't make sense of Homer as he is, and who therefore insists on reading the great poet *backwards*, pasting later "values" onto a time that existed before those "values" themselves did.

Partly as an inevitable result of reading backwards, he is also unable to read Homer in a way that's either real or complete. How can Grudin possibly read Homer whole when he doesn't even read the *shield* whole? After all, only a person who ignores almost all of the contents of the shield's description *except* that it portrays two cities could come up with the remark that Homer's "description of Achilles' shield is an assertion of social consciousness."

Whatever Grudin may understand by the phrase "social con-sciousness," we can be certain that, as he uses it, it's not something in the least familiar to Homer, or, most likely, not something that would be in the least way be welcomed by him.

I suspect that what Grudin means by the phrase "social conscious-ness" is the idea or ideal of doing "good" for everybody universally, as opposed to the Homeric given of "living life as well as is humanly pos-sible, since life is all there is."

What would cause a person to do something like this, imputing concepts to an author who lived and wrote at a time when those con-cepts didn't exist? Well, the answer is a horrible one. We'd better take it step by step.

Part of Grudin's thesis, as he reiterates it near the start of his chap-ter seven, is that "The heart of evil–disregard for humanity and nature–is also the heart of vulgarity."[105] Now we must step carefully. The definition of evil, says Grudin, is that it consists of a "disregard for humanity and nature." Therefore, anyone without a regard for humanity and nature is ipso facto evil. Can you think of anyone who might fit that bill? Well, hang onto your hats, because here comes a whirlwind:

> To see this connection [between "evil" and "disregard for humanity and nature"] in action, we need only look back to a period of history when the modern Judeo-Christian idea of evil was not yet in place: the world of the poet Homer.[106]

What? In *Homer?* A disregard for humanity and nature? Let me put it another way. A disregard for humanity and nature—in *Homer?*

I think it's time for us to look at—and to read out loud if possible—more of the description of the shield: It's time to read all those parts that Grudin apparently *didn't* read:

Hephaistos' creation goes on:

> He made upon it a soft field, the pride of the tilled land,
> wide and triple-ploughed, with many ploughmen upon it
> who wheeled their teams at the turn and drove them in either direction.
> And as these making their turn would reach the end-strip of the field,
> a man would come up to them at this point and hand them a flagon
> of honey-sweet wine, and they would turn again to the furrows
> in their haste to come again to the end-strip of the deep field.
> The earth darkened behind them and looked like earth that has
> > been ploughed
> though it was gold. Such was the wonder of the shield's forging.
>
> He made on it the precinct of a king, where the labourers
> were reaping, with the sharp reaping hooks in their hands. Of the cut swathes
> some fell along the lines of reaping, one after another,

while the sheaf-binders caught up others and tied them with bind-ropes.
There were three sheaf-binders who stood by, and behind them
were children picking up the cut swathes, and filled their arms with them
and carried and gave them always; and by them the king in silence
and holding his staff stood near the line of the reapers, happily.
And apart and under a tree the heralds made a feast ready
and trimmed a great ox they had slaughtered. Meanwhile the women scattered, for the workmen to eat, abundant white barley.

He made on it a great vineyard heavy with clusters,
lovely and in gold, but the grapes upon it were darkened
and the vines themselves stood out through poles of silver. About them
he made a field-ditch of dark metal, and drove all around this
a fence of tin; and there was only one path to the vineyard,
and along it ran the grape-bearers for the vineyard's stripping.
Young girls and young men, in all their light-hearted innocence,
carried the kind, sweet fruit away in their woven baskets,
and in their midst a youth with a singing lyre played charmingly
upon it for them, and sang the beautiful song for Linos
in a light voice, and they followed him, and with singing and whistling
and light dance-steps of their feet kept time to the music. (XVIII, 541-572)

Is there, in any of what we've just read, to be found even the faintest
hint of "disregard for humanity and nature"? Again, the delicacies of
Hephaistos' art—and, therefore, of Homer's art—are so exquisite that
the shield seems actually to come to life: The furrows darken as the
ploughmen make their way forward, and again we hear the "singing
lyre" and watch the "light dance-steps of their feet" keeping "time to
the music." Well and justly is it said "Such was the wonder of the
shield's forging"—words whose double meaning, "such was the wonder of the poet's work," can't conceivably have been lost on Homer as

he himself created the very miracle that he's in awe of. And did anyone notice, as to the charge of "disregard for nature," the unusual quality of the grapes? Why, they're held in such "disregard" that Homer gives them life by *personifying* them: "Young girls and young men, in all their light-hearted innocence, / carried the kind, sweet fruit away in their woven baskets. . ."

There is, of course, still much more of great loveliness and beauty in Hephaistos' forging–there are ox herdsmen, dogs with "shifting feet" (578), "glimmering sheepflocks" (588), a great meadow, lovely clothing, a dance floor where the dancers "on their understanding feet. . . would run very lightly" (599), a world so filled with life that it has in it even "two acrobats" who "led the measures of song and dance" (604-605). Hephaistos, again, has created nothing less than the whole world, and *that's* why his finishing touch is so apt, appropriate, and right:

> He made on it the great strength of the Ocean River
> which ran around the uttermost rim of the shield's strong structure.
> (XVIII, 606-607)

The shield is invaluable, unique, a full-blown treasure that, while giving us–as some have imagined–a kind of complete version of the *Iliad* but in miniature, also gives us the very world itself as Homer saw and knew it–the world also to the *extent* that he knew it, out to the farthest banks of "the Ocean River," beyond which lay only the unknown. Is there violence in this world? Yes, there's a murder, an ambush, an attack, and even the occasion when two lions attack "the great ox, / gulped the black blood and the inward guts, as meanwhile the herdsmen / were in the act of setting and urging the quick dogs on them," although the dogs, "before they would get their teeth in, turned back from the lions" in fear (XVIII, 582-585).

But where is *evil*? Not only where is *evil*, but where is "the *heart* of evil,"[107] as Grudin calls it. To be fair, in his book, Grudin makes a complicated and to my mind quite unconvincing argument that Homer is a kind of transitional figure, a poet who has his back to the "primitive tribalism" of Agamemnon's day and has his *front* toward a different world, one that has in it "social consciousness."

Anyone interested can read the argument and make up his or her own mind about it, though to me it seems confused, forced, off-track, in many ways unfair to Homer, and wildly lacking in evidence. And yet, even without concerning ourselves further with Grudin's Homer-as-window-to-the-future argument, I think we can still rather easily find the umbrella source of his way of thinking–the *central* reason that causes him to misread, misunderstand, and misinterpret both the great poet and the great epic.

As with millions of others–calamitous thought, that there be so many–what makes Grudin unable to read Homer is that he's what you might call a "History Chauvinist," or, perhaps you could say, a "Neo-chauvinist." The terms are my own, and I'm not bragging about them, but what they're supposed to identify are people who actually think–or who fail to *correct* this thinking–that more recent ages are superior to more distant ages, or that the present is automatically superior to the past. They think–or fail *not* to think–that as history goes along, it improves things. They think that as time passes things *get better.*

Any attitude, outlook, or belief of this kind, it hardly need be said, is an absurd and wrong-headed manifestation of nonsense. Still, ruinous and demented outlook though it be, it's one of the most prevalent of views, *certainly* so in our own present-day, desperately under-educated, and anti-educated nation.[108]

As with many sweeping concepts of its sort, there's *some* truth to the insistent belief that modernity is superior to antiquity–though the premise itself remains a half-truth, which is to say, I'm sorry, a falsehood. The bits of undeniable truth in the precept are often seen as having to do with aspects of medical science, the development of antisepsis and of anesthetics, for example. And who could argue–or would want to argue–against those forms of progress? I know very well that I'd rather have an abscessed tooth now than in 1321, or an emergency appendectomy today than in 1923, when my grandmother had hers.

But these kinds of truths are but the tiniest little slivers of evidence inside the massive precept arguing that history brings amelioration of the human condition–tiny little slivers having to do only with the control of physical pain or the prevention of gangrene or sepsis of the blood. Good. But they don't even *begin* to touch on other elements of the question of historical improvement or melioration. They fail, for example, even to begin touching on those aspects of life having to do with the spiritual, intellectual, aesthetic, artistic, political, philosophical, emotional, social, familial, and so on and on.

We've already seen Grudin telling us that "the world of the poet Homer" was a "period of history when the modern Judeo-Christian idea of evil was not yet in place." But what we didn't ask him when we read those words was the simple question, *"So what?"* Twenty-two centuries or so from now, in *The Inferno*, we'll find Dante calling the sun a "planet," since he himself died more than two hundred years before Copernicus, and three hundred or so before Galileo. So shall we call him backward because he didn't know about helio-centrism?

Admittedly, Grudin doesn't think that Christianity did such a great job in all ways–it became corrupted institutionally, he points out, and had the effect of suppressing individual thought instead of opening it up–and yet at the same time he makes clear that in its essence he thinks that Christianity was–is–a very fine thing indeed. Why? Here's the reason, anathema to those who value Homer in great part because he looks directly at life for exactly and really *what it is*:

Christianity reformed and refined Rome, and ultimately all of Europe [Grudin writes], by revealing a second, nonmaterial dimension in life, a spiritual world holding a boundless plenty of togetherness, forgiveness, and love.[109]

Grudin here is introducing the idea of life not for what it is, but for what it *isn't*. Life *isn't*, but the *after* life *is*. The penurious, Hallmark card-like weakness of these words—"togetherness, forgiveness, and love"—is made even more apparent when they're inserted, as here, into discussion of a poet, Homer, whose towering achievements were due in large part precisely to his courageous and unflinching ability to look *at* life and *at* the contrasting components *of* life and to understand and accept them for *exactly what they really were*. And then to hear, further, that a concept developed centuries after Homer—the Platonic concept that the only real and important part of life is the *non*-physical—to hear the idea expressed that Homer's unawareness of such a spiritualist notion is a *debility* to him, that his unawareness of it places him back amidst the darkness and blindness of "primitive tribalism"—well, such an assertion is, to put it bluntly, anathema, backward, illogical, and itself blind.

I don't know about you, but I could use a break. I'm disappointed as hell and mad as hell and need to get over it. I'll see you next time.

DAY SEVEN

Assignment: *Iliad*, Book XXIV

And now, an announcement: It's time for me to make a confession to you and to beg your forgiveness.

If we were in a real classroom, you'd have known long before now that one of my own most often-mentioned and stringently applied classroom rules is that you must *never* trust the instructor.

After all, a good instructor, at least a great deal of the time, should be testing to see whether you're just passively following whatever's being said, or, on the other hand, whether you're actually–and actively–thinking for yourself by making use of available evidence. For example, a good instructor might ask you what I call a "salt or pepper" question–as in "which do you put on your eggs in the morning, salt or pepper?" If a student has been out too late the night before and isn't on full alert but instead is on "full trust ahead," he or she *might* fall for the question by actually trying to answer it. But anyone who's had plenty of sleep *and* has his or her ship's engine-indicator set on "never trust implicitly–*especially* if an instructor is involved"–will see at once that the question is a trap (its "either-or" sets up a false or at least arbitrary dichotomy) and in all likelihood is answerable neither honestly nor accurately within the terms that it permits. In short, the question must be questioned, just as the instructor must always, too, be questioned, or at the very least be held under reasonable suspicion.

We're now approaching the end of our study together of the *Iliad*, and so I'll ask a few more questions that I hope will lead you to see exactly how I deceived you, perhaps even lied to you–though of course only with the very best of intentions.

You can see the huge importance of never fully trusting a classroom instructor any more than you should fully trust a political candidate. The political candidate wants to make you vote for him or her and might tell you all sorts of untruths, half truths, desirable unrealities, and the like. The instructor, if he or she is a good one, wants to get you, yes, to like what you're doing, but even more importantly to get you to think for yourself about it and not, say, merely by imitation. In hoping to achieve his or her end, is it any less likely that the instructor may try to trick you than it is that the political candidate may?

All of that said, let's go back to our horizontal-line-on-the-blackboard experiment and to the different ideas, concepts, phrases, words and the like that we placed either above or below the line. For convenience, I'll reproduce the results here.

Passivity	
Gentleness	Kindness
Beauty	Mothering
Babies	Nurturing
Art	Softness
Craftsmanship	Biting the dust

Sheep herding	Storms approaching
Eyeball on speartip	Killing
Assault	Slaying
Force	Stabbing
Bestiality	Ugliness
Force	Violence
Ugliness	War
Bleeding	Guts spilled

Now. I don't know which parts of the *Iliad* may constitute your own favorites, although mine–not wholly but largely–can be found in the books of the poem that I assigned for our reading here together. Now, though, back at the time when we did our blackboard-and-the-line experiment, you hadn't yet read Book XVIII, with its description of the shield's forging–unless, of course, you were reading ahead of the schedule, in which case the more power to you.

Either way, I think it's important that we now do a "post-shield" repetition of the blackboard experiment.

After all, we now have the shield itself as a model. And on the shield, after all, Homer (aka Hephaistos) placed a great many of the same things we originally made a list of in preparing for our clipboard and then blackboard experiments–as well as placing many *more* on the shield. Here's our own old list:

1. An Eyeball Stuck on a Spear-tip
2. Art
3. Assault
4. Babies
5. Beauty
6. Bestiality
7. Biting the Dust
8 Bleeding
9. Brutality
10. Craftsmanship
11. Cruelty
12. Force
13. Gentleness
14. Gushing blood
15. Guts spilled
16. Killing
17. Kindness

18. Mothering

19. Nurturing

20. Passivity

21. Sheep herding

22. Slaying

23. Softness

24. Spear points

25. Stabbing

26. Storms approaching

27. Terror

28. Ugliness

29. Violence

30. War

Most of the items from this old list would indeed have a natural place on the shield, along with all the ones we left out, including dancing, harvesting, gathering, singing, lute-playing, courting, marrying, being eaten by lions, and more.

Now, our new task is very simple. Our new task is to figure out where to place each item—ours *and* Homer's—not on the blackboard but on the *shield*.

I'm going to put another rest-stop on the page. And, for this rest, I want you to take as much time as you like. No limit. But whenever it is that we do meet on the other side of the black dot, I want you to have identified in exactly what way it was that I deceived you—lied to you, a person might even say—and when it was that I did it. So long as you succeed in identifying it, I'll worry later about begging your forgiveness.

•

I'm going to assume that you found it, that you found it right away, and that you're now madder than hell at me for having been so devious, deceitful, and false–whatever good motive I may have had for being so. On the other hand, if there's any chance that you may have enjoyed the trick, then maybe we'll be able to mend fences and get along very well together again at some later time, maybe even have a drink together.

My deceit took place at the very instant when I drew *this* on the blackboard:

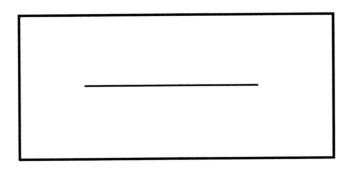

And what *was* that? Aside from its having been a dirty trick that I'm now confessing to having played on you, it is–well, a sign, perhaps a symbol, or, certainly, a metaphor. It represents a division–one that I foully tricked you into accepting as if it were valid and true–between, say, the directions "up" and "down," with "up" being considered superior to "down." It becomes, after Plato (still a few hundred years down the road), a representation of the idea that things made out of any form of materiality are "bad" (and have to be put on the "down" side of the line), while things "made" out of pure spirituality, of immateriality, are "good" (and get to go on the "up" side of the line).

It's a metaphor suggesting the way people see the ranking of things if they, for example, think that the "soul" is "good" while the body is bad. Robert Grudin is a person like that–and he goes so far (like Plato) as to conceive of there being something known as "evil" in the state of physical existence, and that that something-in-existence most definitely must be held to its place below the "line."

What more to say about the "line"? Well, whatever Robert Grudin or any others like him may tell you, it's a concept, viewpoint, outlook, or idea about a kind of division that had never so much as even *occurred* to Homer. Homer would never have thought of or been exposed to so cockamamie an idea as dividing all of existence into the realms of "up" and "down," corresponding to the nice and the not-nice, to the non-physical ("up") and the physical ("down").

This single fact–the fact of his having been a holist rather than a dualist–as much as any other characteristic of Homer's way of seeing, perceiving, thinking, composing, or of representing "life," is the one fact *most* responsible for making what we call "Homeric" seem and feel the way that makes it, to us, Homeric.

Yes, there are faint presences of "up" and "down" even in the *Iliad*, with the "gods" having their place "up" on Mount Olympos, and with the "underworld" being the "place" people go when life has been torn away from them, or when they've been forced against their will to stop inhabiting the *state of* life.[110] It may well be–and this is possibly a question better suited to a cultural anthropologist or historian of ideas than to a literary reader like me–that these faint presences of "up" and "down" are the very *Ur*-concepts that will lead Socrates and others like him to develop what we'll later call Platonism.[111] But even if they *are* such Ur-concepts as that, they remain sufficiently undeveloped in the Homeric period for the poet to see the world in a far, far different way from the way the Platonists or the Grudins do. For Homer, there's nothing unnatural, perverse, unfitting, or unfeeling about the comparison between the mother brushing away the fly and Athene brushing away Pandaros' spear ((IV, 127-133), or about the comparison between Simoeisios' falling forward in death and the falling of a black poplar that will then lie aging, later to be suitable material for the wheelwright. (IV, 473-489)

Nor will there be anything unnatural for Homer to make juxtapositions, as we'll see in a moment, that to a Platonist or a Grudinite–or even to many of *us*–might be taken not merely as extreme or stretching the credible, but possibly as psychotic.

But let's finish with our line before we get to psychosis. Clearly, what we've got to do with the line if we hope to remain true to the Homer of the *Iliad* is, pure and simple, get rid of it, thus:

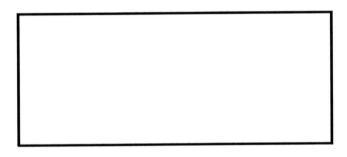

Then, we'll *also* have to get rid of this completely arbitrary four-cornered shape (why *four* corners? why not six? eight? three? why *any*?) and turn the outline of the world, just as in the *Iliad*, and just as was done by so many pre-Columbian Native Americans, into a circle:

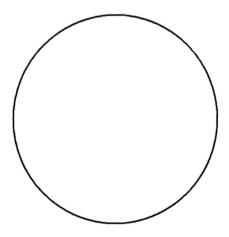

What next? Well, look how foolish our old List of Thirty-One looks if we try to push it into the circle while keeping the *spirit* of the rectangle:

This is like trying to fit a peg into a square hole. But the minute we do as Homer-Hephaistos did, that is, fill the circle without any conception or awareness whatsoever of *there being or ever having been* a horizontal line–*then* we can begin to see the world as Homer saw it: Not dualistically, but *holistically*:

And so we draw to a conclusion in our time here together. Admitted lover and profound admirer of the *Iliad*[112] and its creator that I am, I ask myself what I might want to emphasize, or re-emphasize, before we part. And I answer as follows: I want to emphasize that the poem is and remains great *because* its foundational and most profound subject is *human* character and psychology; and I want to emphasize that the poem is and remains great–and utterly fascinating–not because it or its creator are in any way whatsoever "primitive," but because it is a poem conceived and created in a time when *holism* in human perception and observation of the world still existed, a time when neither the world nor the human intellect had yet been ravaged, fractured, and splintered into two by dualism, by up versus down, by body versus soul.

These are the twin characteristics of the poem that, more than any other, give it both its enormous sophistication, on the one hand, and its ability, on the other, even now, after almost three thousand years, to be as extraordinarily moving as it indeed can be.

An example of the first of those two qualities, that of the poem's foundation being built on and of human psychology, can be seen to absolutely brilliant effect in Book XXIV, with its portrayal of the night-visit of the aged king Priam to the tent of Achilleus in order that Priam can plead in person that he be given the shamelessly abused and mistreated body of his son Hektor.[113]

Just from our own reading, we know only too well the near-impossibility of reaching the small, thinking, responsive core that *is*[114] hidden somewhere very, very deeply inside the otherwise explosive and thickly armored self of Achilleus. But Priam's peerless courage in making his way alone to the tent of Achilleus, in offering himself with utter defenselessness before the most feared warrior in all of the assembled armies–such matchless courage and selfless determination touch Achilleus deeply enough that he responds with these words:

'How could you dare come alone to the ships of the Achaians
and before my eyes, when I am one who have killed in such numbers
such brave sons of yours? The heart in you is iron. Come, then,
and sit down upon this chair, and you and I will even let
our sorrows lie still in the heart for all our grieving.' (XXIV, 519-523)

We can measure all the more vividly the hugeness of what Priam has accomplished[115] by contrasting the doomed Hektor's own inability to have gained so much as one iota of emotional sympathy or responsiveness from the unrelievedly brutal Achilleus.

When Achilleus slew Hektor, he aimed for the place

where the collar-bones hold the neck from the shoulders,
the throat, where death of the soul comes most swiftly; in this place
brilliant Achilleus drove the spear as he came on in fury,
and clean through the soft part of the neck the spearpoint was driven.
Yet the ash spear heavy with bronze did not sever the windpipe,
so that Hektor could still make exchange of words spoken.
But he dropped in the dust, and brilliant Achilleus vaunted above him:
'Hektor, surely you thought as you killed Patroklos you would be
safe, and since I was far away you thought nothing of me,
o fool, for an avenger was left, far greater than he was,
behind him and away of the hollow ships. And it was I;
and I have broken your strength; on you the dogs and the vultures
shall feed and foully rip you; the Achaians will bury Patroklos.'
(XXII, 324-336)

Here we come again to the "feed and foully rip" line that we looked at on our very first day, contrasting it with the lines referring to "the delicate feasting / of dogs, of all birds" (I, 4-5). I hope by now that the seeming inconsistency no longer troubles anyone but is seen instead as a natural aspect of the holistic world-view that's at the very root of all that we now think of as Homeric. *We* are likely to place dogs above or below our imaginary or metaphoric "line," depending largely on whether they happen to be "delicate" or "bestial," nice or nasty, good or bad, sweet or mean. For Homer, dogs are dogs, sometimes bestial, sometimes pets, sometimes workers, sometimes eating at a delicate, bone-picking leisure, at others ripping and tearing in a famished eagerness to fill their bellies. Look closely at our final pictorial version of the shield-circle (p. 192) and see where the two manners of dogs at feed have ended up.

More on all this in a moment, but, first, Achilleus: Here, without any question, we've got the same righteous, injured, rigid, utterly and wholly self-centered and self-absorbed Achilleus that we had all the way back in Book I at the lowest point of the Agamemnon-Achilleus quarrel. Now, admittedly, Hektor is about to die—is dying already—but look at the enormous difference in character, manner, and thought— or even in emotion-thought—between the two great warriors as Hektor supplicates Achilleus, not for his life, which is forfeit already, but simply for a traditional decency in the treatment of his body, a matter of concern to him not only for himself but for "the Trojans / and the wives of the Trojans," who deserve the same decency in the treatment, even in war, of the body of their son:

> In his weakness Hektor of the shining helm spoke to him:
> I entreat you, by your life, by your knees, by your parents,
> Do not let the dogs feed on me by the ships of the Achaians,
> but take yourself the bronze and gold that are there in abundance,
> those gifts that my father and the lady my mother will give you,
> and give my body to be taken home again, so that the Trojans
> and the wives of the Trojans may give me in death my rite of burning.
> (XXII, 337-343)

The dignified, measured, thoughtful words of Hektor couldn't be more unlike those in Achilleus' response, where his extraordinary self-absorption is absolutely clear in his consideration of him*self* as victim, as one who has been more monstrously treated, be this a state of war or not, than anyone else. This is the Achilleus that way back at the beginning I called "evil," albeit with the qualifier, then as now, that I use the word in "quotation marks. . . to show that [I'm] using the word temporarily and for convenience" (p. 24).

Some people think that quoting oneself is bad policy, but I say that if it's useful, go ahead; what can be wrong with it? Here's what we said back then (p. 24), about Achilleus' insubordination to his commander and leader, Agamemnon. Now, he is behaving in a parallel way, but this time toward the dying Hektor:

> And what's wrong with him that makes him "evil". . .?
> Well, let's go back to that hypothetical court martial. Achilleus, in a word, is insubordinate. It's perfectly true that as a *warrior*, he is superior to everyone else in the entirety of the Argive army. As a *warrior*, that is, he is subordinate to no one. But in the matter of being *leader*, he is and must be subordinate to his commander, Agamemnon. And there's something in the temperament and psychology of Achilleus that makes him unable to endure that. He can't *stand* being subordinate to Agamemnon as leader.

The subtlety, depth, and complexity—as well as the dramatic presentation—of the human character and psychology of its characters, again, can be seen as the deepest foundation of the *Iliad*. Helen, Agamemnon, Andromache, Hektor, and of course Achilleus himself are as fully-dimensioned psychologically and as fully realized as any characters in Western literature, and Homer's perceptions into the minds and hearts of these characters will remain the enduring model for the portrayal of these characters will remain the great model for psychological drama, a model that will recur in the worlds of Vergil (70 BC-19 BC), Dante (1265-1321), Chaucer (1343-1400), even Shakespeare (1564-1616). In far more fundamental ways than its "heroic" style and "epic" scope, the Iliad will be the fountainhead of long centuries of literature that will look into and dramatize the human heart, intellect, and psychology.

I'm going to let you read–and be moved by–the great Priam-Achilleus scenes by yourself, without me nattering away over your shoulder. But just consider that *here* is the same vicious and rabid Achilleus whose "heart of iron"[117] the old and frail Priam will soon prove himself able to pierce, finding inside it an even deeper human and responsive place than *we* ever saw or imagined back in Book I when Athene managed to keep Achilleus from murdering Agamemnon,[118] or here, where Achilleus is utterly without pity for Hektor.

Here is Achilleus in action, the hyperbolically and perhaps even delusionally "victimized," rigid, and vengeance-driven warrior whom Priam will prove himself able to humanize, move, and at least half-way tame. After this, some other matters, and then our close:

> But looking darkly at him swift-footed Achilleus answered:
> 'No more entreating of me, you dog, by knees or parents.
> I wish only that my spirit and fury would drive me
> to hack your meat away and eat it raw for the things that
> you have done to me.[119] So there is no one who can hold the dogs off
> from your head, not if they bring here and set before me ten times
> and twenty times the ransom, and promise more in addition,
> not if Priam son of Dardanos should offer to weigh out
> your bulk in gold; not even so shall the lady your mother
> who herself bore you lay on the death-bed and mourn you:
> no, but the dogs and the birds will have you all for their feasting.'
> (XXII, 344-354)

Before this, before the moment of his abject defeat, the great Hektor knew that "'now evil death is close to me, and no longer far away, / and there is no way out'" (XXII, 300-301). Knowing that "'now my death is upon me'" (303), he determined at the least to make a mark:

> 'Let me at least not die without a struggle, inglorious,
>> but do some big thing first, that men to come shall know of it.' (XXII, 304-305)

And the result was Hektor's great "swoop," his absolutely extraordinary armed run at his enemy Achilleus. Splendid in itself, Hektor's swoop offers something more: An opportunity almost as remarkable as the shield-forging scene itself for us to "see" through the eyes of Homer, this great holistic, pre-Platonic, and pre-dualist poet.

Here it is. You'll see that it joins up to the moment we've already seen, when Achilleus thrusts his spear into Hektor's neck:

> So he spoke, and pulling out the sharp sword that was slung
> at the hollow of his side, huge and heavy, and gathering
> himself together, he made his swoop, like a high-flown eagle
> who launches himself out of the murk of the clouds on the flat land
> to catch away a tender lamb or a shivering hare; so
> Hektor made his swoop, swinging his sharp sword, and Achilleus
> Charged, the heart within him loaded with savage fury.
> In front of his chest the beautiful elaborate great shield
> covered him, and with the glittering helm with four horns
> he nodded; the lovely golden fringes were shaken about it
> which Hephaistos had driven close along the horn of the helmet.
> And as a star moved among stars in the night's darkening,
> Hesper, who is the fairest star who stands in the sky, such
> was the shining from the pointed spear Achilleus was shaking
> in his right hand with evil intention toward brilliant Hektor.

He was eyeing Hektor's splendid body, to see where it might best
give way, but all the rest of the skin was held in the armour,
brazen and splendid, he stripped when he cut down the strength of
    Patroklos;
yet showed where the collar-bones hold the neck from the shoulders,
the throat, where death of the soul comes most swiftly; in this place
brilliant Achilleus drove the spear as he came on in fury... (XXII, 306-326)

There are one or two instances of the purely formulaic fixed epithets in the passage–"brilliant Hektor" and "brilliant Achilleus"–and of course the style in general remains largely formulaic. But within the freedoms allowed by formula, just look at what Homer does through the use of adjectives and other kinds of comparison–again and again and again joining or linking or juxtaposing the tender and the fierce, the beautiful and the ferocious, the artistic and the death-dealing, the wondrous and the merciless.

Hektor is "like a high-flown eagle," consistently enough, but Homer bats not an eye at the following "tender lamb" or "shivering hare." Then it's Achilleus' turn to charge, his heart "loaded with savage fury" juxtaposed with the "beautiful elaborate great shield"–which from the start, we mustn't forget, *is* both a weapon of war, though a defensive one, and, as the single most carefully wrought symbolic passage in the poem, itself *also* a work of art. Achilleus' helm is "glittering," while he himself is compared not only to "a star" but specifically to "Hesper,"[120] "who is the fairest star who stands in the sky." And, in spite of the fact that Achilleus is studying it to find his spear-target, Hektor's body nevertheless is "splendid."

The passage gives us something like a miniature version of the shield itself, both it and the shield having or showing no natural inclination whatsoever to separate the violent from the lovely, the artistic from the brutal, the glittering from the death-dealing. *All* are parts of the whole. The *whole* is life. And *life* is the poet's great subject.

Many of those among us, admittedly, and very possibly many among those who are reading this book, can find it difficult to "feel" that the kind of holism that permeates the *Iliad* from first line to last is really quite "natural" or "normal" or even quite "right"–in the sense, conceivably, of "right in the head."

I can well understand reactions of this kind, since every person among us, believer or atheist, cynic or sentimentalist, highly educated or slightly so, has swum in the waters of dualism, breathed the atmosphere of dualism, and been exposed to the assumptions of dualism for his or her entire life. Go to New York City and ask yourself why the buildings are so tall. Well, part of the reason is economic, yes, but even more of it is because of the near-religious assumption that the direction "up" is so superior to the direction "down" that the two are more than merely opposites but are virtual anathema one to the other. Or church spires–no economics there, presumably, but ever-up remains the infinitely preferred direction.

Let's look together at a passage that, even more than others we've looked at, may bring about in many readers, not surprisingly, a certain disbelief, and, in other readers, the possibility of a real disgust. Of the passages that I know at all well in the *Iliad*, this one may be the single most vivid dramatization of the natural fact or reality of holism, one of the most concise examples of what it really means to be free of the horizontal line that separates entire aspects of life one from another, the immaterial and spiritual from the physical and earthly. In this case, you'll see that their holistic way of seeing frees the Achaian warriors from any hint of what will become our own all-but-absolute separation of "beauty" and "brutality," of the "attractive" and the "repulsive." For those still living in a world defined by holism rather than by dualism, no such arbitrary separation existed.

Here's the passage, beginning with Achilleus pulling his spear from

Hektor's body:

> He spoke, and pulled the brazen spear from the body, and laid it
> on one side, and stripped away from the shoulders the bloody
> armour. And the other sons of the Achaians came running about him,
> and gazed upon the stature and on the imposing beauty
> of Hektor; and none stood beside him who did not stab him;
> and thus they would speak one to another, each looking at his neighbor:
> 'See now, Hektor is much softer to handle that he was
> When he set the ships ablaze with the burning firebrand.'
> So as they stood beside him they would speak, and stab him. (XXII, 367-375)

The greatest error we can make, I think, is to respond to Homer–to any aspect either of the contemporary world he portrays or of the historic-legendary world of the Trojan war that he recalls–by looking down on it from what we wrongly believe to be a "superior" historical vantage point, and by denigrating what we see, hear, and read as being "primitive," or "tribal," or "uncivilized," by giving it these or any other "designating-of-inferiority-to-us" labels of the kind given it by the Grudinians among us, the Platonists or neo-Platonists among us, by almost all of the *practicing* mono-theists among us, by the Cartesians, and, not least, by the capitalist strivers for global empire, who are themselves so absolutely sequestered by the thick horizontal line of dualism[121] that they are entirely blinded to the wholeness of the world and are able to see only a narrow and splinter-thin part of it–which they, of course, like men in that deep pit we spoke of, take for the whole.

Which of us, after all, is in actuality the more primitive–those in Homer's world, or those of us in our own world governed by the global capitalists? We know that the global capitalists–perhaps because of their splinter-thin range of sight, perhaps for other reasons as well–have revealed themselves to be fond of using various methods of torture on other human beings.[122] This fondness extends, at least of late, all the way from the highest levels of globally ambitious leadership–the likes of David Rockefeller or Henry Kissinger–down through such puppets of those leaders as the Prime Minister of England and the President of the United States, and then even further down, through the Houses of Lords and Commons, through the House of Representatives and the United States Senate, then up again to the more powerful levels of the corporate directorships, leadership of the intelligence agencies, and the leadership of the corporate-military complexes that are directed from places like the Pentagon.

In the *Iliad*, though, I'm not aware of torture being used or taking place. I'm not aware of any allusion to it or mention of it. I'm not aware of there being even a thought of it.

There's brutality, there's suffering, there's gore, there's blood, there are agony, pain, and death, there's even slavery–in ancient Greece, if not in the *Iliad*–but there's not torture.[123] Many might consider that the words I've just now listed themselves obviate any question of torture, the words indicating so generalized an absence of consideration for the pain of others as to make the torture question moot. We agreed long ago that Homer's world is brutal and violent. I ask only, before we claim any general superiority of our age over his, that we look clearly, closely, and with open conscience, at our own.

An extremely important word in the *Iliad* is the word "pity." The absence of pity–as in the absence of it so much of the time in Achilleus himself–results in failure. The restoration of it results in success. And careful readers, those who understand that Homer builds his poetry on a foundation of human psychology, human feeling, and human consciousness, know exactly and solely where the responsibility for avoiding such failure and for achieving such success lies–solely and only within human beings, since they, along with nature–their earthly mother–are the only two things that exist, have ever existed, or ever *will* exist.

Homer, Shakespeare, Chaucer–not very many among the great Western writers are able to look at these facts of our human existence *more* clearly or *more* steadily or *more* uncompromisingly than Homer is able to do in the *Iliad*.

Ironically, the great speech about success and failure comes from Achilleus himself, though only after Priam has performed an act of courage as great as any of Achilleus' or Hektor's own in making his night-visit to the enemy's tent. "'I put my lips to the hands of the man who has killed my children,'" Priam says (XXIV, 506), with the result that the iron Achilleus is, in fact, actually touched by pity:

> Thereafter he rose from his chair, and took the old man by the hand,
> and set him on his feet again, in pity for the grey head and the grey beard,
> and spoke to him and addressed him in winged words: 'Ah, unlucky,
> surely you have had much evil to endure in your spirit.
> How could you dare to come alone to the ships of the Achaians
> and before my eyes, when I am one who have killed in such numbers
> such brave sons of yours? The heart in you is iron. Come, then,
> and sit down upon this chair, and you and I will let
> our sorrows lie still in the heart for all our grieving.' (XXIV, 514-523)

We've looked at these lines before, or at part of them. But the additional words of Achilleus that they lead into now–these we haven't looked at. They bring us very close to the end of our study.

I'll repeat a small amount from the previous citation in order to smooth the transition into the new, and even more important, part of the speech:

> 'The heart in you is iron. Come, then,
> and sit down upon this chair, and you and I will even let

our sorrows lie still in the heart for all our grieving.[124] There is not

any advantage to be won from grim lamentation.

Such is the way the gods spun life for unfortunate mortals,

That we live in unhappiness, but the gods themselves have no sorrows.

There are two urns that stand on the door-sill of Zeus. They are unlike

for the gifts they bestow: an urn of evils, an urn of blessings.

If Zeus who delights in thunder mingles these and bestows them

on man, he shifts, and moves now in evil, again in good fortune.

But when Zeus bestows from the urn of sorrows, he makes a failure

of man, and the evil hunger drives him over the shining

earth, and he wanders respected neither of gods nor mortals.'

(XXIV, 531-533)

Just how helpful is Achilleus' counsel so far? His estimation of Priam's purposefulness and great courage is certainly just, true, and accurate–and the bond that comes into existence between the two men, and the two enemies, is just as certainly understandable within the bounds of human psychology–including the fact that the bond is shaky and also including the fact that Achilleus shows signs of flaring up into the same old righteousness, insubordination, and anger as before ("'No longer stir me up, old sir. I myself am minded / to give Hektor back to you,'" he tells Priam (560-561), insisting that *he* be the order-giver; and then he frightens the poor doddering king with the threat of physical danger ("'you must not further make my spirit move in my sorrows / for fear, old sir, I might not let you alone in my shelter, / suppliant as you are; and be guilty before the god's orders'" (568-570).

Those who have stuck with me all the way through this little book know that I myself both prefer and recommend reading the *Iliad* as if the gods "weren't in it." *And* those readers know that I do so because I can find no evidence anywhere in the poem that Homer–himself every bit as confident, powerful, and sophisticated in his own understanding of human motivation, psychology, and feeling as the gods ever might be–considered them, either, in any way other than as very ancient and highly conventional fantasies that indeed reflected the human mind and the human condition but in no way controlled them.

That, however, doesn't mean that Homer's *characters* may not have believed literally in the gods, to degrees greater or less, nor does it mean that his *listeners* very likely, if not most likely, did too. Not, if I may allude to Jerry Seinfeld, that there's anything wrong with *that*. In the case of Achilleus, certainly we can leave him with his apparently literal belief in Zeus, in the doorsill of Zeus, and in the two urns that stand on that doorsill, one of evils and one of blessings. And yet at the same time, if *we* don't believe in Zeus, aren't we every bit as entitled– in fact, aren't we required[125]–to leave him *out* every bit as much as Achilleus is entitled to keep him *in*?

My feelings on this subject are strong, and I do think that we're every bit as entitled on *our* side as Achilleus is on *his*. What this means, in practical terms, is that we non-believers are free to reduce Zeus–no, are under the necessity of reducing him–to a being who exists solely and only within the realm and boundary of metaphor in its purest form.

And if we *do* do that, it's only appropriate and right to ask what that metaphor will be a metaphor *of*. And the answer, here just as it will be in every case having to do with the gods, is that the metaphor will be a metaphor either of *natural* force or of *human* psychology, feeling, and behavior.

Now, allowing Achilleus his view of things, let's take a look at ours. What are these urns, really? Well, for one thing, they're metaphors representing good luck and bad luck, the same thing, really, as what Achilleus calls "evils" and "blessings."

To this extent, to the extent that they "mean" good and bad luck, the urns are really nothing more than metaphors for natural forces–since luck, in its purest form, is determined solely by the laws of nature.

Things get more complicated, though, and more interesting, if we go on to other matters than pure chance–specifically, to matters of *human choice.*

After all, with Zeus out of the picture, who is left to dip into either the urn of evils or the urn of blessings, whether to "bestow" their contents just about evenly, on the one hand, or to scoop more deeply and to "bestow" more widely from just *one* of the urns or the other?

And the answer is, of course, that who is left to do this kind of choosing–since that's exactly what it is: choice–is solely and only human beings themselves. What the *Iliad* demonstrates as bountifully and as vividly and as deeply as any other work of literature we have is that aside from "choice" of the kind dictated by nature–whether Pompeii will or won't be buried, for example–the only thing that determines the nature of the world or the nature of existence in it is in turn the nature of the choices made *by* the human beings who live in that world and who therefore experience the nature of existence *in* it.

With chance set aside, the very concept of "fate," as we've said before, is definable as being nothing other than whatever it may be that human beings *do.* Achilleus tells us that it's *Zeus* who's the actor and who, by sprinkling out dust preponderantly from the "urn of sorrows," "makes a failure / of man" (XXIV, 531-532), with the result that man "wanders respected neither of gods nor mortals" (XXIV, 533).

But the Trojan war itself, like all wars, came about because of what *people* did.[126] It came about because of what Helen did, because of what Alexandros did, because of what Agamemnon and Menelaos did, what Hektor did, and, certainly, because of what Achilleus did. All wars are caused by human beings–what else could conceivably cause them? And, by the same token–again, with nature-driven chance set aside–all wars have been *ended* by human beings.[127]

Achilleus both does and doesn't know what he's talking about–he's like one of the "unreliable narrators" that English professors in the mid-twentieth century will begin talking about when they analyze novels. It can certainly be argued ("Sing, goddess, the anger of Peleus' son Achilleus / and its devastation. . .") that if the *Iliad* could be said to have a central character, that character would arguably be Achilleus. But the *Iliad* is neither a novel nor a play (though it has in it the seeds of both), and, no, it does not have a central character in anything like our conventional sense of that term. I said earlier that Achilleus is a bit like the irritant around which a pearl forms. I still think that that comparison is useful, *and* I also think that Achilleus remains a certain kind of problem for Homer throughout the poem. Like all the other characters, he came to Homer as what you might call "inherited goods," not as something *chosen* by the poet but, instead, as another part of the already-existing story as it came down *to* the poet.

In that way, Achilleus is no different from any of the other major figures in the poem. But he does differ from all the rest in a certain different and important way: Central though he may be, Achilleus, of all the major figures, has the *least* insight of any, and the *least* capacity for self-understanding.

Remember Helen in Book III, as she virtually psychoanalyzes herself, and even Alexandros, in the same book, showing an understanding of what he *is* when he castigates the great Hektor for failing to value his powerful erotic human quality ("Never to be cast away are the gifts of the gods, magnificent, / which they give of their own will, no man could have them for wanting them" [III, 65-66]). Agamemnon early on understands the dangers of his own anger—and, in demonstrating his ability to suppress and control that anger, and avert its danger, shows a fitness for leadership *far* superior to any equivalent thing in Achilleus. Hektor may not be entirely flexible in his understanding of himself and the workings of his own mind, but he is *firm*:

Hektor will do the best he is capable of, even if that means returning to battle carrying his inward conviction that his city, his wife, and his son are all going to be lost–and, of course, himself. Even Andromache comes alive with a wonderful psychological complexity when, as fearful of defeat as Hektor is, she nevertheless pleads with him to remain out of the battle ("'Hektor, thus you are father to me, and my honoured mother, / you are my brother, and you it is who are my young husband'" [VI, 429-430]).

But Achilleus? I can remember three times when he shows himself to be thoughtful–and in none of the three is his thought *quite* in keeping with his character. In all three, it seems as though someone else should or could be speaking, or should or could be doing what Achilleus is doing. And in none of the three does Achilleus reveal any change in himself that *lasts*, or any hint that he himself *understands* what's happening to him.

Nevertheless, Homer does the very best he possibly can with this burdensome and intractable inheritance, the character of Achilleus.

One of Achilleus' "thoughtful" moments, as we saw, comes in Book I, when he decides not to draw his sword and murder Agamemnon on the spot. Now, for a more psycho-emotionally mature character, such a decision is unlikely even to have arisen. In this case, though, the pouty and adolescent Achilleus says to Athene, after she has grabbed him from behind by the hair, that "'it is necessary that I obey'" you and Hera. His reason? "'So[128] it will be better.'" But *why* will it be? Well, because "'If any man obeys the gods, they listen to him also'" (I, 215-218).

It is most inviting to think that Achilleus is doing something here along the lines of what Helen does in Book III when she both understands and analyzes her own contradictory sexual impulses, demonstrates both her liking and her *resentment* of them, then first rebels against one side of them but quickly retreats to find protection by embracing the *other* side (III, 428-436).

In other words, it is inviting to imagine that Achilleus is saying that the achieving of self-knowledge (like, say, the knowledge Agamemnon has achieved about *his* own anger) can become a guide for the making of later and better decisions.

But if a major part of what "humanism" means is the understanding that human beings, and the best abilities and capacities of human beings, are the only source we have for guidance, judgment, understanding, and even for *meaning*–well, then Achilleus doesn't really do so very well functioning in the humanist world of Homer. It simply doesn't seem that he *or* his judgment *or* his self-control *or* his capacity for pity improves in him, there being no real indication in the rest of the poem–in the space between his brief conversation with "Athene" in Book I and his later meeting with Priam in Book XXIV–of any *lasting* increase in self-understanding taking place within him.

It's fascinating that Homer gives Achilleus some of the very best lines in the poem–even though the psychology of the speaker seems both too thin and too shallow to support the thematic greatness and significance of those lines. What better example of great dramatic verse is there than the passage in Book IX, when Achilleus gives his reasons for turning down the wondrous gifts offered him by Agamemnon if only Achilleus will rejoin the fighting?

Here again–at least *I* can't help but see this as being the case–we see a disjuncture between the material that Homer has been "given" or has "inherited" and what he actually needs in order to make the best and richest use of it dramatically and poetically. With Helen, with Andromache, with Hektor, with Agamemnon, he's fine, and all goes well. Each of those characters has introspection, each has depth, each has *some* kind and degree of self-recognition and self-understanding–whether or not it brings them ease or peace. But not so with Achilleus–who nevertheless is absolutely central to the entire drama, and who therefore is very likely to be relied upon for the expression of some of that drama's central understandings, realizations, or perceptions. And so it is that Achilleus, as said, gets some of the poem's best lines. But Homer is put in a position of having to force those great lines into a psychological vessel neither deep nor large enough to sustain or support them in any truly believable psychological way. As a result, Homer is forced into doing something the equivalent of giving the lines of Hamlet's soliloquies to—well, Falstaff, maybe, or, even more aptly, Hotspur.

Nevertheless, the lines are high, fine, dramatic, moving, and, above all, expressive of what I can't help but take as the central tenet of the Homeric—and the ancient humanist—view of human existence and of the nature, weight, and requirements *of* that existence.

The lines, which we've seen before, speak for themselves: They say that *Life is all there is.* A reader has to be willing to pardon the fact that the speaker of them himself seems unlikely to be generative of such thoughts. For the poetry given him by Homer speaks clearly, fervently, accurately, and for the ages:

> For not worth the value of my life are all the possessions they fable
> were won for Ilion, that strong-founded citadel, in the old days
> when there was peace, before the coming of the sons of the Achaians;
> not all that the stone doorsill of the Archer holds fast within it
> of Phoibos Apollo in Pytho of the rocks. Of possessions
> cattle and fat sheep are things to be had for the lifting,
> but a man's life cannot come back again, it cannot be lifted
> nor captured again by force, once it has crossed the teeth's barrier.
> (IX, 400-409)

And the third occasion when that shallow vessel, Achilleus, is used as a container for the most profound, deep, far-reaching, and revelatory of ideas and thoughts governing and delineating the very nature of the humanism that Homer understands as defining human life within the world as he sees it–this third occasion comes in the night-meeting between Achilleus and the aged Priam.

We've looked at this vitally important section of the *Iliad* already, but now we need to complete that look. Homer has put into the mouth of the innocent, shallow, and un-introspective Achilleus the brave, noble, and responsibility-bearing words that when human beings make poor decisions instead of *best* decisions, they "[make] a failure of man," who, as a consequence, "wanders respected neither of gods nor mortals."

Achilleus then diverges from his main theme to talk about–appropriately enough–himself, but doing so in some of the more insipid, un-energetic, and poetically uninspired lines in the entire poem–lines in which Achilleus talks about himself not psychologically but only in regard to his family history. It's impossible not to think that even Homer felt these to be obligatory lines, structurally required by the architecture of the poem, a means by which he could *somehow* bring to a close this scene of the great, steadfast, and courageous Priam as he is portrayed here in opposition to the shallow, adolescent, non-introspective and unpredictable Achilleus, who nevertheless must be acknowledged if only for the large centrality of his role in the poem. And so we get a series of tiresome lines :

'Such were the shining gifts given by the gods to Peleus
from his birth, who outshone all men beside for his riches
and pride of possession, and was lord over the Myrmidons. Thereto
the gods bestowed an immortal wife on him, who was not mortal.
But even on him the god piled evil also. There was not
any generation of strong sons born to him in his great house
but a single all-untimely child he had, and I give him
no care[129] as he grows old, since far from the land of my fathers

> I sit here in Troy, and bring nothing but sorrow to you and your children.
>
> And you, old sir, we are told you prospered once; for as much
>
> as Lesbos, Makar's hold, confines to the north above it
>
> and Phrygia from the north confines, and enormous Hellespont,
>
> of these, old sir, you were lord once in your wealth and your children.
>
> But now the Uranian gods brought us, an affliction upon you,
>
> forever there is fighting about your city, and men killed. (XXIV, 533-548)

Perhaps I'm too hard on Achilleus, though he does remain stalwartly the least introspective of the chief characters in the poem. Still, toward the close of the lines just cited, he does begin, however faintly, to show signs that he has begun to think instead of simply to recite. If, as we're entitled and in my own view *required* to do,[130] we "remove" the "gods" from this line ("But now the Uranian gods brought us, an affliction upon you. . ."), its real meaning is allowed to emerge.

In other words, Achilleus, whether wittingly or not, is referring to "fate," and since we know that "fate" is what people *do*, he is actually saying to Priam "But now *we* came to you, an affliction upon you. . ." Again, whether *he*, as the character named Achilleus, is aware that this is what he's really saying, we can't know. But we do know that *we* are aware of it–and we also know, at least so far as my own memory of the poem serves, that this is only the third of three places where Achilleus shows any sign of psychological, or psycho-emotional, dialogue with himself–the first being the episode in Book I where he keeps himself from slaying Agamemnon, and the second the moment when he says to his mother, "I wish that strife would vanish away from among gods and mortals, / and gall, which makes a man grow angry for all his great mind, / that gall of anger that swarms like smoke inside of a man's heart / and becomes a thing sweeter to him by far than the dripping of honey" (XVIII, 107-110).

In any case, such is the immeasurably subtle genius of Homer–or of the Homeric poet or poets–that this faint emerging of even so small a degree of real introspection or of actual *thinking* in the character of Achilleus leads at once, naturally and directly, to three lines that may be the most specifically and concretely revelatory of any others in the poem as to what the Homeric view, attitude, and vision toward the nature of life and toward the nature of existence *within* life really is. That they come from the limited Achilleus rather than from, say, the far more complex and thoughtful Hektor or Agamemnon or Helen, makes them only the more memorable and–well, the more precious. It's almost as though the poem itself, or certainly the experience of Priam's visit, has had the effect, virtually, of *surprising* this physically gifted but callow adolescent into blurting out, as *advice* to the old king, Priam, what may be the three most profound lines in the *Iliad*:

> 'But bear up, nor mourn endlessly in your heart, for there is not
> anything to be gained from grief for your son; you will never
> bring him back; sooner you must go through yet another sorrow.'
> (XXIV, 449-451)

"But bear up."

Life *is*. And, for those human beings existing inside life, life must be borne. As I've suggested, that these three lines come from Achilleus rather than from someone else may seem to bring to them a debility. On the other hand, perhaps it brings to them an authenticity–and *certainly* a deep melancholy–in that they are coming from the young man who earlier "destroyed pity" and who now advises his grief-stricken elder that "there is not / anything to be gained from grief for your son; you will never / bring him back," as though, if nothing else, he, too, recognizes the absoluteness of what he has done and of what he has caused to be lost.

"Absoluteness" may be the word, if we were forced to pick out only one, that best suggests what the Homeric eye sees when it looks out into the world. And is it possible that even Achilleus grew able to understand that absoluteness, before the end?

We'll never know. But is it possible that the last line of the poem is a hint one way or the other? That line, after all–plain, unadorned, uninflected, un-emphasized–may be among the most melancholy poetic lines of all poetic lines that exist. Or it may be one of the most non-judgmental, impartial, and objective. Or, in the unflinching clarity, steadiness, and absoluteness of the eye of the poet who conceived of it, it may be one of the most humane and courageous of lines ever written:

> **Such was their burial of Hektor, breaker of horses.**

We'll never know. And that, need it be said, is a very, very great part of the reason why we will never, ever, stop *wanting* to know.

–Eric Larsen
–*May 3, 2009*

Back Matter

Course One

Books Required:
Homer, *The Iliad*, tr. Lattimore
Aeschylus, *The Oresteia*, tr. Fagles
Sophocles, *The Oedipus Cycle*, tr. Fitts & Fitzgerald
Euripides, *Three Plays*, tr. Roche
Plato, *Great Dialogues*, tr. W. H. D. Rouse
Virgil, *The Aeneid*, tr. Mandelbaum
St. Augustine, *Confessions*, tr. Rex Warner

Assignments in the *Iliad*:
Day 01	*Iliad* I, lines 1-7
Day 02	*Iliad* I (Quiz 1, on Bk. I)
Day 03	*Iliad* III, IV (Quiz 2, on Bks. III, IV)
Day 04	*Iliad* VI, IX (Quiz 3, on Bks. VI, IX)
Day 05	*Iliad* XIV, XVIII
Day 06	*Iliad*, XXI, XXII (Quiz 4, bks. XIV, XVIII)
Day 07	*Iliad*, XXIV

The Twenty Four Books of the *Illiad*

Book I–The Quarrel
Book II–The Forces–Are Displayed
Book IIIA–Truce And A Duel
Book IV–Pandarus Breaks The Truce
Book V–Diomedes Fights The Gods
Book VI–Hector And Andromache
Book VII–Aias Fights Hector
Book VIII–The Trojans Reach The Wall
Book IX–Overtures To Achilleus
Book X–Night Interlude
Book XI–Achilleus Takes Notice
Book XII–Hektor Storms The Wall
Book XIII–The Battle At The Ships
Book XIV–Zeus Out-Manoeuvred
Book XV–The Achaians At Bay
Book XVI–Patroklos Fights And Dies
Book XVII–The Struggle Over Patroklos
Book XVIII–Armour For Achilleus
Book XIX–The Feud Is Ended
Book XX–The Gods Go To War
Book XXI–Achilleus Fights The River
Book XXII–The Death Of Hektor
Book XXIII–The Funeral And The Games
Book XXIV–Priam And Achilleus

Footnotes

[1] Find a course outline on p. 215.

[2] The date given by Herodotus and roughly accepted by Lattimore (see Lattimore's Introduction, p. 18). It appears now, however, that Lattimore may have been wrong. For a hint of the scholarship on Homer's dates, see http://en.wikipedia.org/wiki/Homer and carry on from there if interest leads you. Lattimore's date may be as much as a century too early.

[3] *The Iliad of Homer, Translated with an Introduction by Richmond Lattimore*, The University of Chicago Press, 1951. (ISBN: 0226469-409) We're using the paperback edition, which first appeared in 1961. My own personal copy is the twenty-first paperback impression, dated 1971.

[4] See Lattimore's Introduction, pp. 14-16, for a good summary of the whole story.

[5] Another name for Troy is "Ilium." So "Iliad" means "song of Troy," similar to the way "Odyssey" means "song of Odysseus," Odysseus being the Greek name for Ulysses.

[6] In Book VI, "Hektor and Andromache," we'll get to meet—*very* personally—not only Hektor and his extraordinary wife, Andromache, but also the great Helen "of Troy" herself, along with her Trojan husband-abductor (husband *or* abductor, depending on what stories you go by), the vain and fascinating Paris.

[7] In line one of Book I, for example, the glossary will show you that "Peleus" is pronounced "PEL ee us," with the accent on the first syllable. In the same way, you'll find that "Achilleus" is "ach ILL ee us," the emphasis on the *second* syllable.

[8] Lattimore, Introduction, p. 14.

[9] If you want to find out how Umberto Eco accounts for the disappearance of the comedy portion of the *Poetics*, read *The Name of the Rose* (1980). You'll never guess Eco's explanation—but you *may* be convinced by it.

[10] And there's no way of replacing the enormity of the loss when the great library at Alexandria burned down, along with the totality of its holdings. You can get some introductory information about this disaster here: http://en.wikipedia.org/wiki/Library_of_Alexandria

[11] If one literally "believes" in the gods, then the plague did come from the arrows of the angry Apollo. Another view might be that, since the viral or bac-

terial onset of the disease–of any disease–was invisible and a mystery, metaphors like this one of the angry god's arrows coming "from afar" arose as explanations of natural phenomena otherwise not understandable.

[12] If your volume of the Lattimore *Iliad* doesn't supply running heads for identifying the "titles" of the twenty-four books of the poem (as mine doesn't), the list of their titles (on p. 216) might be worth putting a bookmark in.

[13] No semester went by without someone raising the question as to whether Achilleus and Patroklos were sexual lovers. I don't know. Maybe. Maybe not. The whole subject of male homosexuality among the ancients is out of my ken–and more or less of my interest, too. Still, something so simple as reading Plato requires at least *some* serious entertainment of the question, nor am I about to say that I don't think the question is a serious one. It is. I just don't think it's essentially a literary question. No less a figure than Alexander the Great is portrayed as gay by Peter Green, in *Alexander of Macedon, 356-323 BC* (1991). Though Green's book is a scholarly biography, a student once said that reading it was like reading "an adventure novel." On the subjects of male gayness and of Alexander, here are two more suggestions: Mary Renault's *The Nature of Alexander* (1975), which is Renault's historical biography of the great figure. It's shorter than Peter Green's book (less battle detail). But be sure to read Renault's biography *after* reading her novel *The Persian Boy*.

[14] That is, Achilleus took time to brag and crow about his achievement in showing himself superior in arms to Hektor. To us, this convention of "vaunting" at such times may seem crude, primitive, even barbaric. But is it? And is Homer himself "crude, primitive, barbaric"? These questions are among the greatest of those to be raised–and answered–in our reading of *The Iliad*.

[15] That is, far greater than Patroklos was.

[16] Here is as good a place as any to acknowledge and lament one's own ignorance–of Homeric Greek, that is. In such ignorance as this, a person–unless he or she actually knows a person like Richmond Lattimore!–can at least compare other translators' decisions to get an idea of where the range of choice lies. Here, for example, first read by me back in 1960, is E. V. Rieu's prose translation of Achilleus' vaunting over Hektor:

> "Achilleus saw that Hector's body was completely covered by the fine bronze armour he had taken from the great Patroclus when he killed him, except for an opening at the gullet where the collar bones lead over from the shoulders to the neck, the easiest place to kill a man. As Hector charged him, Prince Achilles drove at this point with his lance; and the point went right through the tender flesh of Hector's neck,

though the heavy bronze head did not cut his windpipe, and left him able to address his conqueror. Hector came down in the dust and the great Achilles triumphed over him. 'Hector,' he said, 'no doubt you fancied as you stripped Patroclus that you would be safe. You never thought of me: I was too far away. You were a fool. Down by the hollow ships there was a man far better than Patroclus in reserve, the man who has brought you low. So now the dogs and birds of prey are going to maul and mangle you, while we Achaeans hold Patroclus' funeral'" (pp. 405-406, Penguin Books, 1950 [my own copy was reprinted in 1958]). For any who might find these matters interesting, here is Rieu's prose version of the first seven lines of Bk. I: "The Wrath of Achilles is my theme, that fatal wrath which, in fulfilment of the will of Zeus, brought the Achaeans so much suffering and sent the gallant souls of many noblemen to Hades, leaving their bodies as carrion for the dogs and passing birds. Let us begin, goddess of song, with the angry parting that took place between Agamemnon King of Men and the great Achilles son of Peleus. Which of the gods was it that made them quarrel?" (p. 23) Rieu uses "as carrion" for "delicate feasting," though his later "maul and mangle" more closely reflects Lattimore's "foully rip."

[17] Johnson's full paragraph: "But original deficience cannot be supplied. The want of human interest is always felt. *Paradise Lost* is one of the books which the reader admires and lays down, and forgets to take up again. None ever wished it longer than it is. Its perusal is a duty rather than a pleasure. We read Milton for instruction, retired harassed and overburdened, and look elsewhere for recreation; we desert our master and seek for companions." One can't lightly disagree with the great Johnson, and in this case not even I myself disagree entirely. But I do disagree in large part. My first extended experience of Milton came under the spirited and wonderfully elegant guidance of Scott Elledge (at Carleton College, spring 1960), and Elledge, who loved Milton powerfully, left me with the great gift of having absorbed some part of that same love. To tell the truth, I can hardly wait until, in this series of books, we reach *Paradise Lost.* We'll not only have a grand and fascinating time of it then, but, thanks to the invaluable legacy left by Scott Elledge, we'll find that the want of human interest is *never* felt. We won't, however, unlike Johnson, be reading the entire epic.

[18] Or certainly indisputable among the likes of us, living as we do in our sped-up and "entertainment-fed" era. Back a couple of centuries, though, it was a different thing to Stephen Maturin. Maturin is ship's physician aboard *HMS Surprise* under the command of Captain Jack Aubrey in Lord Nelson's navy. In *The Far Side of the World*, a volume in Patrick O'Brian's great series of Aubrey/Maturin historical novels, you'll find this masterful and wondrous

paragraph: "Even if she [the *Surprise*'s quarry] were already in the Marquesas she would not be so very far away by now, as these were reckoned in the prodigious expanse of the Pacific, where something in the nature of a thousand miles seemed the natural unit. Another unit might be a poem: Stephen was reading [first-officer] Mowett's *Iliad* and he was keeping to one book a day, no more, to make his pleasure last; he had begun a little while after leaving the Galapagos and he was now in book twelve, and he reckoned that at the present rate of sailing he would finish just before they reached the Marquesas. He did his reading in the afternoons, for now that the days were calm and untroubled, with the necessary weeks of their western passage taken out of time as it were, a self-contained whole, he and Jack filled the evening with the music [played on their stringed instruments] they had been obliged to forgo in more demanding waters." (*The Far Side of the World*, 1984)

[19] When I first read the Homeric epics, as a student, I made a point of writing in the margins, against the first line of any speech, the name of the speaker, followed by a colon. At line 59, thus, I've got "Achilleus:" in my margin, as Achilleus addresses Agamemnon. Enormous elements of the poems consist of speeches, almost as if they were in part stage-dramas. Identifying the speakers in this way helps make clear what's going on, and it makes for extremely efficient review later on of what you've read earlier. You know, review for exams and the like.

[20] If you look up "Danaans" in Lattimore's glossary, you'll find that Achaians, Danaans, and Argives are all used interchangeably.

[21] "Host" means huge number, as in "a host of angels." Readers curious about symmetries in the poem might be struck by the fact that on the *tenth day* Achilleus comes forth, hoping to do good. And it's now, in the tenth *year* of the Trojan war, that, by withdrawing from the fighting, he's about to exert an effect as ill as that of the plague.

[22] "An ancient Greek or Roman sacrifice of 100 oxen or cattle" (http://www.merriam-webster.com/dictionary/hecatomb).

[23] Achilleus' word, "claims," with its less-than-subtle touch, at least to *our* ears, of sarcasm, carries a heavy burden at this point in the poem and in the psycho-emotional battle that's about to erupt between Achilleus and Agamemnon. I don't know Greek. Is Achilleus' sarcasm evident in the original? Well, here's E. V. Rieu's translation of the same passage, from which we might get at least some idea: "'Dismiss your fears,' said the swift Achilles, 'and tell us anything you may have learnt from Heaven. For by Apollo Son of Zeus, the very god, Calchas, in whose name you reveal your oracles, I swear that as long as I am alive and in possession of my senses not a Danaan of them all,

here by the hollow ships, shall hurt you, not even if the man you mean is Agamemnon, who bears the title of our overlord.'" (p. 25) Is there sarcasm in "bears the title"? In the original Greek? In Lattimore's "claims to be"?

[24] E. V. Rieu: "Calchas sat down, and the noble son of Atreus, imperial Agamemnon, leapt up in anger. His heart was seething with black passion and his eyes were like points of flame. He rounded first on Calchas, full of menace" (p. 25). Lattimore's choice of "but" seems to me a stroke of genius.

[25] Some will remember Richard Nixon's vice-president, Spiro Agnew, who bitterly castigated the press for never running any "good news" but only "bad."

[26] Readers of *Slaughterhouse Five* will remember Kurt Vonnegut's wonderful rendering of the young punk, for whom, when his ego suffers injury, the only thing that's really "sweet" is "revenge." In his case, he gets revenge on a neighbor by giving the neighbor's dog chopped meat that has ground glass mixed in with it.

[27] "Leda and the Swan," W. B. Yeats (1924)

> A sudden blow: the great wings beating still
> Above the staggering girl, her thighs caressed
> By the dark webs, her nape caught in his bill,
> He holds her helpless breast upon his breast.
>
> How can those terrified vague fingers push
> The feathered glory from her loosening thighs?
> And how can body, laid in that white rush,
> But feel the strange heart beating where it lies?
>
> A shudder in the loins engenders there
> The broken wall, the burning roof and tower
> And Agamemnon dead.
>
> Being so caught up,
> So mastered by the brute blood of the air,
> Did she put on his knowledge with his power
> Before the indifferent beak could let her drop?

[28] G. M. Kirkwood, *A Short Guide to Classical Mythology* (1959), p.33. This little book, barely over a hundred pages, is the single book out of all reference books on classical mythology that I'd recommend over any and all others for conciseness, ease of use, and thoroughness.

[29] When I was there in 1969, a local entrepreneur had brick-sized blocks of wood for sale, labeled as remains of the great Trojan Horse (an object that goes unmentioned in the *Iliad*).

[30] However, do see Lattimore's Introduction, pp. 53-54, "The Gods in the Iliad." Lattimore disagrees on the matter of Zeus as being subject to fate, arguing that he's *not* subject to it.

[31] "A needless repetition of an idea, statement, or word" (http://www.merriam-webster.com/dictionary/tautology)

[32] Meaning "hold back."

[33] Meaning "stop," "arrest," or "keep from moving."

[34] "a combination of contradictory or incongruous words (as *cruel kindness*)" (http://www.merriam-webster.com/dictionary/oxymoron)

[35] Take a look at http://en.wikipedia.org/wiki/Catalogue_of_Ships to find a wonderful map showing graphically all who are named in the Catalogue and identifying where they came from.

[36] Alexandros is Paris, and vice-versa.

[37] A useful site for information about the "Trojan War" is at http://en.wikipedia.org/wiki/Trojan_War#Dates_of_the_Trojan_War. And http://en.wikipedia.org/wiki/Heinrich_Schliemann is useful for information about Heinrich Schliemann and his tremendously important archaeological work at Troy.

[38] "Greave," by the way, means "armor for the shin" http://www.merriam-webster.com/dictionary/greaves

[39] A remark like this one mustn't be allowed to go by without at least some corrective qualification. If truth be told, we're every bit as arbitrarily set in our own ideas of what characteristics and devices do or don't represent "the real" as Homer may have been, or was, set in his. In my own opinion, in fact, we're at a point in human history where more people are probably more lacking in consciousness or understanding of what the "real" is, let alone how to portray it, than ever before. This is, clearly, another idea to be continued later. Anyone interested in it, might read my book *A Nation Gone Blind: America in an Age of Simplification and Deceit* (2006).

[40] "Book II opens a great and eventful day of fighting, which does not end until Book 18," Lattimore points out in his Introduction "p. 15)

[41] There are hardly any metaphors in Homer, amid the cornucopia of simi-

les, which we haven't yet looked at. But here's a metaphor, in Helen's description of Aias. I'll italicize it. "'That one is gigantic Aias, *wall of the Achaians,* / and beyond him there is Ideomeneus like a god standing / among the Kretans, and the lords of Krete are gathered about him.'" (III, 229-231)

[42] Meaning "son of Atreus" and used more often for Agamemnon. See glossary.

[43] A third, it could be argued, is the power of nature. But since the events of nature per se are governed so overwhelmingly by chance–chance that the storm will arise, the earthquake occur–that I remain comfortable, at least for the time being, with allowing chance (or fate) and nature to be considered one. Later–when we get, say, to William Blake and to the romantics who follow him, an adjustment will very clearly be needed.

[44] Or so we agreed, back on p. 46.

[45] "**Psychomachia** is a literary concept named for a Latin poem by Prudentius. The poem dealt with the inner conflict within one's soul, between virtue and vice, through allegorical representations. This concept of an inner struggle became key to the developing Christian religion, and was refined dramatically in the medieval morality plays. Works such as *Everyman*, *Piers Plowman*, and *Faust* featured protagonists struggling with temptation, literally personified through the seven deadly sins (gluttony, lust, et. al). A variation of this involved the use of a 'Good Angel' and 'Evil Angel,' one to encourage the tormented soul and the other to push the protagonist further along the path to ruination." (http://muppet.wikia.com/wiki/Psychomachia)

[46] A word I've chosen purposely. I mean it the same way "terrible" was meant in the lines we saw earlier. Human psychology, as we all know well, and as Homer also knew, is both *awful* and *terrible*.

[47] You can read about *Gilgamesh* at http://en.wikipedia.org/wiki/Epic_of_Gilgamesh

[48] Both Helen and Clytemnestra, like Achilleus himself, are mortals, having been born from one mortal parent (Leda) and one immortal (Zeus). Helen must and will die, even though a daughter of Zeus.

[49] Pages 15-16 in my Harvest paperback.

[50] Those interested in the metaphor of rose as love-object can read about– or maybe even *read–Roman de la Rose*, or *The Romaunce of the Rose*, the French medieval (ca. 1230) allegorical poem, its first few thousand lines written by Guillaume de Lorris, then 17,000 or so additional ones written by Jean de

Meun. You don't have to read the whole thing to get a taste–and an understanding–of the allegorical method, where the rose stands "as a symbol of female sexuality in general," and the chivalric lover seeks her. ohttp://en.wikipedia.org/wiki/Roman_de_la_Rose

[51] III, 229

[52] IV, 312, for one of hundreds of examples.

[53] There's a notable little metaphor: "a cloud of foot-soldiers."

[54] Unlike the authorship question in the case of Shakespeare. Doubters that Shakespeare of Avon was actually the writer of the plays have been scorned, ridiculed, and impugned by establishment figures almost forever–especially by figures in the *academic* establishment. My own view is that the rigor of their rejection suggests the weakness of their case. If you're interested in exploring the powerful argument for Edward de Vere, Fourteenth Earl of Oxford, as the real writer of the plays, you can't make a better start than with Mark Anderson's fascinating and fine *"Shakespeare" by Another Name*: http://shakespearebyanothername.com/

[55] The sharp eye here will notice the little tiny simile nested within the larger one.

[56] Lattimore, Introduction, p. 42.

[57] Lattimore, Introduction, p. 43.

[58] Please don't be shocked at my use of this word. I mean it neutrally and always point out that of all disabilities, ignorance is the most responsive to cure and most easily remedied. Effort is the primary and most effective antibody in its cure, especially if accompanied by a bit of guidance. This little book, for example. If a person reads the assignments and then follows through with the guidance–well, that person will no longer be in the dark as to "Homer real." One more thing is salutary in dealing with ignorance–and that's to be free and open in admitting one's own. I point out both readily and frequently the great depths of my ignorance–of particle physics, mathematics, Carolingian history, most languages, and so on. I'm not proud of it, but on the other hand recognition and *acknowledgement* of ignorance are powerful aids not only in promoting honesty but in helping remove the sting–and also the danger–from this disability, ignorance.

[59] Page 24

[60] Or white phosphorus, as used by the U.S. in Falluja and by Israel in Gaza.

[61] An interesting question about consistency may be in order here. Agamemnon is said to have spoken "justice" when he urged that of the Trojans "not a one of them go free of sudden / death and our hands." The word "justice" is at line 62. Then at line 119 begins the long background history mentioned earlier, leading to the discovery by Glaukos and Diomedes of their distant relationship and thus to their "[exchanging] the promise of friendship." According to Agamemnon's earlier declaration, the only "just" thing would be for Diomedes to slay Glaukos. Is this a case where the old phrase "even Homer nods" applies? Or is it–for those of us in search of Homer "real"– something more? Wikipedia, as of this writing, has a fine piece on the subject of the Homeric "nod": http://en.wikipedia.org/wiki/Homeric_nod

[62] There's our complicated Helen again! She may have said to Priam "I wish bitter death had been what I wanted, when I came hither / following your son" (III, 173-174), but now, under quite different circumstances, she's not hesitant to change the story for Hektor's ears, putting the blame on Alexandros alone, whose "blind act" certainly *sounds* like a passion-driven act of abduction. What a great lawyer Helen would make!

[63] If any reader of these pages does in fact pray daily to Zeus, Hera, Athene, Aphrodite, Apollo and the others, that worshipper can be made exempt from the others of us who do not so pray and who *do* therefore enjoy "good and free conscience" in giving *human beings* in the *Iliad* the responsibility for events–other than for purely "natural" events like earthquakes–rather than allowing that such matters were determined by the "gods." In tolerance, I beg the pardon of any true believers and active worshippers.

[64] Hera borrows Aphrodite's "magically" seductive waist-wrap so she'll be irresistible to Zeus who, she knows perfectly well, will, like all men, fall asleep after making love–thus giving *her* a chance to influence the battle in favor of her beloved Danaans over Zeus' beloved Trojans. When Hera appears before him, he finds her so irresistible that he's inspired, before submitting to her charms, to cite for Hera's benefit *all* of his prior love-conquests–not the kind of pick-up line that guys in *our* "real" world might find as successful for them as it is for Zeus. Here's the line: "Then in turn Zeus who gathers the clouds answered her: / 'Hera, there will be a time afterwards when you can go there [to visit Okeanos] / as well. But now let us go to bed and turn to love-making. / For never before has love for any goddess or woman / so melted about the heart inside me, broken it to submission, / as now: not that time when I loved the wife of Ixion / who bore me Peirithoös, equal of the gods in counsel, / nor when I loved Akrisios' daughter, sweet-stepping Danaë, / who bore Perseus to me, pre-eminent among all men, / nor when I loved the daughter of far-renowned Phoinix, Europa / who bore Minos to me, and

Rhadamanthys the godlike; / not when I loved Semele, or Alkmene in Thebe, / when Alkmene bore me a son, Herakles the strong-hearted, / while Semele's son was Dionysos, the pleasure of mortals; not when I loved the queen Demeter of the lovely tresses, / not when it was glorious Leto, nor yourself, so much / as now I love you, and the sweet passion has taken hold of me.'" (XIV, 312-328)

[65] That is, not of low birth or of a family below the nobility.

[66] "To a Friend"

> Who prop, thou ask'st, in these bad days, my mind?–
> He much, the old man, who, clearest-souled of men,
> Saw The Wide prospect, and the Asian Fen,
> And Tmolus hill, and Smyrna bay, though blind.
>
> Much he, whose friendship I not long since won,
> That halting slave, who in Nicopolis
> Taught Arrian, when Vespasian's brutal son
> Cleared Rom of what most shamed him. But be his
>
> My special thanks, whose even-balanced soul,
> From first youth tested up to extreme old age,
> Business could not make dull, nor passion wild;
>
> Who saw life steadily and saw it whole;
> The mellow glory of the Attic stage,
> Singer of sweet Colonus, and its child.

Written by Matthew Arnold, 1849. The references are to Homer, Epictetus, then Sophocles. More detail is provided in *The Norton Anthology of English Literature*, Fourth Edition, pp. 1359-1360.

[67] Anyone interested in my characterizations here might well be interested in Leonard Schlain's absolutely fascinating *The Alphabet Versus the Goddess* (Viking, 1998). In Schlain's overview of history from the fertile crescent on up, there are bushel baskets-full of major figures to despise. Schlain's book is likely to remind readers of Stephen Dedalus' famous comment in the second chapter of *Ulysses* that "History. . . is a nightmare from which I am trying to awake."

[68] http://en.wikipedia.org/wiki/Poetics_(Aristotle)

[69] 428/427 BC–348/347 BC http://en.wikipedia.org/wiki/Plato

[70] In the *Odyssey*, when Odysseus enters the underworld and visits the dead Achilles, Achilles famously gives expression to the idea that life is all there is, and that death is only the *absence* of that immeasurably superior state when he says "O shining Odysseus, never try to console me for dying. / I would rather follow the plow as thrall to another / man, one with no land allotted to him and not much to live on, / than be a king over all the perished dead." Book Eleven, 487-491, trans. Richmond Lattimore.

[71] That is, after the 1859 publication of *The Origins of Species*.

[72] Geology, for example, and, although not strictly speaking a "science," the Higher Criticism. See http://en.wikipedia.org/wiki/Higher_criticism

[73] Jean-Paul Sartre's famous line, that "existence precedes essence," expresses the same idea: That life holds no innate meaning (people are born into mere "existence") and, if it is to *gain* meaning (essence), that meaning will have to be created by the existing person. Read more about Sartre (1905-1980) at http://en.wikipedia.org/wiki/Jean-Paul_Sartre

[74] And to do so also *within the confines dictated by* the life they existed inside of.

[75] Rieu: "'But if I hid myself like a coward and refused to fight, I could never face the Trojans and the Trojan ladies in their trailing gowns. Besides, it would go against the grain, for I have trained myself always, like a good soldier, to take my place in the front line and win glory for my father and myself'" (pp. 128-129).

[76] "'I have come down to stay your anger–but will you obey me?'" (I, 207-208)

[77] Most of the popular ones–the ones you'll remember if, say, you were introduced to the story of Troy somewhere in junior high–are missing in the *Iliad*. Achilleus' destined short life, as said, is hardly central, and there's no mention anywhere of Thetis dipping her son by the heel, as a baby, into the Styx. There's no Trojan Horse–nor even any end to the war–and the so-called Judgment of Paris is heard of only faintly (XXIV, 22-30). The exact psycho-emotional details of who "took" whom when Helen and Paris left Argos together (see Book III) remain less prophecy-driven than they do complex, contradictory, shifting, and altogether (and captivatingly) human questions. You can look all these stories up in G. M. Kirkwood, *A Short Guide to Classical Mythology* (1959). See again note 28.

[78] Anyone interested in why it's so ruinously hard to find, get, or create grown-up readers in America should run, not walk, to get hold of a copy of John Taylor Gatto's *Weapons of Mass Instruction: A Schoolteacher's Journey*

through the Dark World of Compulsory Schooling (New Society, 2009)

[79] Terms, again, that she must therefore live within the confines *of.*

[80] We'll see it first in Aeschylus (ca. 525-456 BC), "the father of tragedy" http://en.wikipedia.org/wiki/Aeschylus

[81] **Suspension of disbelief** or 'willing suspension of disbelief' was a formula devised by the poet and aesthetic philosopher Samuel Taylor Coleridge to justify the use of fantastic or non-realistic elements in literature." http://en.wikipedia.org/wiki/Suspension_of_disbelief

[82] We'll come back to this point later, but those who suspect that nothing determines fate other than fate itself–that is, that "fate" and "chance" are synonymous–will certainly be interested in how it comes about, in Book XXIII, that Hektor's death-day has arrived instead of Achilleus'. Who decides? Well, *nobody*. Even Zeus has to rely on a toss of the cards: "But brilliant Achilleus kept shaking his head at his own people / and would not let them throw their bitter projectiles at Hektor / for fear the thrower might win the glory, and himself come second. / But when for the fourth time they had come around to the well springs / then the Father balanced his golden scales, and in them / he set two fateful portions of death, which lays men prostrate, / one for Achilleus, and one for Hektor, breaker of horses, / and balanced it by the middle; and Hektor's death-day was heavier / and dragged downward toward death, and Phoibos Apollo forsook him" (XXIII, 205-213). Still, in spite of Zeus' scales, and in spite of *my* doubts, Lattimore himself insists that "Zeus is *not* subject to fate" (Introduction, p. 54, emphasis in original).

[83] Anyone interested in this idea–that we ourselves must form our own world and its meaning–can continue examining it from a slightly different perspective in Paul Levy's fascinating and penetrating *The Madness of George W. Bush: A Reflection of Our Collective* Psychosis (2006).

[84] From *Existentialism and Humanism* (1946), translated by Bernard Frechtman; quoted by me from "Choice in a World Without God," in *The World of Short Fiction*, ed. Robert C. Albrecht (The Free Press, 1969).

[85] Prince Hal, in *King Henry the Fourth, Part One*, II, iv, 91.

[86] Life, it was thought, passed out of the body with the last breath–"expiration." Hence mention of "the teeth's barrier," since, especially if one were dying in agony, the teeth would be clenched against the pain–and also in an attempt to keep that last breath still inside.

[87] Since the word "mad," as chosen by Lattimore, may tend to be taken am-

biguously by us, I offer E. V. Rieu's choices for comparison: "'My venerable lord,' replied Agamemnon King of Men, 'the account of my blind folly that you have given us is wholly true. Blinded I was–I do not deny it myself. The man whom Zeus has taken to his heart and honours as he does Achilles, to the point of crushing the Achaeans for his sake, is worth an army. But since I did give in to a lamentable impulse and commit this act of folly, I am willing to go back on it and propitiate him with a handsome indemnity'" (p. 164).

[88] Rieu: "'Fewer Achaeans would then have bitten the dust of this wide world, slaughtered by the enemy while I sat aloof in my anger.'" (p. 355)

[89] That is, creative of *meaning.*

[90] See IX, 114-120, quoted on p. 147.

[91] I mean, of course, "even Non-Apollo himself grows angry at his fellow non-gods."

[92] Or not, certainly, what it's *wholly* about.

[93] The real ones used to be made up of forty-five.

[94] There are lots of exceptions here, as we'll find out when we come to Plato– whose opinion of art, for example, was not what you would call high .

[95] *There's* a good example of Homer's rare use of metaphor: the arrow "leapt away, furious. . ."

[96] That is, Ares drove the Trojans while Athene drove the Achaians.

[97] That is, Achilleus will be the second of the two to die.

[98] Rieu: "So then, Patroclus, since I too am going below, but after you, I shall not hold your funeral till I have brought back here the amour and the head of Hector, who slaughtered you, my noble-hearted friend. And at your pyre I will cut the throats of a dozen of the highborn youths of Troy, to vent my wrath on them for killing you. Till then, you shall lie as you are by my beaked ships, wailed and wept for day and night by the Trojan women and the deep-bosomed daughters of Dardanus whom we captured after much toil, with our own hands and our long spears, when we sacked rich cities full of men." (pp. 345-346)

[99] For the story, look him up in your G. M. Kirkwood *Short Guide to Classical Mythology.*

[100] The word "talk" reminds me to mention that the entire forging of the shield is one of the passages in the *Iliad* that begs most rightly and justly to

be read aloud–and that will most fully, profoundly, and poetically reward whoever gives it his or her best effort at doing so.

[101] Shoemaker & Hoard, 2006.

[102] "And what's wrong with him that makes him 'evil' (the quotation marks are to show that we're using the word temporarily and for convenience)?" (p. 24)

[103] Grudin, p. 87.

[104] Dear Mr. Grudin: Two questions. In our modern and enlightened modern society, do we or do we not fight wars? The answer, of course, is yes, we do. The second question, then, follows: Are we "sane," or are we "insane"? I believe that an answer is owed us.

[105] Grudin, p. 79.

[106] Grudin, p. 79.

[107] Emphasis mine.

[108] Again, those struck by this rather denunciatory tone might be interested in *A Nation Gone Blind*, where my reasons for being considerably less than optimistic on the subject of education in America can be found.

[109] Grudin, p. 84.

[110] And it mustn't be forgotten that there are plenty of divinities *down there*, too.

[111] I do know that we'll be talking about these concepts a great deal more when we get to Aeschylus, Sophocles, and Euripides in the next volume of this series. Apollo, for example, in *The Oresteia*, will be very proud of himself because he thinks he is associated with the mind, brain, and *eyes*–those parts of the body that reside in the "upper" parts of the human person. And he will be scornful–oh, *how* scornful–of the Furies or the Choephoroi, later to be known as the Eumenides or "the Kindly Ones." But what are they that Apollo should scorn them so? Well, they dwell in darkness, are shriveled, and ooze strange fluids–or are, if you wish, the womb. For Apollo, as later for Platonists, the motto could be "Eyes-and-brains good, wombs bad."

[112] Even though that doesn't mean a lover of the *whole* poem *all* the time. Having now read *ten* books of the *Iliad*, you might possibly find it interesting to look back at our discussion in the early part of Day Two about reading great works in abridged form–or not. There's much, much great stuff in the *Iliad* that our assignments left out.

[113] Remember Apollo's disgusted and cautionary note about Achilleus' treatment of Hektor's slain body: "'Great as he is, let him take care not to make us angry; / For see, he does dishonour to the dumb earth in his fury.'" (XXIV, 39-54)

[114] Athene touched it all the way back in Book I, though with great uncertainty that even she could succeed, asking herself "'But will you obey me?'" (I, 207) Now, Priam is able to make his way far more deeply into the core of Achilleus' psychology—a core that Achilleus himself may not even quite know is there.

[115] "'I put my lips to the hands of the man who has killed my children,'" he says (XXIV, 506) in one of the greatest and finest scenes in all of literature outside of Shakespeare.

[116] Speaking of Shakespeare, I myself am an Oxfordian, meaning that I think that Edward DeVere, the 17th Earl of Oxford (1550-1604) is the one who actually wrote the Shakespeare canon. If you're interested, far and away the best *recent* book among the many on this subject is Mark Anderson's *Shakespeare by Another Name* (Gotham Books/Penguin Group USA, 2005).

[117] Hektor's words (XXII, 357)

[118] "Then in answer again spoke Achilleus of the swift feet: / 'Goddess, it is necessary that I obey the word of you two, / Angry though I am in my heart. So it will be better. / If any man obeys the gods, they listen to him also.' (I, 215-218)

[119] Are these really worse than the things Achilleus has done to Hektor, either directly or indirectly? Re-read Andromache's pathetically gripping plea to Hektor in Book VI, where, because of her entire family having been slain by Achilleus, she laments to her husband: "'Hektor, thus you are father to me, and my honoured mother, / you are my brother, and you it is who are my young husband.'" (429-430)

[120] What we call "the Evening Star"

[121] So little do they know about either the whole of themselves or about the whole of the world that they both *see* themselves as being and *believe* themselves to be *above* the line.

[122] See http://www.informationclearinghouse.info/article22529.htm for a related article, "Children as Unlamented Victims of Bush's War Crimes," by Michael Haas. Haas' book, *George W. Bush, War Criminal? The Bush Administration's Liability for 269 War Crimes*, is available from Greenwood Press at

this site: http://www.greenwood.com/ books/printFlyer. aspx?sku= C36499

[123] As for the infamous institution of slavery, we'd hardly be free to call ourselves superior on that issue, either, except for the fact that both as law and institution it is now is a thing of the past. New forms of it, however, seem to be advancing, as with, say, the privatizing of prisons, where the way to greater profit is greater numbers of prisoners. A person could ask how the turning of imprisonment into an industry like this differs fundamentally from creating a slave class.

[124] Achilleus' meaning seems to be, "We will be calm together, no matter how much sorrow we are feeling." Rieu: "You have a heart of iron. But pray be seated now, here on this chair, and let us leave our sorrows, bitter though they are, locked up in our own hearts, for weeping is cold comfort and does little good." (p. 451)

[125] That is, required to "leave them out," in the sense we're talking about, *if* we're to remain true to our own psycho-intellectual view of the nature of existence and of truth. Anyone who does indeed pray to Zeus and worship him regularly should of course leave him "in" the story and read him literally. Anyone who *does not* do those things and yet leaves Zeus *in* and continues reading him literally, as a figure who makes decisions and influences human affairs–such a person, it seems to me, is naïve as a reader and thinker, and, worse, a self-caused (forgive me for the fearsomeness of such a word) hypocrite.

[126] Everyone understands, I'm sure, that *failing* to do something is, or certainly can be, the same as doing something. Take Achilleus again: By failing to contain or suppress his self-righteous anger and his jealousy of Agamemnon, he causes the deaths of many warriors. And by failing, again, to contain or suppress his self-righteousness, self-satisfaction, and residual anger *after* slaying Hektor, what he does do is "'[destroy] pity'" and bring "'dishonour to the dumb earth in his fury'" (Apollo's words, XXIV, 44, 54).

[127] For the influence of nature-driven chance on wars, and especially on the *ends* of wars, see Hans Zinsser's riveting and lively *Rats, Lice, and History* (1935). Zinsser himself said that the book was "a biography" of typhus, but you'll find it to be much, much more than only that.

[128] We might re-punctuate this as "So, it will be better," meaning "This way, it will be better."

[129] The sense is that Achilleus, being in Troy, is unable to provide care or comfort to the aging Peleus.

[130] Except, as must always be pointed out, for readers who in fact remain practicing worshippers of and believers in the Homeric gods.

LaVergne, TN USA
24 January 2010
171023LV00004B/158/P